The Complete Options Trader

Michael C. Thomsett

The Complete Options Trader

A Strategic Reference for Derivatives Profits

palgrave
macmillan

Michael C. Thomsett
https://thomsettsguide.com/
Spring Hill, TN, USA

ISBN 978-3-030-09506-2 ISBN 978-3-319-76505-1 (eBook)
https://doi.org/10.1007/978-3-319-76505-1

Softcover re-print of the Hardcover 1st edition 2018

Cover design by Tjaša Krivec

Printed on acid-free paper

This Palgrave Macmillan imprint is published by the registered company Springer International Publishing AG part of Springer Nature.
The registered company address is: Gewerbestrasse 11, 6330 Cham, Switzerland

Contents

Introduction	1
Market Overview	5
Market Risks	25
Option Strategies	55
Option Glossary	137
Elements of Value	199
Return Calculations	213
Options and Stock Selection	227
Option Taxation	237
Index	243

List of Figures

Market Overview

Fig. 1	Total options contract volume, 1973–2015	9
Fig. 2	Option contract volume by exchange, 2015	9
Fig. 3	Visualizing historical volatility	18
Fig. 4	Moneyness of the option	19

Market Risks

Fig. 1	Consumer Price Index (CPI), 1987–2017	37
Fig. 2	Equifax stock chart	48
Fig. 3	Monsanto stock chart	50

Option Strategies

Fig. 1	Bear call spread	57
Fig. 2	Bear put ladder	58
Fig. 3	Bear put spread	59
Fig. 4	Box spread (debit)	61
Fig. 5	Box spread (credit)	62
Fig. 6	Bull call ladder	64
Fig. 7	Bull call spread	65
Fig. 8	Bull put ladder	66
Fig. 9	Bull put spread	67
Fig. 10	Butterfly spread	69
Fig. 11	Calendar spread	71
Fig. 12	Collar	72
Fig. 13	Condor	74
Fig. 14	Conversion	76
Fig. 15	Covered call	79
Fig. 16	Covered strangle	81
Fig. 17	Types of spreads	83

Fig. 18	Gut strangle (long)	84
Fig. 19	Gut strangle (short)	85
Fig. 20	Iron butterfly (long)	87
Fig. 21	Iron butterfly (short)	88
Fig. 22	Long call	90
Fig. 23	Long call condor	92
Fig. 24	Long iron butterfly	93
Fig. 25	Long put	95
Fig. 26	Long put butterfly	96
Fig. 27	Long put condor	97
Fig. 28	Long stock (synthetic)	99
Fig. 29	Long straddle	100
Fig. 30	Married put	101
Fig. 31	Put ratio backspread	105
Fig. 32	Ratio backspread (call)	106
Fig. 33	Ratio backspread (put)	107
Fig. 34	Ratio calendar combination spread	108
Fig. 35	Ratio calendar spread (call)	110
Fig. 36	Ratio calendar spread (put)	111
Fig. 37	Ratio call spread	112
Fig. 38	Ratio put spread	114
Fig. 39	Ratio write	115
Fig. 40	Reverse hedge	118
Fig. 41	Short call butterfly	121
Fig. 42	Short call condor	122
Fig. 43	Short iron butterfly	123
Fig. 44	Short put butterfly	125
Fig. 45	Short put condor	126
Fig. 46	Short stock (synthetic)	127
Fig. 47	Short straddle (covered)	129
Fig. 48	Short straddle (naked)	130
Fig. 49	Short strangle	131
Fig. 50	Strap	134
Fig. 51	Strip	135

List of Tables

Market Risks
Table 1 Breakeven rates 39

Option Taxation
Table 1 Qualified covered calls 239

Introduction

Options: This highly specialized and complex industry should be all about risk analysis, hedging, and management of an equity portfolio. All too often, the attributes of options trading are poorly understood, risk is ignored or simplified, hedging is not folded into a strategic evaluation, and options traders shun the value of holding equity positions.

This book evaluates a range of strategies not only in the context of their potential rewards, but also in the degree of risk they involve. The purpose is to demonstrate how a broad approach to analytically using options—as part of a larger investing policy—can and does enhance portfolio profits with lower levels of risk.

The options market in its current configuration has been in existence only since 1973. However, over this brief period of time, it has expanded substantially. This has occurred in terms of the volume of trading, exchanges, variety of strategies, new terminology, trading rules, and understanding of risks. The rate of growth has been impressive.

In 1973, only 1.1 million contracts were traded. The latest published statistics, for 2015, reported 4.1 billion, an increase of over 3700% and involving $604 billion per year.[1]

The number of strategies alone has represented a significant part of the expansion in the options market. In 1973, only one type of option—the call—was traded and only on a limited number of underlying stocks. Over the years, puts have been added, not only doubling the type of option, but exploding the potential forms of combinations and hedges. The underlying security has also expanded beyond stocks, to include indices, exchange-traded funds (ETFs), interest rates, credit, and futures.

M. C. Thomsett, *The Complete Options Trader*,
https://doi.org/10.1007/978-3-319-76505-1_1

With the expansion of exchanges, underlying securities, and the types of option strategies traded, the options industry has become complex and expansive, growing every year and gradually becoming an international market where it once was restricted to exchanges in the United States alone. The introduction of the Internet has created the global options market, and the development of low-cost online discount brokerage has made the options world available to every trader. In the past, access and cost were prohibitive, but today this no longer is an issue. However, this widespread access introduces not only opportunity, but also a broader range of risks. An options trader today is faced with the challenge of mastering a complex and rapidly changing market. Even with years of experience in equity investing and trading, the potential in trading options introduces new concepts and new ways of observing markets.

Options enable speculation for those seeking fast profits and willing to expose themselves to high risks of equally high losses, but there is more. With increasing volume of trading, the use of options to hedge market risk in equity positions is becoming the dominant strategic use for options. Today, an investor in equity can reduce and even eliminate market risk with the use of hedging. The options market has always been understood as one avenue for enhancing profits and for managing risks, making options exciting and potentially risky at the same time; when the potential for risk hedging is added to the equation, even the most conservative trader or portfolio manager is able to generate profits and reduce equity risks.

This expanded role for options has been made possible by broadening the universe of strategies. The scope of these strategies can be overwhelming for an options trader. The basic trades—buying calls or puts for speculation—are only the most obvious uses of options. They can be used in a broad range of expanded strategic applications not only to speculate, but also to hedge. This is a rich and diverse range. Some strategies are very high risk, and others are very conservative.

One of the most popular strategies is the covered call, which involves selling one call against 100 shares of stock owned. A covered call seller (also called a writer) receives a premium when the option is sold, and that premium is profit if the call ends up expiring worthless. The short position can also be closed at any time, or held until exercise. In any of these outcomes, the trader continues to earn dividends on the stock, and controls the outcome to a degree. A properly selected covered call can easily create double-digit profits in any of the possible outcomes. This makes the strategy practical for a range of investors and traders interested in expanding beyond the well-known and basic strategy of buying value stocks and earning dividends.

On the far side of the spectrum is the practice of selling naked calls. When traders do this, they receive premium income, but they also risk exercise and potential losses. Many variations of naked option writing mitigate the market risk. In between the very conservative and the very high risk are numerous other strategies.

This book is a comprehensive reference for the entire options market, exploring all aspects of options trading, risk, and potential for consistent profits. Most people prefer to focus on the listed options available on individual stocks, and this is the focus of the examples in the *Option Strategies* chapter. In 1973, knowledge (or, at least, awareness) of options was limited and only a few traders had heard anything about them. There was practically no source for education on the topic and most stockbrokers were ill-equipped to advise clients about trading options. Today, traders go online to get immediate information, but "online" did not exist in 1973. The Internet as a widespread tool for the market was two decades away. Today, however, the entire options market has become mainstream and a growing number of people are recognizing that options can provide many roles within a portfolio and can be used to manage a broad range of risks. Online sites also offer a diverse level of education and free examples of trades.

The modern options market would not be possible without the Internet. Unlike the past, when traders had to rely on stockbrokers for quotes and order placement, and information was exchanged over the phone, today's market allows everyone to see in an instant what the pricing is for thousands of options. Trades can be executed by traders themselves for a very small transaction fee, and with nearly immediate order filling. The stockbroker has become obsolete in the options industry. This does not mean that financial planning is not of great value. However, an options trader should possess a level of knowledge about risk and should be able to make trading decisions without relying on an advisor. For longer-term financial and tax planning, financial planners offer specific value; for short-term trading decisions, traders should make their own decisions.

The concept of asking a broker's advice for an options trade is contrary for three reasons. First, stockbrokers are not necessarily skilled in the options market, even if they are licensed to execute options trades. Second, options trading demands on-going tracking of both options and the stocks they refer to, often minute by minute. Third, paying commissions to a full-service brokerage firm erodes profits from options trades, making many strategies marginal or impractical.

This book is designed for the skilled market trader and investor who has not necessarily been exposed to options. These investors are more likely than average to employ a discount brokerage service, to make their own decisions, and to monitor their investments. Full-commission brokerage is appropriate only for clients who are worried about risk, less knowledgeable about markets, and who trust their broker to give them sound advice. It is also designed to provide value to the portfolio manager who may be involved with equity and debt securities and may discover hedging opportunities with the added utility of options. In fact, portfolio risks can be reduced dramatically with options-based hedging tools.

For both individual investors and portfolio managers, options expand the profit universe by enabling the mitigation and elimination of risk. In the past, options have been viewed by "the crowd" of Wall Street as an oddity, a side-bet, or a separate market, appropriate only for speculators. But as new products and new strategies have been developed, this outlook has evolved. Today, retail and institutional investors use options to (a) insure long portfolio positions, (b) hedge short risks, (c) exploit short-term market price swings, and (d) enhance profits. Even in the most basic of portfolios, all of these applications of options make them valuable management and risk-reduction tools. The most basic speculation in options is an entry strategy for many options traders, but it becomes less important over time. Today, the options market has grown into a means for taking much of the risk out of the investment equation.

This book provides a market overview and discussion of risks, in addition to a comprehensive listing of strategies. Most of these strategies are accompanied by tables and illustrations identifying profit and loss zones as well as breakeven points.

This book also provides a comprehensive explanation of the many strategies, including profit, loss, and breakeven analysis complete with examples and payoff diagrams. It also has a complete glossary of terms used in the options industry: elements of value, calculation of returns from option and stock trading, how stocks are picked for options trading, taxation of the options market, and online and print resources for further research.

Note

1. Source: Chicago Board Options Exchange (CBOE), at http://www.cboe.com/data/market-statistics-2015.pdf. Retrieved September 27, 2017.

Market Overview

The options market is highly specialized, intricate, and often misunderstood. The reputation of options as high risk is only partially deserved. In fact, options products may be structured to suit any investment profile, from very high risk to very conservative, or to be used strictly to hedge risks in equity positions.

Today, options are more popular than ever and have become portfolio tools used to enhance profits, diversify, and reduce risk through hedging strategies. In the recent past, a small number of insiders and speculators used options, and the mainstream investor did not have practical methods available for efficient or affordable trading. Most stockbrokers were ill-equipped to help their customers make options trades in a timely manner, placing the retail investor at a great disadvantage. With today's Internet access and widespread discount brokerage service, virtually anyone with an online hook-up can track the markets and trade options. Many online resources are also available for training and clarification about many options topics.

The History of Options Trading

There is nothing new about options. They can be traced back at least to the mid-fourth century B.C. In 350 B.C., in *Politics* Aristotle wrote about Thales and his use of options:

> There is the anecdote of Thales the Milesian … he knew by his skill in the stars while it was yet winter that there would be a great harvest of olives in the coming year; so, having a little money, he gave deposits for the use of all the

M. C. Thomsett, *The Complete Options Trader*,
https://doi.org/10.1007/978-3-319-76505-1_2

> olive-presses in Chios and Miletus, which he hired at a low price because no one bid against him. When the harvest-time came, and many were wanted all at once and of a sudden, he let them out at any rate which he pleased, and made a quantity of money. Thus he showed the world that philosophers can easily be rich if they like, but that their ambition is of another sort. He is supposed to have given a striking proof of his wisdom, but, as I was saying, his device for getting wealth is of universal application, and is nothing but the creation of a monopoly. It is an art often practiced by cities when they are want of money; they make a monopoly of provisions.[1]

In this example, the deposit created a contract for future use. When that contract gained value, the option owner (Thales) proved to be more than a philosopher. He was also a shrewd trader.

Options allow traders to leverage relatively small amounts of capital to create the potential to earn future profits or, at least, to accept risks in the hope that those options will become profitable later. This all relies on the movement of prices in the underlying security. Thales relied on supply and demand for olive presses, and today options are popularly used to estimate future movement in the prices of stocks. The concept is the same, although the product is different.

A similar event occurred in seventeenth-century Holland, where interest in tulip bulb options sparked a mania and demonstrated how irrationality and speculation can destroy fortunes. The tulip had become a symbol of wealth and prestige and the prices of tulip bulb options went off the charts. By 1637, prices had risen in these options to the point that people were investing their life savings to control options in single tulip bulbs. The craze ended suddenly and many lost everything overnight. Banks failed and a selling panic pushed the high level of prices into a fast crash. There is a valuable lesson in this "tulipmania" for everyone trading options today. In an orderly market, prices of stocks and options rise and fall logically. The reasoning is sound because the tangible supply and demand factors make sense. In a market craze or panic, prices change quickly and irrationally. In the tulipmania example, there was no rational reason for anyone to invest everything in tulip bulb options—other than the fact that everyone else was doing it, and it seemed that everyone else was getting rich in the process. Prices rose quickly, and fell even more quickly.[2]

The difference between Thales and the Dutch was one of common sense. Thales saw an opportunity and invested with a clear vision of how profits would ensue. He was correct and he made a profit. In the tulipmania, greed blinded people and the reckless actions brought about the crash. Symptoms included the rapidly growing prices, expansion of the market, and the failure to realize that the prices were simply too high and, in fact, irrational.

For many decades after the Dutch experience, public sentiment about speculation was unfavorable. Of course, there were numerous examples of market speculation, which never seems to disappear altogether. However, incidents like tulipmania, without doubt, have added to the negative reputation of speculators as gamblers and reckless traders. In fact, many speculators accept the high risks of their approach to the options market, in exchange for the high opportunities speculation offers:

> The speculator who is not an investor (nor a "bear") is one who makes a purchase in the expectation of profiting from an increase in the value of the property rather than through its being made productive … When the appellation "gamblers" is applied to those who deal in this manner, it may express the private view of the person using the term; but in law and in fact such transactions do not constitute gambling.[3]

Options have suffered from their reputation as high-risk devices appropriate only for speculators. Thus, three factors—the combined complexity of options, perception of high risk, and association with speculators—have all combined to create a widespread negative view of this field. Complicating the matter even more, options trading in the public markets is a relatively recent development. A formalized system has been in place only since the early 1970s. Many decades earlier, an initial effort at creating a formal options market occurred.

In the late nineteenth century, a businessman named Russell Sage developed the first modern examples of calls and puts. He made money on the venture and bought a seat on the New York Stock Exchange (NYSE) two years later. His career was successful but spotted with occasional scandals. In 1869 he had been convicted under New York usury laws, and was later associated with Jay Gould, the infamous market manipulator. Gould had tried to corner the gold market at one point, and later invested in the railroad industry, along with Sage and many others.

The Sage options lacked standardized terms (type of option, underlying security, strike price and expiration), making it difficult to expand the market beyond the initial buyer and seller. However, it started a trend that never ended. These over-the-counter contracts remained available to a few insiders in the exchanges and, without an actual options exchange, the market was limited to only those with access to the stock exchange. In this respect, the Sage options were not publicly available, and had limited appeal due to the uncertainty in terms beyond an initial agreement between buyer and seller. This remained unchanged until the 1970s.

The Chicago Board of Trade (CBOT) recognized early on—by the beginning of the twentieth century—that diversification of public markets was desirable for both buyers and sellers and that a healthy balance between the two sides would be beneficial. The CBOT and its role were well defined in an article in 1911 that remained accurate 60 years later:

> The primary function of boards of trade is to facilitate the marketing of products and merchandise, and to provide facilities for their distribution to the consumer in different sections of the country and in different parts of the world. Boards of trade are not established in the interest of the buyer exclusively, or the seller exclusively, but in the interest of buyer, seller, and producer and consumer alike. They have no private interests to promote; they gather information, statistical and otherwise, for the benefit of all concerned; they are absolutely and emphatically identified with the public welfare.[4]

With these standards of operation serving as a core philosophy of the CBOT, the desire to support diversification to bolster trading in the larger investment market eventually led to formulation of an options industry available to the public at large. CBOT established a new organization in 1973, the Chicago Board Options Exchange (CBOE). On April 26, 1973, CBOE initiated the first options market with guaranteed settlement and standardization of price, expiration, and contract size for call options. The Options Clearing Corporation (OCC) was also created to act as guarantor of all option contracts. (This means that the OCC acts as buyer to each seller and as seller to each buyer, ensuring liquidity for every option contract.) Trading in calls became available, but only on 16 listed companies.[5]

By 1977, when put option trading was first allowed, the market had exploded to over 39 million contracts traded (in 1973, only 1.1 million traded). Trading began taking place not only through the CBOE system, but also on the American, Pacific, and Philadelphia Exchanges. Today, volume is higher than ever before and spread beyond the CBOE to the American, Philadelphia, New York, International, and Boston Exchanges. A chart summarizing the expansion of options contract trading from 1973 to 2015 is shown in Fig. 1. From the initial 1.1 million contracts traded per year, the latest available summary reveals more than 4 billion options traded per year.

The once limited market currently trades using many different exchanges. The 2015 breakdown by exchange is summarized in Fig. 2.

In 1982, a new concept was introduced beyond the use of calls and puts on stocks. Index options were originated by the Kansas City Board of Trade with options on the Value Line stocks. This Value Line Index was followed in 1983 by the CBOE introduction of the Standard & Poor's 100 index (OEX), (com-

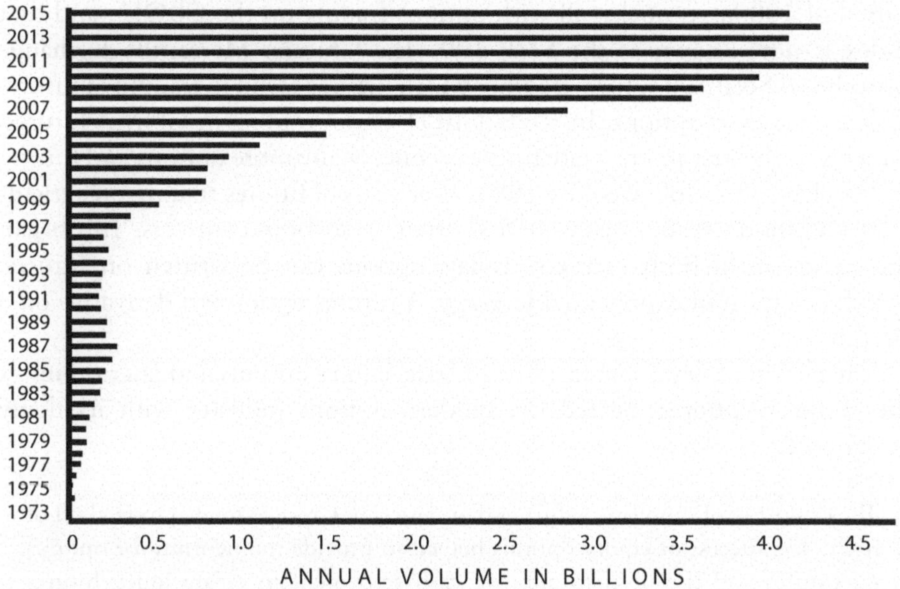

Fig. 1 Total options contract volume, 1973–2015

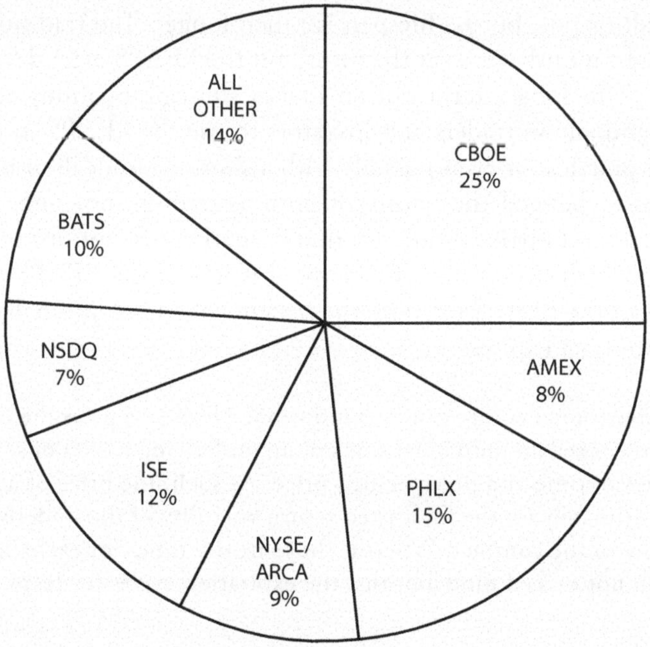

Fig. 2 Option contract volume by exchange, 2015

prised of 100 large stocks, all with options trading on the CBOE), and that index is now known as the S&P 100. The Chicago Mercantile Exchange introduced S&P 500 futures trading, which began a trend in trading of futures indices as well as options. In 1976, CBOT began trading in GNMA futures, which was the first interest rate futures venue. Many more options and futures indices have since followed. By 1984, after years of futures trading on agricultural commodities, options were first listed on soybean contracts. This began an expansion of both markets. Today, options can be written on futures, which is a form of exponential leverage. A futures option is a derivative on a derivative.

The period of development, first of basic equity options and later on index and futures options, created the modern options industry with its many variations:

> The explosion of innovation during that period in Chicago tended to feed off of itself. The success of equity options helped to provide momentum for options on futures and the need to approve cash settlement to create index futures allowed for greater innovation in the equity options space.[6]

In 1990, the CBOE introduced a new type of options, the long-term equity anticipation securities option, or LEAPS. The LEAPS is exactly the same as the listed call or put, but its lifespan is much longer. The traditional option lasts only eight months or so at the most, but the LEAPS extends out as far as 30 months. This longer-term option makes strategic planning much more interesting and allows traders and investors to use the LEAPS in many ways that are not practical or even possible with a shorter-term call or put.

The LEAPS changed the nature of options trading, not only due to the longer time period involved but also due to market perceptions of long-term volatility and high time value. To many, this makes the LEAPS overpriced, but the cost of the LEAPS includes the benefits of an exceptionally long time before the contract expires:

> Like a conventional equity call or put option, a leap (*sic*) gives the owner the right to buy or sell an individual stock or an underlying basket of stocks at or within a given time at a pre-specified price. As such, the price of a leap (*sic*) depends intimately on the forecasted return volatility of the underlying asset over the life of the contract. Whereas the maturity times for exchange traded options do not exceed nine months, the expiration cycles for leaps range up to 3 yr.[7]

Today's options market looks much different than the market of a few decades ago. It has expanded and continues to expand. In the future, additional forms of expansion will continue to broaden the influence of options into many more markets, with the introduction of new and potentially profitable options strategies.

Basics of Options—Standardized Terms

Today, all listed options include standardized terms. These are the type of option (call or put), the underlying security on which options are bought or sold, the strike price, and the expiration date. These are *standardized* in the sense that they cannot be exchanged or replaced. Once an option exists, its terms remain unchanged until the contract expires. Standardization brings order and certainty to the market.

Types: Calls and Puts

A call grants its owner the right, but not the obligation to buy 100 shares of the underlying stock, at a fixed strike price per share and on or before a specific expiration date. The owner of the call acquires these rights in exchange for a premium paid for the option. The value of the option rises if the terms become more attractive before expiration. If the market value moves higher than the fixed strike price, the option value rises; if it remains at or below the fixed strike price, the premium value falls.

The call buyer is not obligated to exercise the option. There are three choices. The option may be allowed to expire worthless, which occurs if the current market value remains below the strike. The contract can also be closed at a profit or loss, and sold on the exchange. The sale may occur at a loss; the option trader may realize that the position is not going to become profitable, and taking a partial loss is preferable to letting the contract expire, meaning the value would go to zero. Finally, the option owner can exercise that option and buy 100 shares at the fixed strike price. For example, if the strike is 50 and current value per share is $56, exercise gets 100 shares at the fixed price of $50 per share, or $6 per share lower than current market value.

The call seller does not pay a premium, but receives it. When a trader sells an option, the trading sequence is reversed. Rather than the well-known long position of buy-hold-sell, a short position has the sequence sell-hold-buy. When a trader sells a call, this grants the rights under the option contract to a buyer. The seller and buyer usually do not meet face to face, because all options trading is done through the OCC, which facilitates the market (acting as seller to each buyer and as buyer to each seller). When exercise occurs, the OCC matches the transaction and assigns the exercise to an options writer. In the case of a short call, the seller is obligated to sell 100 shares of the underlying stock at the fixed strike price. For example, if the strike is 50 and current market value per share is $56, a seller is obligated to sell shares at the fixed strike even if that means having to buy the same number of shares at $56 per share, or for a loss of six points ($600 for 100 shares).

A put is the opposite of a call. This option grants its owner the right, but not the obligation, to sell 100 shares of stock at a fixed strike price, or on before a specific expiration date. Just as a call owner hopes the value of the stock will rise, a put owner hopes the value will fall. The more the price falls, the more valuable the put becomes.

A put buyer may take one of three actions before expiration. The put can be closed at its premium value, and a profit or loss taken. The put can also be allowed to expire worthless, which occurs if the underlying stock is at or above the strike price at the time of expiration. Finally, the put can be exercised. This means the owner is allowed to sell 100 shares of the underlying stock at the fixed strike price. For example, if a trader owns 100 shares purchased at $50 per share and also buys a 50 put, exercise will occur at that price. If the stock's value falls to $41 per share before expiration, the put owner can exercise the put and sell 100 shares for $50 per share, even though current market value is nine points ($900) lower.

A put seller grants the option rights to a buyer. So if a trader sells a put, it means that they may be obligated to accept 100 shares of the underlying stock at the fixed strike. If the strike is 50 and the current market value of stock falls to $41 per share, the put will be exercised. The put seller will have 100 shares put to them at the fixed price of $50 per share, or nine points above current market value.

The Underlying Security

The underlying security is fixed and cannot be changed. Options are traditionally opened on a single stock, but today the underlying security may be an index, future, currency, commodity, or ETF. Many creative expansions and variations of the options market have been developed and continue to be introduced. Examples in this book focus on options on stock, as the best-understood and most popular form of options trading.

Every stock option refers to the rights on 100 shares of stock. A single option grants rights to those 100 shares, either to buy (call) or sell (put). The option's current premium value is expressed on a per-share basis, however. For example, if an option is currently valued at 4.60, that means it is worth $4.60 per share, or $460.00 (per 100 shares).

An on-going debate between traditional stock investors and options traders is based not only on perception of risk, but also on the relative value and suitability of one of the other (stock purchase versus options trading). In options trading, the underlying serves as one of four standardized terms, but many traders make the mistake of viewing the underlying only as a vehicle for risk-reduction, or as a less than important attribute of a trading tactic. In fact, selection of an underlying security as a first step in trading often determines the degree of risk in the options trade. The underlying security, once quantified, largely determines the risks associated with subsequent options trading. So a trader who buys 100 shares primarily to enter strategies such as covered calls may easily ignore the risks of selecting securities without also judging their risk. Because highly volatile stocks present higher market risks than lower volatility stocks, their options are likely to be richer as well. So selection of an underlying based on attractive option premium may be contrary to the trader's risk profile.

A related concept, *price discovery*, is a means for determining how fairly (or unfairly) priced a security may be, including both shares of stock and options contracts. This complicates the role of the underlying security. When the question of how the security is priced enters into the equation, it may distort how options are valued:

> Some markets such as the underlying stock are more suitable for price discovery during ordinary time periods, so that the usual information flow is gradually and smoothly impounded into prices. Other types of markets, such as options contracts, may play an informative role at times of severe information asymmetry and in advance of extreme events.[8]

An extreme event may come in many forms. A known extreme event such as an earnings report (with its potential for either positive or negative surprises) is one of those times when options volatility is likely to depart from smooth price discovery. The timing may indicate the wisdom of waiting for the surprise to occur, or may also indicate the speculative opportunity to take up a position *before* the extreme event, in order to profit from it (or to lose if the underlying price moves in the "wrong" direction).

Strike Price

The value at which options can be exercised is called the strike price (also known as striking price or exercise price). For example, if the strike is 50, it means the option will be exercised at $50 per share if and when exercise occurs. The proximity between strike price and current market value determines the option's value, along with the amount of time remaining until expiration.

When the underlying stock's current value is higher than a call, the call is in the money (ITM). When the price is lower than the strike, the call is out of the money (OTM). When it is exactly equal to the strike, the call is at the money (ATM).

For puts, this is opposite. When the stock's price is higher than the put strike, it is out of the money, and when the stock price is lower than the fixed strike, that put is in the money.

Expiration

Every option is scheduled to expire in the future. The farther away the expiration date, the higher the option's value. With options, traders coordinate time with proximity and price. The closer the strike to current market value of the underlying stock, the more price reacts to price changes; and the closer the expiration date, the more the option's premium value reacts to price movement.

When a trader opens an option, the time remaining until expiration affects the decision about which specific contract to buy or to sell. Time to expiration affects the value of the option and defines risk. For sellers of options, the longer the time until expiration, the greater the risk of exercise. Exposure to this risk is one of the most important factors in comparing option prices. Exercise is most likely to occur on the last trading day, but it can occur at any time during the life of the option. For those buying options, a long time until expiration is both a positive and a negative. It is positive because with more time, there is an increased chance of movement in the price of the underlying stock. A desirable change in value (upward for call buyers or downward for put buyers) defines whether options will be profitable or not. The negative is that greater time also means higher cost. The more a trader pays for an option, the more difficult it will be to create future profits.

The Option Premium and Its Components

The premium—the cost of the option—varies over time, based on three factors. These are time to expiration, volatility, and intrinsic value.

Time Value

The longer the time until expiration, the higher the "time value" of the option. Time value tends to change very little for exceptionally long-term options. For example, for a LEAPS option, which has as long as 30 months to expiration, changes in the underlying stock's price will have little or no effect on time value. As time approaches expiration, however, its decline accelerates. At the point of expiration, time value will have declined to zero.

The tendency for time value to accelerate as expiration approaches affects the timing of trades, especially for short positions in options. Long options do not become profitable if the underlying price does not move, mainly due to declining time value. However, short option traders (sellers) know that time value creates profits. As time value evaporates, the option loses premium value. And because short traders go through the sequences of sell-buy-hold instead of the opposite, reduction in value equals profits. So the short trader sells to open and then when value has fallen, buys to close at a lower premium level. This is where time value works for the seller.

Volatility

The most elusive and hard to understand part of premium value is due to the level of volatility in the underlying stock as well as in the value of each option. This volatility is an expression of market risk. Stocks with relatively narrow trading ranges are less risky (but they also offer less opportunity for profits in the stock or in options). Stocks with broad trading ranges and rapid changes in price are high risk but also offer greater profit opportunities. The option premium level is directly affected by this price volatility. The level of unpredictability in a stock's current and future price level defines an option's premium value.

Some analysts include this volatility effect as part of time value, but this only confuses the analysis of options. Time value by itself is predictable and, if it could be isolated, could be easily tracked over the course of time. Time value tends to change very little with many months to go, but as expiration nears, the rate of decline in time value accelerates and ends up at zero on the day of expiration. But time value cannot be separated from the other elements of value, so it is often seen as part of the same price feature. Time and volatility values, combined, are often described as a single version of "time value premium." If these two elements are separated, option analysis is much more logical.

The portion attributed to volatility may be accurately named "extrinsic value." This is the portion of an option's premium beyond pure time value, but excluding intrinsic value (the portion of premium caused by the option being in the money). Extrinsic value can be tracked and estimated based on a comparison between premium trends and stock volatility. This is referred to as implied volatility of the option.

To understand how volatility works for the underlying stock, a few technical tools are required. The trading range (highest and lowest priced in the current price trend) is easily quantified for most stocks. A study and comparison of stocks reveals that trading ranges vary considerably. The greater the breadth of the range, the more extrinsic value exists in option premium. To accurately track and predict extrinsic value, you need to adjust the method for calculating volatility for the underlying stock. This is called historical volatility and is based on the breadth of trading over time in the underlying security. Because option values are derived from changing value and volatility in the underlying security, it makes sense to track volatility based on the underlying price behavior. This is why options are also referred to as *derivatives*—their valuation is derived from price behavior in the underlying security.

Volatility does not always account for the occasional price spike. In statistics, one principle required to get an accurate average is to exclude any unusual spikes in a field of values. This should apply to stock prices as well, but the adjustment is rarely made. Applying a basic statistical rule that spikes should be removed, volatility for many underlying securities would be far lower than with the spike included. The definition of a spike is that it takes price above or below the trading range *and* that following the spike, prices return to the normal range without repeated the spike again.

Determining the level of extrinsic value (volatility value) requires considerable technical analysis of the stock's price *and* its trend. No current value should be studied as fixed in time, but rather takes on meaning when its change is part of the analysis. The trend affects recent changes in option extrinsic value, and may also point to how that trend is going to continue to change in the future.

Beyond historical volatility in the underlying security, some options traders prefer to track *implied volatility*. This is an estimate of how option premium will change in the future. Whereas historical volatility can be calculated precisely based on recent price behavior, implied volatility is an estimate, and it requires imposition of many assumptions. Since option valuation is directly a factor of the underlying (historical) volatility, the accuracy of relying on implied volatility as an estimate of future premium levels is questionable. A trader can visualize levels of volatility in the underlying simply by observing price movement over time on a stock chart. This provides an immediate view of any unusual price movement or distortion. It also demonstrates that implied volatility of an option's future value is not as useful as historical volatility of the underlying security:

> At first glance, the options market may seem to be an inappropriate place to look for price distortions. Standard arbitrage considerations dictate that option prices must be closely tied both to each other and to the underlying stock prices. Any large deviations from "fair values" should be quickly eliminated. However, under real-world market conditions, option values can deviate from fair values by significant amounts without creating riskless-arbitrage opportunities.[9]

This is precisely the point of relying on underlying price volatility as a timing device for options timing. Distortions in option pricing point to advantages in either buying or selling and how those decisions are timed. It is the underlying price behavior that reveals potential timing opportunities. Of interest in the timing of trades is the question of whether historical volatility is expanding or contracting. To time either long or short options trades, this is a crucial observation. Volatility tends to move in cycles, so the timing of trades is related directly to this tendency. A short entry (selling an option) is likely to be most profitable when volatility is highest. At such times, premium levels tend to be higher. So a seller will receive more premium if the sale is timed with high volatility; and because volatility is cyclical, the chances for a rapid decline in option premium are higher as well, and will occur as volatility contracts. For a long trader (buying an option), it makes sense to time a trade when historical volatility is low, because the premium level of an option will be at their lowest point, and likely to increase as volatility expands.

An example of different volatility levels is shown on the stock chart in Fig. 3.

The chart highlights two periods, both framed by Bollinger Bands. The first reveals a period of low volatility (range between the upper and lower bands), with approximately three points. The second reveals a period of high volatility, with a volatility range as high as 14 points. For a trader timing entry and exit based on historical volatility, timing for a long trade (buying an option either to open or to close) would be best at the lowest volatility level. Selling would be maximized at the high volatility level.

Fig. 3 Visualizing historical volatility

This visualization using the overlay of Bollinger Bands makes it easy to spot volatility. The indicator consists of three bands. The middle band (a dotted line) is a 20-day simple moving average. The upper and lower bands are calculated at two standard deviations away from the middle band. This sets up the levels of volatility. More valuable, however, is that it also makes it possible to see when volatility is expanding or contracting.

Without needing to perform any independent calculations or impose assumptions (as is required to calculate implied volatility), the simple device of overlaying Bollinger Bands on the stock chart helps options traders to time trades based on ever-changing levels of volatility.

Intrinsic Value

The final portion of the option's premium is the most easily explained and understood. Intrinsic value is that portion of the premium attributed to ITM status of the option. When an option is ATM, meaning strike is equal to the underlying price, there is no intrinsic value. When the option is OTM, meaning the call strike is higher than the current underlying price or put strike is lower than current stock price, there is no intrinsic value. The only time intrinsic value exists is when the option is in the money.

The relationship between price and option strike is broadly referred to as the *moneyness* of the option. To illustrate this principle, Fig. 4 summarizes ITM, ATM, and OTM status for an option with a strike of 81.

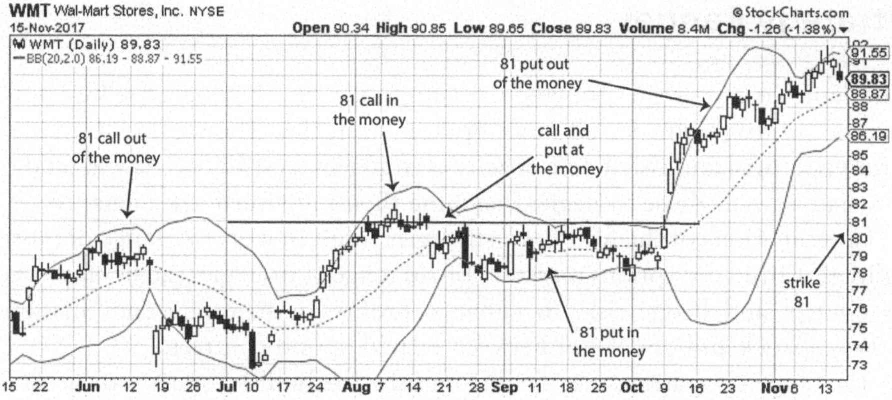

Chart courtesy of StockCharts.com

Fig. 4 Moneyness of the option

The strike in this example is 81, meaning that exercise would always occur at $81 per share. When the price of the underlying is exactly $81 per share, the option is ATM. When the price is higher than $81 per share, the 81 call is ITM and the 81 put is OTM. When the underlying price is lower than $81 per share, the 81 call is OTM and the 81 put is ITM.

In describing existing options, the moneyness is important. Intrinsic value only exists for options in the money, and at that time, as the level of ITM grows, so will the option premium. For the owner of an option, this is desirable; the higher the level of premium, the more profitable the long call (as the underlying price moves up) or the long put (as the underlying price moves down). On the opposite scale, the seller of an option will have a greater profit when the option is OTM. The farther away from the strike the underlying price moves (downward for a short call or upward for a short put), the more profitable a short trade becomes.

Intrinsic value of the option also is associated with price efficiency in the underlying security. Studies of market trends and pricing appear to support this assumption:

> A strong set of results pertains to the effect of the intrinsic value of the option on liquidity and price efficiency in the market for the stock. When the intrinsic value of the option is positive, convergence to intrinsic value in the stock is faster, liquidity trader losses are smaller, and the volatility of transactions prices is lower than when the option's intrinsic value is zero. This appears due to the greater information content of trades in the option market in this case: this information is used by the dealers in the stock to more rapidly pinpoint intrinsic value.[10]

Strategy Ranges

The four basic strategies (buying or selling calls, and buying or selling puts) are the starting point for all other options strategies. The varying degrees of profit potential and risk define dozens of strategies, and all traders will tend to gravitate toward those strategies matching their individual risk tolerance.

Combinations of the four basic strategies result in a diverse range of possibilities. Within the options market, a broad range of strategies can be employed to control and hedge risk, to enhance profits, or to create combinations between stock and options or between related option contracts.

The range of strategies can be distinguished as bullish, bearish, or neutral. A bullish strategy will produce profits if the price of the underlying stock rises. A bearish strategy becomes profitable when the stock price falls. And a neutral strategy does best when the underlying stock's price remains within a narrow price range. The classifications of strategies can also be broken down into a few broad types:

Single-Option Speculative Strategies

The speculator uses options simply to exploit how the underlying stock price moves in the future. Long positions benefit when the price of the stock rises (for long calls) or falls (for long puts). Short speculative strategies, also called uncovered or naked writes, assume higher risk positions. While the holder of a long position will never lose more than the cost of opening the position, naked short selling may include potentially higher risks. A naked call writer has potentially unlimited risk based on the possibility that a stock's price could rise indefinitely. A naked put writer faces a downside risk; if the stock value falls the put will be exercised at the fixed strike price, and the writer will be required to buy shares at a price above market value.

In modern trading strategies, speculation often is recognized as scientific when based on analysis of technical signals and confirmation. A less enlightened view from more than 100 years ago viewed speculation as impulsive and a form of recklessness:

> *Speculators.*- That a considerable portion of the population is either permanently or temporarily identified with this class is a fact as well known (*sic*) as it is regrettable. At one time or another nearly every one succumbs to the insidious at- tack of the "get-rich-quick" microbe … The effort to speculate, for the most part unrecognized and often almost unconscious, and in its temporary effect upon demand practically indistinguishable from actual consumption, permeates in varying degrees the entire social structure.[11]

Speculative strategies—in spite of the opinion in the negative often seen in the past and also in the present—serve a purpose in many broader market tactics, such as swing trading or day trading. These timing strategies are based on timing to the top or bottom of short-term price swings. Rather than using shares of stock for swing trading, using long options provides three major advantages. First, it involves less capital so a swing trading strategy can be expanded. Second, risk is limited to the cost of the long option, which is significantly lower than buying shares of stock. Third, using long puts at the top of a short-term price range is easier and less risky than shorting stock.

Swing and day traders also may use short options for swing trading and day trading. In this approach, short puts are opened at the bottom of a swing and closed as the price rises, and as time decay sets in. Short calls are opened when prices peak, and are closed when price declines and time decay lowers the premium value. The use of short options is based on the opposite sequence of events from long trades. The long trade follows the sequence "buy-hold-sell" and the short trade is based on "sell-hold-buy."

Single options are also used to insure other positions. For example, traders may buy one put to protect current paper profits in long stock positions. They may also buy calls to mitigate the risks of being short on stock. Insurance of other positions, or hedging those positions, has become one of the most important ways to manage portfolio risk.

Covered Calls

One of the most popular strategies is the covered call. When a trader owns 100 shares of the underlying stock and sells a call, the market risk faced by the naked writer is eliminated. If the call is exercised, the writer is required to deliver those 100 shares of stock at the strike price. Although the market value at that time will be higher, the covered call writer receives a premium for selling the call, and continues earning dividends until the position is exercised, closed, or expired. As long as the strike selected was higher than the price initially paid for the 100 shares, the covered call writer also earns a capital gain upon exercise. So covered calls produce three sources of income: option premium, dividends, and capital gains.

Even with the attractive three sources of income, covered calls are far from foolproof. The "lost opportunity" risk of covered calls—which occurs when the underlying price rises far above the call's strike and shares are called away—is a very real risk, and traders should engage in covered calls only when fully aware of this risk. This was a point raised by Fischer Black, the well-known co-author of the Black-Scholes pricing model:

> It is sometimes said ... that covered option writers almost always gain more than they lose by writing options. This statement focuses on the premium income, and downplays the possible loss of appreciation on the stock if the option is exercised. In fact, careful study shows that an investor who writes call options against his stock will often end up with a worse position than the one he started with.[12]

A variation of covered call writing that varies the risk level is the ratio write. This strategy involves selling more calls than full coverage allows. For example, a trader who owns 200 shares and sells three calls has entered a 3:2 ratio write. Yet another variation is the naked put, which has the same market risk as the covered call, but does not include ownership of 100 shares of the underlying.

Spreads

Then spread involves buying or selling options at different strikes, or with different expirations, or both. Variations include calendar, butterfly, ratio, and reverse spreads. These are among the most popular of option strategies, because profits and losses can be controlled and limited in the structure of the spread.

In the spread, a long and short call and opened, or a long and short put are opened, at the same time. The concept is based on paying for a long position with premium income from a short position, in order to limit risk while introducing the possibility of profits. There probably are more variations of spreads than any other classification of trades, as one study concluded:

> Since calls and puts differ by both strike price and time-to-expiration and may be either bought or sold, there are a large number of possible combinations—a total of 36 possibilities when there are only two possible strike prices and two times-to-expiration. If we add the underlying asset or consider combinations of three or more options, the set of possibilities is much larger. Although only a subset of these are recognized, named, and discussed in the options literature, the number of named combinations is still large. For instance, we found one website which defined 74 different combinations ...[13]

Straddles

The straddle involves buying or selling dissimilar options with the same strike. Risks may be greater and creating profits is often more difficult than with spreads, but many variations make straddles interesting and appealing. Because one of the two sides can be closed profitably at any time, straddle risks can be reduced over time, especially for short positions or for the strangle, a variety of straddle.

Synthetic Positions

Some strategies are designed to create profit and risk profiles equal to other positions; these are called synthetics. For example, opening a long call and a short put at the same strike creates synthetic long stock; and a long put with a short call at the same strike creates synthetic short stock. The appeal to synthetic positions is that they can be opened for less capital than the mirrored position, and often with identical or lower risk.

Anyone embarking on the use of options in their portfolio will appreciate the various levels of risk to any particular strategy. The next chapter explains how risk varies among the different option strategies.

Notes

1. Aristotle, *Politics*, Book One, Part XI, c. 350 B.C.
2. Tobias, A. & Mackay, C. (1995 reprint edition). *Extraordinary Popular Delusions and the Madness of Crowds.* New York NY: Broadway Books, pp. 92–101.
3. Stevens, A. C. (September, 1892). The Utility of Speculation in Modern Commerce. *Political Science Quarterly*, Vol. 7, No. 3, pp. 419–430.
4. Stone, G. F. (September, 1911). Board of Trade of the City of Chicago. *The Annals of the American Academy of Political and Social Science*, Vol. 38, No. 2, pp. 189–205.
5. The original 16 companies on which call options were traded in 1973 were AT&T, Atlantic Richfield, Brunswick, Eastman Kodak, Ford, Gulf & Western, Loews, McDonalds, Merck, Northwest Airlines, Pennzoil, Polaroid, Sperry Rand, Texas Instruments, Upjohn, and Xerox.
6. Collins, D. P. (August 16, 2016). Listed Options: A Brief History. *Futures Magazine*.
7. Bollerslev, T. & Mikkelsen, H. O. (1999). Long-term Equity Anticipation Securities and Stock Market Volatility Dynamics. *Journal of Econometrics*, Vol. 92, pp. 75–99.
8. Cao, C., Chen, Z. & Griffin, J. M. (May, 2005). Informational Content of Option Volume Prior to Takeovers. *The Journal of Business*, Vol. 78, No. 3, pp. 1073–1109.

9. Amin, K., Coval, J. D. & Seyhun, H. N. (October, 2004). Index Option Prices and Stock Market Momentum. *The Journal of Business*, Vol. 77, No. 4, pp. 835–874.
10. De Jong, C., Koediik, K. G. & Schnitzlein, C. R. (July, 2006). Stock Market Quality in the Presence of a Traded Option. *The Journal of Business*, Vol. 79, No. 4, pp. 2243–2274.
11. Selden, G. C. (February, 1902). Trade Cycles and the Effort to Anticipate. *The Quarterly Journal of Economics*, Vol. 16, No. 2, pp. 293–310.
12. Black, F. (July/August, 1975). Fact and Fantasy in the Use of Options. *Financial Analysts Journal*, Vol. 31, No. 4, pp. 36–41.
13. Chaput, J. S. & Ederington, L. H. (Summer, 2003). Option Spread and Combination Trading. *The Journal of Derivatives*, Vol. 10, No. 4, pp. 70–88.

Market Risks

Are options high-risk trading devices? Many who invest or trade avoid options in the belief that they are speculative, exotic, and even dangerous. However, as the options industry has evolved over the years, it has outgrown its reputation as a speculative, "shoot from the hip" form of leveraged trading. The modern options industry has many faces, from the speculative trader willing to accept extraordinary levels of risk, all the way to the most conservative investor or portfolio manager seeking safe risk hedges.

In any trading strategy, risk is too often overlooked, with focus on profit opportunities without considering the totality of the risk/profit universe. The value of an investment and its potential for profits can be compared and evaluated only when reviewed in a broader context of how much risk is involved, given the profit potential. In the past, too many traders fell into the trap of focusing on profit alone, while ignoring or even being unaware of the risks involved. The selection of a strategy that takes both profit potential and risk exposure into consideration has an improved chance for success.

Options traders face the same risks as all investors, and these are caused by well-known factors, both within the market and outside. Risks come from economic causes as well as market-driven ones such as the most basic and ever changing supply and demand, or the more complex sentiments and belief systems among investors. The domestic political cycle as well as geopolitical changes all affect markets. Today, with improved communications and Internet access, markets have become global in a real sense. In the past, references to a global economy or global market were often future-looking but not practical. Today, the markets have merged and anyone can trade in foreign stock, futures, currency, precious metals, and other markets, all online and

M. C. Thomsett, *The Complete Options Trader*,
https://doi.org/10.1007/978-3-319-76505-1_3

instantaneously. In the past, investing on a foreign-listed stock was both cumbersome and expensive, not to mention cost prohibitive. Today, the lines of international trade have blurred and investors are no longer limited to only companies listed on domestic exchanges.

This new reality has also increased profit potential *and* risk. These two—profit potential and risk exposure—cannot be separated because they are different aspects of the same feature of investing and trading. The connection applies whether in a particular market sector, economic cycle, or type of product. Options, as products, have greater risks of some kinds and less of others. For example, there is less market risk in taking positions in options because less money is required to open a position. Any trader can control 100 shares of stock by buying a single call, and its cost will be a fraction of the cost of buying 100 shares. Furthermore, this ability is not limited to buying a call (the equivalent benefit of owning 100 shares). It also enables a bearish investor to control outcomes by buying puts, not to mention the expansion of these ideas through selling options or transacting combinations of the basic buy/sell and call/put choices. This advantage has an accompanying disadvantage: options expire.

Options mitigate risks and also enable investors and traders to control shares of the underlying security, which becomes significant when considering the high price per share of many stocks. With options available at a small fraction of the cost for 100 shares, options open up markets in ways not possible when limited to equity positions. This is also possible without substantially higher levels of market risk:

> In addition to efficient allocation of risk, derivatives offer another important benefit: they can provide investors with opportunities that would otherwise be unavailable to them at any price. That is, derivatives can provide payoffs that simply cannot be obtained with other, existing assets.[1]

At the same time that benefits are created by leverage, options come with an equally serious set of risks. Leverage creates greater potential for profits and for losses. For example, if a trader spends $10,000 in buying stock, the market risk is isolated to the risk of a declining value. However, if the same trader places $10,000 into long option positions, it becomes possible to acquire many times more control over underlying price movement, which means much greater profit potential. It also means the position is exposed to greater risks. So you cannot escape risk entirely. In fact, when you exchange one risk for another, it may also mean changing the risk *level.* If a position creates greater opportunity for profit, the risk level will invariably be greater as well.

With this in mind, risk analysis is best performed with a view of the overall levels of risk exposure as well as levels of profit potential.

The informed risk manager risk requires a thorough appreciation of which levels apply to a particular position or mix of positions within a portfolio. Options can be used to reduce the well-known market risks; however, the appropriate use of options should be designed as portfolio management tools and with an understanding of option risks as separate attributes.

Market and Volatility Risk

Stock investors think about market risk in terms of how stock prices rise and fall; this often is the sole focus for the "buy and hold" approach to investing as well as the stock-based speculative or swing trade of short duration. Focus on overall markets and indices most often defines the market mood at any given time and, as a result, also defines levels of market risk.

Option traders tend to consider market risk in two aspects. First is the market risk of option trading itself; second is the variation of risk levels among different option trading strategies. Although this is a broader view of the risk universe, option traders are also likely to overlook fundamental risk. Even when traders are fully aware that fundamental trends affect the value of the company, and thus, long-term prospects of stock prices, they may choose to focus only on the option-based risks. This is a mistake, since fundamental risk ultimately determines technical attributes of stock prices as well as options. Specifically, high-beta stocks (with price movement more volatile than the overall market) reflect cash management and cash flow attributes of the company, so that price movement is affected directly by fundamentals and their trends. A study of this theory suggests that:

> the high annual betas of growth stocks with the market's discount-rate shocks, and of value stocks with the market's cash-flow shocks, are determined by the cash-flow fundamentals of growth and value companies. Thus, growth stocks are not merely "glamour stocks" whose systematic risks are purely driven by investor sentiment.[2]

Market Risk of Option Trading

Option-based market risk is most often called volatility. The likelihood of acceleration of deceleration in option value is invariably the result of changing volatility in the underlying stock, thus the term *derivative* to describe the nature of an option. Many speculators and traders employ volatility as the means for identifying entry and exit points in swing trading and similar programs. Using options in place of shares of stock provides many advantages, including limited market risk, high leverage, and the ability to maximize sell signals with the use of long puts rather than with short stock. Trading on volatility instead of on price provides additional advantages, notably when the underlying stock is exceptionally volatile. The combination of volatility trading and advantageous use of time value premium near to expiration makes volatility trading a practical method for using market risk (volatility) effectively.

Implied volatility, or an option's prediction about the volatility of the underlying stock, is in a sense the opposite of option selection based on the stock's own market risk. Implied volatility is intended to predict near-term stock volatility. If trading begins with observation of the stock's historical volatility, it leads to timing and selection of option trades. If trading begins with an observation of the option's implied volatility, then option trends are assumed to determine the timing of stock trades. In some respects this is true:

> Clearly, investors trade options for reasons other than possessing private information about the volatility of underlying stocks (e.g., for hedging or for liquidity reasons). In general, this fact should just make it more difficult to detect a relationship between option market demand for volatility and the future volatility of underlying stocks. It does, however, seem important to control for investors trading in the option market on private information that the underlying stock price will increase or decrease … it is possible that a positive relation between non-market maker net demand for volatility and future stock price volatility could be driven by investors trading on directional information in the option market.[3]

Any speculation concerning a relationship between option implied volatility and underlying price movement has to be based on a belief that options influence is substantial on the equity market. This belief is suspect, because the generators of stock price movement are more closely related to large institution equity trading decisions, high-frequency trading, and retail supply and demand for a company's shares. It should be recalled that options are *derivative* products, meaning their value and volatility are derived from price behavior in the underlying security, and that the underlying does not act and react based on behavior in option contracts.

Implied volatility also requires an estimation of future changes in volatility of the option. The assumption is based on current volatility, making the calculation much less reliable than the more reliable and specific historical volatility. Because this is based on recent price range and movement, it is precise and known. Implied volatility is based on the assumption that changes in volatility can be determined scientifically when, in fact, those changes cannot be known. The uncertainty itself is what makes options trading potentially profitable. The unknown—volatility—is by nature not subject to accurate calculation.

Implied volatility is the isolated and unknown portion of an option's market risk. In fact, it is the only segment of the option premium that is not known in advance. The intrinsic value (degree the option is in the money) of the option premium is the easiest to calculate, because that value is equal to a specific number of points. Time value (that portion attributable solely to time) is also predictable, and the loss of time value is known to evaporate with increasing speed as expiration approaches. The extrinsic (volatility) portion of the premium is not known in advance and has to be estimated. That estimate may be based on the assumptions going into calculation of implied volatility, or it can be based on the study of price patterns and signals, volume, momentum, and moving averages—all observed on a stock chart.

A side-by-side analysis of two stocks demonstrates how the volatility variable works. Given the same price level of the underlying, option strike, dividend, and time until expiration, option traders observe differences in total option premium and yield. This is the non-intrinsic, non-time value portion of premium, or the *quantified* implied volatility of the option. Some otherwise unexplained spikes in implied volatility can be caused by insider trading or by publicly known rumors. Even so, the popular pricing models, notably Black Scholes, do not track volume spikes accurately. Black Scholes is based on an assumed flat implied volatility; however, the occurrence of implied volatility spikes throws the model off and demonstrates that traders, especially option traders, need to rely on both fundamental and technical developments to time trades based on unexpected price movement. In this model, Black Scholes is not capable of explaining spikes, whereas analysis of historical volatility trends is more accurate. In fact, no pricing models can explain underlying spikes and implied volatility spikes.[4]

More reliable is a series of easily observed fundamental events. These include news of potential mergers, anticipated earnings surprises, delayed filings of SEC financial statements, changes in management, or impending missed dividends are only a few examples of the rumors or events that tend to aggravate implied volatility.

Even in highly volatile underlying stocks, the longer the time until expiration, the less volatility will be observed in the option premium. As a consequence, LEAPS implied volatility when expiration is more than two years away is likely to be close to zero—even when the underlying stock is highly volatile. The tendency for long-term options is to have low implied volatility when expiration is many months away, with those levels increasing to more expected levels of implied volatility as expiration approaches. In this regard, implied volatility of the LEAPS is influenced by time, which explains why it is often included with and described as part of time value. The two influences on premium value are vastly different, but the degree of volatility is less responsive when more time remains until expiration. This facet of implied volatility may be thought of as the "time value of volatility," although it has nothing to do with the predictable decay associated with the approach of an expiration date. The fact remains that time does influence implied volatility, but in ways that are far less predictable than time value premium.

One risk involving volatility is in how well option traders predict change over time—in other words, the question should be: Do implied and historical volatility merge as expiration nears? In practice, some backward-looking analysis reveals that a two-part analysis is a good predictor of implied/historical trends and volatility factors. But this is not universal. In some cases, predicting a merger between volatility levels is not reliable at all. Implied volatility tends to become more reactive as the time horizon shortens. Implied volatility is probably less variable as a means for judging relative risk of options. Historical volatility also has a degree of varying reliability because stock pricing tends to be highly chaotic in the short term, and over-reactive to the very latest news, rumor, or market perceptions. As a consequence, the evened-out moving averages of historical volatility are sound indicators, but historical volatility in the short term (i.e., the last three months of an option's life cycle) is less reliable. This is why the use of moving averages is popular; even as lagging indicators, moving averages reveal a great deal when studied in the context of convergence and crossover.

Variation of Option Strategy Risk Levels

The analysis of options based on implied or historical volatility is an elusive exercise. Although intended as a method for quantifying market risk, historical volatility is based on past performance and cannot always accurately predict the future. It can add value to the understanding of price behavior in the underlying, however. The duration of high and low volatility, the rapidity of change, and the current direction of volatility (increasing or decreasing) is all easily observed on a stock chart. However, even with an understanding of how volatility defines option risks, the strategy selected ultimately determines a trader's exposure.

Covered Call Risks

On the conservative side, the covered call is the safest and most profitable of all option strategies, although it is not without risk. A study of possible outcomes reveals that a properly structured covered call yields double-digit returns (when annualized) even in the worst-case scenario. A "properly structured" covered call contained specific attributes:

1. It is written on stock whose net basis is below the strike price of the short call. This creates a net capital gain in stock if and when the short call is exercised. At the same time, the short call should be out of the money to maximize the advantageous position regarding decline in time value premium.
2. Dividend yield is greater than average, to increase overall net return when all sources are considered in the equation (dividend yield, capital gains, option premium).
3. The turnover rate is high, meaning that selection of shorter-term covered calls will experience accelerated decay in time value, increasing the changes for expiration or, in the alternative, for rapidly declining premium value so that the position can be closed at a profit.
4. The ability to roll forward and up to avoid exercise if the call is in the money as expiration becomes close. This rolling decision provides a net credit in the exchange of the two positions, while also increasing the exercise price by one increment (thus increasing capital gain in the underlying when exercise does occur).

The covered call is popular among conservative traders because it consistently produces profits with a fairly low risk of exercise. Covered call writers may profit from loss of intrinsic value when they write ITM short calls. However, it is more conservative and potentially more profitable to seek positions between two and five points out of the money. This maximizes the chances of declining premium value in the short option even when the underlying price rises and approaches or even surpasses the strike.

Covered call writers avoid exercise by rolling forward if and when the call is in the money close to expiration. This not only defers the expiration date and escapes the potential for exercise; it also creates an additional credit in the position. The extended period of exposure is a disadvantage; however, if the trader rolls forward and up to a higher strike, that achieves two benefits. First, it avoids exercise and second, it alters the strike price so that if and when exercise does occur, there will be additional profits earned equal to the difference between original and rolled strike prices.

One danger of rolling occurs when tax consequences are not included in the decision to roll forward. This can be especially costly for anyone who has owned the underlying stock for less than one year and when the original basis far below current market value. The assumption is that if the covered call is exercised, the profit on the underlying will be taxed at long-term capital gains rates. That is true only if the trader writes a call that is at the money, out of the money, or within a very limited range in the money. If the call is too deep in the money (see chapter "Option Taxation" for a discussion of "qualified" covered calls) the long-term counting period may be tolled, so that even a holding period over one year may result in a short-term capital gain in the underlying. The original covered call may be qualified under this rule, only to roll out of the money to a deeper level, unintentionally creating an unqualified call. So the original covered call may have been out of the money, but given today's underlying market value, a rolled call complicates the tax consequences. From the trader's point of view, the forward roll is merely a strategic replacement of one call with another. But from the tax point of view, each short call is treated as a separate position. So the original, closed at a loss, will result in a current-year short-term capital loss, and the new call may be treated as a new and unqualified covered call. If that is exercised, the underlying stock may be taxed at higher short-term rates.

Lost Opportunity Risk

The tax risk of rolling covered calls makes it essential that any rolling for covered calls should keep the tax rules in mind. Ignoring this could result in much greater tax liabilities due to loss of the favorable long-term tax rate on the underlying stock.

Beyond the tax consequences, covered calls involve two specific forms of risk. First is the risk most options traders think about as a primary concern, which is the *lost opportunity risk* of covered calls. If the underlying price moves higher than the call's strike, the risk of exercise becomes apparent, especially near expiration. If the trader takes no action (closing the position or roiling forward), the ITM call will be exercised. The lost opportunity is equal to the net difference between the strike of the short call and the current market value per share at the time of exercise. The greater the difference, the greater the loss. For example, a covered call's strike is 65 and it is exercised when the underlying price has risen to 72. The seven points (72–65) is the lost opportunity.

The second form of risk is often overlooked by traders. If the value per share in the underlying falls below the net basis, a paper loss results (and is realized only if shares are sold). For example, the purchase price of stock was $64 per share, and a 65 call was sold for 3 ($300). The net basis is $61 per share (64–3). If the underlying price falls below the net basis of $61 per share, the position is at a loss.

Both of these forms of risk (lost opportunity and paper loss) are unrealized losses. The lost opportunity exists only in the sense of a profit that could have been realized if a call had not been written. The paper loss exists but becomes realized only if and when shares are sold at that net loss level. Quantifying the risk level for covered calls should include both of these forms of loss, with the understanding that the loss is not the same as realized losses in other positions.

Beyond covered calls, traders use options in other conservative strategies. These include the use of puts to insure long portfolio positions, or long calls to hedge short stock risks. These insurance trades reduce or eliminate risk at and beyond the long option's strike. Ratio writes, or the use of partially uncovered short calls against a long stock position, are considered conservative trades even with the added short option exposure. Even though risk cannot be avoided in this variation, it remains relatively low as long as the ratio itself is not extreme. For example, a 2:1 ratio write consists of one covered and one naked call. In comparison, a 3:2–4:3 ratio (three calls against 200 shares or, even safer, four calls against 300 shares) are increasingly lower-risk. The ratio write is a sensible method for using multiple option contracts to increase cash flow without greatly increasing market risk.

Moderate and Neutral Strategies

Moderate strategies include those programmed to guarantee limited profit in exchange for limited risk. Any outcome will be minimal in either event. So positions like the butterfly spread may be used to estimate short-term price movement or volatility. If volatility estimates are low, positions are appropriate that will become profitable within a narrow price range (with losses minimally fixed and to occur either above or below the profit zone). If volatility is expected to be high, the opposite position can be designed, to provide a narrow mid-range fixed or narrow-range loss, with fixed profits either above or below.

Slightly greater risks occur in positions with fixed middle-zone losses and increasing profit ranges either above or below that middle zone. These positions may be synthetic as they reproduce price action in the underlying stock, but for a highly leveraged cost structure.

A greater level of risk occurs in the simple but widely practiced single-option long position. Ironically, long option positions are normally the entry level allowed by brokerage firms for new option traders. Three-quarters of these positions held to expiration will expire worthless. However, the true risk is far less than it seems at first glance. Only those options held to expiration suffer the three-quarter level of loss. A majority of long options are closed well before expiration, so the true loss exposure is much lower. The actual statistics reveal that the often-cited 75% loss statistic is misleading. The actual outcomes:

- 10% of option contracts are exercised
- 55%–60% of option contracts are closed prior to expiration
- 30%–35% of option contracts expire worthless (out-of-the-money with no intrinsic value)[5]

The advantage of buying calls or puts is that the dollar amount is small compared to the purchase of stock, and losses are always limited to the amount paid for premium at the time positions are opened. Considering the need to overcome time value decay while building intrinsic value in a long position, long options are moderately risky. The long position trader relies on a combination of profitable volatility plus rapid price change in the underlying before expiration.

High-risk strategies include naked options, especially when positions involve multiple contracts. The naked put has limited risk because a stock's price can only fall so far, and the naked put's actual market risk is identical to the market risk of the covered call. When a naked put is in the money, exercise can be avoided by rolling forward. A roll forward and down also reduces potential losses by lowering the eventual price of stock. The ideal forward-down roll creates a net credit while exchanging an ITM short put for an OTM short put. Exercise can occur at any time, but it is most likely to occur right before expiration or on the last trading day. So the short put writer has an advantage in the majority of instances, because exercise can be avoided through the forward roll or by closing the position.

The short call is higher risk than the short put because a stock's price, in theory at least, can rise indefinitely. The unknown highest possible price of a stock is potentially an expensive problem, because the call seller has to make up the difference between strike and market value. Naked call risks are considerable, but they can be mitigated or limited by purchasing higher-strike calls or purchasing shares of the underlying. While these mitigating trades cost money, they also cut or stop the risk from growing further. Naked call writing risks are mitigated by timing decisions to coincide with upside price spikes above the prevailing trading range, especially when the spike has gapped strongly and a reversal is expected. The risk is further reduced when the time to expiration is short (under 10 days), so that time decay will be at its highest.

Naked (uncovered) call writers can avoid exercise with a forward roll. Rolling to the same strike avoids exercise while creating a net credit in the exchange of one option for another. However, rolling forward and up reduces the potential loss if and when exercised. In theory, exercise can be avoided indefinitely through a series of forward rolls. However, margin requirements should also be considered. The higher the potential exercise cost (growing as underlying market value moves farther from the fixed strike), the higher the margin requirement will be; so traders with limited funds may need to sell other holdings simply to maintain the short call position. The ideal roll forward and up creates a net credit while also replacing an ITM short call with an OTM short call position. This represents an exchange of intrinsic value for time value, which can be profitable as long as the underlying remains at or below the strike. When that occurs, the premium value will decay rapidly as expiration approaches; but the short call position remains high-risk as long as the underlying stock is volatile or when the situation is evolving and difficult to predict.

The greatest option market risks occur in short positions involving multiple contracts. Even if margin requirements can be met to keep these positions in good status with the broker standards and federal requirements, the market risk may change rapidly as prices of the underlying evolve. Rolling achieves a delay in exercise and, in many cases, avoidance. However, some short option traders have been taken by surprise when early exercise creates losses far greater than their premium income, or when the price performance of the underlying maintains option premium value due to implied volatility trends. Early exercise is most likely immediately before ex-dividend date, resulting from a dividend capture strategy, gaining a quarterly dividend with a holding period of only a few days (owning long calls with the intention of exercise before ex-dividend and then selling shares soon after). Depending solely on time decay is not adequate. If option writers tend toward the more volatile issues, the decay in time value may be offset easily with extrinsic value premium, even as expiration approaches.

Inflation and Tax Risk

Inflation Risk

Inflation is the loss of purchasing power, although it is more often thought of as rising prices, which is the opposite side of the same inflationary trend. One investment and trading goal is to offset lost purchasing power from inflation, through profits. To understand how this affects capital value, a highly conservative and risk-sensitive approach might be to make no trades at all; but this only gives way to the eroding force of declining purchasing power. The problem all investors and traders face is balancing risk tolerance with the need to outperform inflation.

The role of inflation in true investment returns is not a settled matter; considerable controversy makes inflation more complex than it appears at first glance. Between 1965 and 1981, the New York Stock Exchange Index declined by 68%, including average returns and dividends. Most experts assign the cause of this net negative return to inflation.[6]

However, beyond inflation by itself, others have pointed to the combined impact of inflation and taxes, which together drastically increase the net return required to break even.[7]

An analysis of this inflation and tax impact begins with a summary of inflation over a 30-year period. From 1987 to 2017, the Consumer Price Index (CPI) grew from 113.6 to 244.786.[8] This index is based on the starting point in 1982–1984 where the index began at a value of 100. A complete chart showing growth in the CPI since 1987 is shown in Fig. 1.

This analysis reveals that one dollar in 1987 had an inflated value of $113.60, and by 2017 the same dollar had increased to $244.79. For investors, this means that $244.79 was required in 2017 to match the purchasing power of a 1987 dollar valued at $113.60 (or a 1982–1984 dollar valued at $1.00).

The ramification for investors is that net profit has to beat the growth in inflation just to maintain purchasing power from one year to the next. So if inflation averages 2% per year, a 2% return on investment is only a breakeven rate. Inflation has reduced the value of a 2% return to zero, based on an equivalent 2% inflation rate. The risk of earning less than the rate of inflation may also be termed purchasing power risk.

Tax Risk

Closely related to inflation are the tax issues involved with options trading, where two types of tax risk have to be considered. Chapter "Option Taxation" describes the tax rules for option traders, including how long-term capital gains rates may be lost with certain kinds of trading activity. The following explains how tax planning may reduce liabilities by timing current-year losses, versus gains in future years.

The first tax consideration for options involves the timing of profits and losses. A seller (such as a covered call writer) receives the premium income in the tax year that the position is opened. But the profit is not taxed until the tax year when the position is closed or expires. Similar advantages may be gained by opening synthetic positions involving the sale of a put at the same time

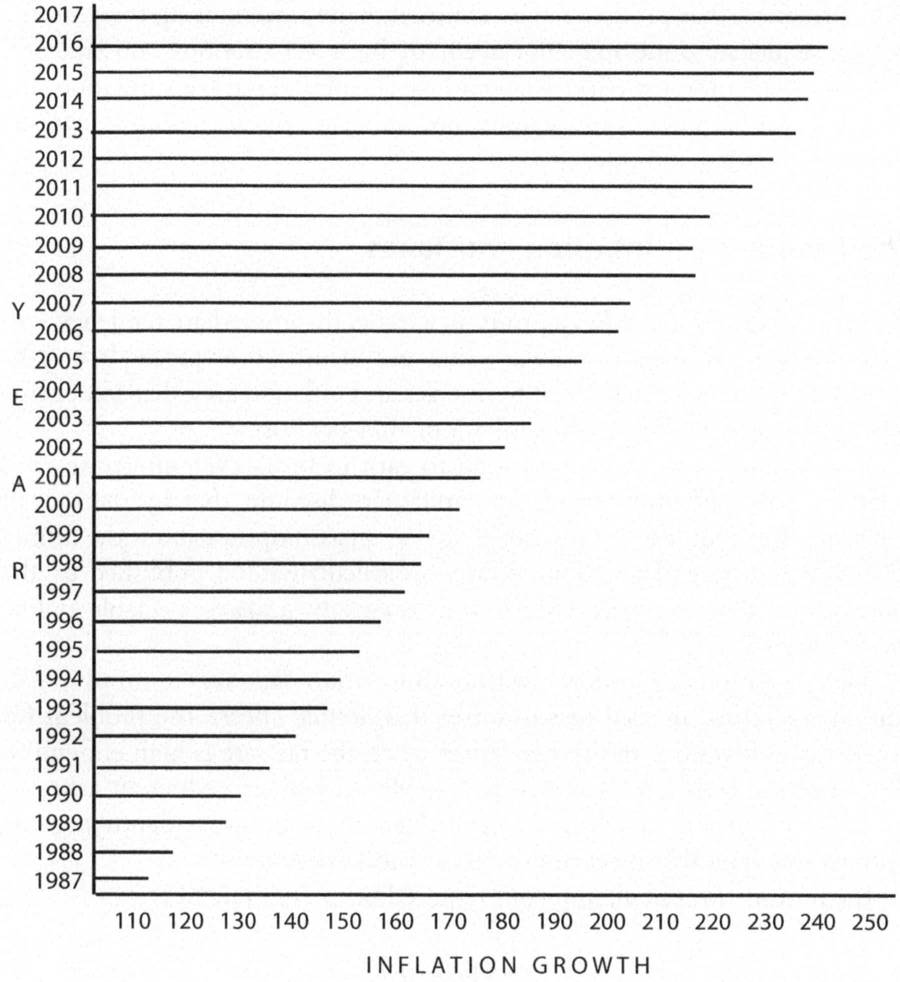

Fig. 1 Consumer Price Index (CPI), 1987–2017

stock is sold. The sale of stock may be timed to create a tax loss in the current year, and the put used to create a synthetic replacement position. From the tax point of view, this will be treated as a wash sale if the short put is exercised within 30 days, and the desired current-year tax loss will not be allowed. So tax risk has to include as part of a planning and timing system a complete understanding of tax rules and penalties under some circumstances.

Another version of tax risk is the discounting of profits based on tax liabilities. For example, if your combined federal and state effective tax rate (the rate charged on taxable income) is 40%, then only 60% of pretax profits can be counted accurately as after-tax net gains.

Considering that profits may be churned many times during the year, the tax consequence alone may not seem to be a very serious consequence. However, when the tax effect is taken into account along with inflation, the situation can be much more serious, not only for option trading but for all forms of investing and trading.

The Double Hit—Inflation *and* Taxes

When an option trader takes a profit on a trade, the immediate tendency is to mentally count it at its full dollar value and identify it as profit. It may be surprising to discover that when both taxes and inflation are calculated, some profits may actually be net after-inflation, after-tax losses.

To determine how much you need to earn to break even after taxes and inflation, calculate after-tax income and then discount that by the rate of inflation. This requires an estimate as well as an assumption about the immediate inflation rate. These annual rates are calculated and published by the Bureau of Labor Statistics (BLS), with quarterly updates available online (www.bls.gov).

The calculation of breakeven with both inflation and taxes in mind reveals the rate of return needed just to offset this double effect. The problem for conservative investors and traders arises when the tax rate is high enough so that the breakeven rate of return is possible only by exceeding an assumed personal risk profile. A solution to this dilemma is found in identifying safe options strategies that meet or exceed the breakeven rate.

The formula for calculating your required breakeven rate of return is:

$$I \div (100 - T)$$

I = inflation rate
T = effective rat rate

For example, if the current inflation rate is 3% and your effective tax rate (combining both federal and state) is 40%, your breakeven is:

$$3\% \div (100 - 40) = 5\%$$

You need to earn 5% on your overall investing and trading just to break even after taxes and inflation. That rate of return preserves your purchasing power but creates zero profit. So you have to exceed 5% overall rate of return to earn any real net profits.

Table 1 Breakeven rates

Effective tax rate	Inflation rate 1%	2%	3%	4%	5%	6%
14%	1.2%	2.3%	3.5%	4.7%	5.8%	7.0%
16%	1.2	2.4	3.6	4.8	6.0	7.1
18%	1.2	2.4	3.7	4.9	6.1	7.3
20%	1.3	2.5	3.8	5.0	6.3	7.5
22%	1.3	2.6	3.8	5.1	6.4	7/7
24%	1.3%	2.6%	3/9%	5.3%	6.6%	7.9%
26%	1.4	2.7	4.1	5.4	6.8	8.1
28%	1.4	2.8	4.2	5.6	6.9	8.3
30%	1.4	2.9	4.3	5.7	7.1	8.6
32%	1.5	2.9	4.4	5.9	7.4	8.8
34%	1.5%	3.0%	4.5%	6.1%	7.6%	9.1%
36%	1.6	3.1	4.7	6.3	7.8	9.4
38%	1.6	3.2	4.8	6.5	8.1	9.7
40%	1.6	3.2	5.0	6.7	8.3	10.0
42%	1.7	3.4	5.2	6.9	8.6	10.3

This is where option returns become so valuable. Many traders discover that they cannot earn their breakeven rate in their portfolio without raising their acceptable risk level. However, with option strategies such as covered calls, this risk element can be overcome. The returns from covered call writing, which are low risk but high-yield, can be used to enhance an otherwise average rate of return in a portfolio.

To calculate a breakeven requirement in your portfolio, check Table 1.

The higher your effective tax rate and the rate of inflation, the higher your breakeven rate is going to be. If you earn less than the breakeven rate, you are losing money after inflation and taxes. Inflation and tax risk is difficult to overcome without employing high-return but conservative options strategies.

Portfolio Risks

Stock investors spend considerable time and energy in trying to allocate their portfolio exposure, reduce losses, and anticipate future trends within the market. Emphasis is placed on diversification, asset allocation, and leverage. Within all of these concerns, options are effective for reducing and managing risk. However, the use of options as portfolio management tools also brings up the problems of two other kinds of risk: collateral and margin risk, and liquidity risk. Many practical strategies will be inappropriate for a trader whose understanding of these risk variations is minimal.

Collateral and Margin Risk

The fact that collateral is required for some forms of options trading is confusing, due to the use of the term "margin." The rules for stock and options are not identical. Trading stock on margin requires 50% payment, with the remaining 50% financed by your brokerage firm within the margin account. This form of leverage increases the potential of profit, but it also increases risks. For example, a $10,000 stock purchase on margin combines $5000 cash with $5000 borrowed. If the stock's value rises to $14,000 and then is sold, the $5000 is repaid to the brokerage firm and the investor receives $9000. This represents an 80% return before calculating interest paid to the brokerage firm:

Cash paid	$5000
Net proceeds	$9000
Net profit	$4000
Return	*$4000 ÷ $5000 = 80%*

However, in the same investment, assume the stock value declines from $10,000 down to $7000. In this case, the $5000 borrowed is repaid to the brokerage, and the remaining $2000 belongs to the investor. This represents a 60% net loss:

Cash paid	$5000
Net proceeds	$2000
Net loss	$3000
Negative return	*−$3000 ÷ $5000 = −60%*

The benefits of leverage cannot be ignored, but neither should the risk. Buying and selling shares of stock on margin contains the elements of opportunity and risk, but the risk side is overlooked easily. For many who are unaware of the leverage risk, the ability to finance one-half of a stock purchase is attractive, and this is enticing; but it ignores the risk exposure in the same trade.

For options, margin works differently. It does not represent borrowed money, but varying levels of collateral that option traders are required to have in the margin account. A purchase of a long option requires 100% cash payment at the time of the trade. A short position requires deposit in the margin account of 20% of the strike value, adjusted by the amount of premium received. A combination of long and short positions with the same expiration requires calculation of the net difference in strikes, and then a level of collateral based on the risk this involves.

Valuable resources: To study the rules of options collateral requirements, download the free *Margin Manual* from the CBOE, at http://www.cboe.com/LearnCenter/pdf/margin2-00.pdf. Also download the free margin calculator, also from the CBOE, at http://www.cboe.com/trading-tools/calculators/margin-calculator.

Liquidity Risk

Every trader needs to determine when and why to execute trades. One of the great risks for the stock portfolio is easily resolved with the use of options. This portfolio risk arises when stockholders decide to take profits.

The tendency in this scenario is to sell holdings as soon as profits are earned. These paper profits may disappear if prices reverse, so the profits are taken to avoid loss, even when the investor would prefer to continue owning shares. Applied throughout the portfolio, this decision has the result of selling off all of the winners and keeping all of the laggards. This risk, which may also be called liquidity risk, is one in which all investment capital ends up in underperforming issues. Money cannot be transferred out without taking losses. Thus, liquidity risk can also be called lost opportunity risk. With capital committed in this manner, it is impossible to move capital quickly when market conditions present bargains.

An option-based solution eliminates liquidity risk. Assuming that a stockholder prefers to hold stock for the long term, it is illogical to take profits early and dispose of stock. However, with the use of options, it is possible to maintain a portfolio and take profits without selling shares of stock. When prices rise rapidly creating an unexpected higher value, stockholders can take those profits by writing covered calls to generate cash, or by buying long puts to insure paper profits. If the stock's price retreats, either of these positions will become profitable. These are forms of hedging based on the use of options.

With the covered call is that as a short position, the trader receives the premium at the time the position is opened. Time favors the short position so that the chances of a profitable outcome are high. Ideally, the covered call should expire within a short period of time (two weeks or less) and the strike should be at least one increment out of the money. Because the call is covered, no collateral is required as long as 100 shares are also held.

The advantage in the long call is that shares cannot be called away. The disadvantage is that as a long position, a premium must be paid. It also requires movement in the underlying stock's price to create a profit. The purpose of the covered call is significantly different. It is set up only partially to create profits. The greater purpose is to create potential profits if and when the underlying stock's price declines.

A related version of liquidity risk is the selection of covered calls that end up in the money, producing net return of limited dollars. If you have to hold short positions open in this scenario until expiration, it also means the underlying stock cannot be sold, as it has to be kept intact to cover the potential exercise of the short call. The solution to this problem is to limit covered call writing to fairly short-term positions (two weeks or less), so that time value evaporates at its greatest speed. In addition, while exercise has to be acceptable as one possible outcome, conditions change. It may be worthwhile to close short option positions at a loss and replace them with other short calls, sell the stock, or wait and see how the stock behaves.

Knowledge and Experience Risk

Additional forms of risk relate to a trader's knowledge and experience. Brokerage firms are required to determine that a trader has adequate knowledge and experience before allowing an option trading account to be opened. This usually is limited, however, to filling out an application form and funding a margin account. Approval consists mainly in ensuring that adequate funds are available to cover initial margin, and that the individual has at least made a claim to having some knowledge and experience in option trading. Brokerage firms further impose varying trading approval levels to control investor and trader risks. This application process protects the brokerage firm in the event an investor experiences losses and then claims that the brokerage firm should not have allowed trading with unknown risks.

The initial, lowest approval level is restricted to taking up long positions only. As each level is advanced, more complex strategies (and greater risk levels) are allowed. In the highest level, traders are allowed to write short straddles and spreads, or to sell naked options. This all assumes adequate available cash and securities are on hand for margin requirements. Ironically, many advanced spreads and combinations are lower-risk than the more basic long call or put. However, approval levels are set so that a new options trader starts out trading the easiest to understand positions. More experienced traders know this, and tend to focus on short volatility positions (selling versus buying options). As a result, these experienced traders:

> use spreads and combinations to construct portfolios which are highly sensitive to some risk factors and much less sensitive to other risk factors. The most popular combination designs are those yielding portfolios which are quite sensitive to

> volatility and less sensitive to directional changes in the underlying asset value—though they are often not completely delta neutral. Among these, combinations which are short volatility significantly out-number those which were long.[9]

It may be assumed from this analysis that experienced traders gravitate to short volatility trades because positive outcomes are more likely. However, this strategic understanding has to be based on knowledge of not only potential profits, but also higher risk levels. Any complex strategy requires both knowledge and experience, logically. Traders cannot fully appreciate the levels of risk they are entering without these attributes, and knowledge and experience often are gained in an expensive manner. Knowledge is acquired through extensive reading, research, and observation of how markets work. Many websites (notably the Chicago Board Options Exchange) offer free paper trading links. This allows less experienced traders to try out options trading without real money placed at risk. A paper trade is different from a trade with real money, but it provides the new trader with some insight about how a trade actually works and what can go wrong.

Experience is gained in one respect by losing money in the market. Unfortunately, human beings do not learn as much from success as from failure. A stock portfolio can be nicely enhanced with a well-chosen range of options strategies; to gain experience in these, new traders need to move cautiously and slowly. Some basic trading guidelines need to be agreed upon and followed. For example, as conservative a strategy as a covered call is, the trader should be sure to understand exactly what happens when a call is exercised. For each exercise, 100 shares of stock are called away at the strike price. The covered call writer will see 100 shares taken from the portfolio and paid for at the strike at a time when the market value is higher than the call's strike. This has to be an acceptable outcome in order for covered call writing to make sense. Too many covered call writers enjoy receiving cash when they sell the call, but are upset, even surprised, when their 100 shares are called away. At this point, investors also experience the lost opportunity arising from selling 100 shares below current market value.

As the new trader gains experience, techniques improve as well. Picking the best possible call in terms of strike proximity to current market value, time to expiration, and premium income levels, all become matters learned with experience. Covered call writers learn, for example, that with higher volatility, the return is greater but market risks for the underlying stock are higher as well. Options are best selected on stocks of appropriate risk levels (meaning fundamentally strong companies), and not that stocks based on how rich the option premium is at the moment. Experienced covered call writers also gain skill at the timing of rolling forward to avoid exercise, and in the selection of appropriate replacement calls in a forward roll.

Diversification and Asset Allocation Risk

Another form of experience and knowledge is gained from diversifying risk. The focus on diversification easily overlooks the importance of ensuring that diversification is effective. Options provides one form of diversification in portfolios with many different risk profiles.

For many, diversification means distributing capital among several different stocks. This is a very basic form of diversification, but it may not be enough. If all of the stocks in a portfolio react to market trends in the same way, diversification is not effective. Owning stocks in the same industry sector is one common problem, but even owning stocks subject to the same economic cycles presents the same ineffective diversification attributes. Diversification should extend far beyond spreading money among different stocks.

It also makes sense to diversify in terms of risk exposure. Buying insurance puts to offset possible losses in long stock positions is a form of diversification as well as a hedging strategy. Using options for a range of risks while limiting capital exposure is also effective.

Hedging, however, contains risks of its own. In some forms of option hedging, the practice might lead to changes in value from external events and even the creation of unintended and unexpected losses:

> Option hedging contains significant operational risk, for instance, due to the high volume of activity involved there can exist risks due to (for example) accounting reconciliation, data entry, and failed reporting, thus increasing probability of making errors in the process of rebalancing … option hedging contains significant operational risk … it is theoretically or fundamentally difficult to reduce it without incurring hedging errors. Furthermore, the operational risk of option hedging can be amplified due to the low margin requirements in option trading.[10]

Thus, hedging may be perceived as a cure-all but beyond the basic value—creating offsetting positions to reduce or eliminate market risk in equity positions—a hedge, if relied upon excessively, might not be as effective as initially assumed. For example, purchasing long puts for insurance against market risk places an additional inhibiting factor on what is required for breakeven or profit. Not only must the equity value exceed the cost of the put to justify the hedge; it also must move farther in order to yield profits and avoid net losses. In the event of decline in the underlying value, the net insurance protection is reduced by the cost of the put trade. And so, in entering a hedge using options, the net protection *and* exposure need to be well understood in advance, to ensure that the hedge strategy is realistic and reasonable.

If hedging is a replacement for diversification, it may be an effective method for controlling market risk. However, beyond shares of stock as equity positions, investors may also wish to distribute their portfolio among different types of investments, a form of diversification also called asset allocation. Some percentage of capital is placed in stocks, debt securities, highly liquid accounts, real estate, and futures as an example of broad asset allocation.

Just as a portfolio can be under-diversified, it can also be over-diversified. If investment capital is spread too thinly, the overall rate of return is going to perform at average rates of return for the market, at best. This usually means that considering inflation and taxes, the portfolio returns will not even reach the breakeven point. In spite of the popularity of mutual funds over many decades, the industry average has under-performed the overall market, due to fees charged to investors, and to over-diversification: "On the whole, the average mutual fund returns about 2 percentage points less per year to its shareholders than the general stock market does."[11]

To outperform the market in a broadly diversified portfolio, investors need to either raise their acceptable risk level or find an alternative to just buying stocks. Safe option strategies, notably the covered call, solve some over-diversification problems. It is more profitable to limit diversification and to use carefully selected options to improve net return.

Other Forms of Risk

Beyond the forms of risk often discussed in any publication concerning either stock or option trading, some forms of risk are less frequently brought up. These include leverage risk and the risks articulated through alpha and beta.

Leverage Risk

By definition, options are a form of leverage. However, this does not mean that all options represent high levels of risk.

The methods of using capital define the overall rate of return. Leverage models often claim great potential but fail to address the risks involved in a particular approach. So over-leverage invariably will involve cash flow issues, such as the need to fund borrowings on margin; margin calls when values decline in long positions or increase in short positions; and potentially higher losses than the trader's risk tolerance finds acceptable. However, the cash flow question raises even greater risk issues. Use of capital has to take into account how future cash flows are estimated. This is not a precise version of probability:

> The imprecision we encounter when judging or estimating future cash flows is not stochastic in nature, and the use of probability theory gives us a misleading level of precision and a notion that consequences somehow are repetitive. This is not the case, the uncertainty is genuine, i.e. we simply do not know the exact levels of future cash flows.[12]

This points out that leverage risk is not limited to the simple analysis of how to best use capital to expand exposure (to profit or loss). It raises the question of speculation and involves leverage for both speculation and risk hedging. Leverage risk is especially severe when traders speculate with stock. Using margin accounts to maximum allowable levels in order to swing trade is not necessary risky in terms of market risk, but is likely to be severely high-risk in terms of leverage. Borrowed funds have to be repaid from profits or, if losses occur, additionally funded to maintain minimum margin. This presents a significant risk for stock investors.

A solution to the common leverage problems speculators face is to not use stock in strategic approaches like day trading or swing trading, but to use options instead. The leverage value of options in place of stock is considerable, and for a small fraction of the cost of buying 100 shares, a single option facilitates control of 100 shares with much lower risks. Swing trading involves buying at the bottom and selling at the top in its most basic form; thus, a sell set-up for swing trading is risky if it involves going short on stock. However, instead of buying and selling shares, swing traders may buy calls at the bottom and buy puts at the top of the swing cycle. This further reduces market risk exposure while employing option-based leverage to minimize and replace margin-based leverage.

Option traders need to manage specific risks inherent in the options market itself. However, options can also be used to mitigate, reduce, or completely eliminate many stock-based market and portfolio risks. When used appropriately, options are effective hedging tools. The more conservative, long-term value investor can also use options to improve cash income, take profits without having to sell stock, and reduce the risks of swing trading speculation as part of the stock-based portfolio.

Alpha and Beta Risk

Two calculated attributes of investing have to be included in the range of portfolio risks. These are *alpha* and *beta* risk.

Alpha measures performance of an investment and represents the net difference between return on one security versus returns on a market index or other benchmark. For example, if an investment earns 5% and during the same period, the Dow Jones Industrial Average (DJIA) earns 4%, the investment's alpha is 25 (5% ÷ 4% = 1.25, or 25%). If the investment had earned 2.5%, alpha on a 5% benchmark outcome would be −50%. A benchmark may be a market index like the DJIA, a Treasury Bill return, or any number of other broader market indicators. Investment managers, notably in mutual funds, cite alpha to demonstrate broadly how a fund has performed.

The beta coefficient measures the volatility of an investment relative to the overall market or a benchmark. A beta of 1 reveals that an investment is performing exactly at the same level as the market. When beta is less than 1, is means the investment is under-performing, and a beta above 1 reveals that an investment is outperforming.

Alpha and beta are useful for taking the temperature of a portfolio, and quantifying the performance of actual investments versus expectations. Because the performance of individual securities is subject to volatility due to an array of causes, the use of options to insure or hedge positions helps to keep alpha and beta close to market average performance and outcomes.

Fundamental Risk

The typical risks investors and traders focus on are technical in nature. These risks relate to a security's price behavior and the many ways that risks arise after a position has been opened. Beyond the technical, a range of fundamental risks—those risks associated with the organization and its profitability, cash controls, or unplanned events—also affect the technical side, so that prices of stocks and options are influenced directly.

Acquisition and Merger Risk

Among these fundamental risks, the acquisition or merger may immediately affect a security's price with no advance warning. In some instances, an announcement is made that one organization is planning to make an offer to acquire another; however, the price is not announced. In other cases, by the time the deal is announced, it is a done deal.

For example, Whole Foods was trading at $33 per share when the announcement was made that Amazon.com was buying the company for $42 per share, a jump of 27%. The stock price moved as expected, and other retailers, such as Sprouts, Kroger and Wal-Mart, all declined the same day. Any trader holding shares of Whole Foods (or of those other retailers) would have seen the immediate effect of the announcement. Anyone holding options would also experience unexpected profits or losses, depending on whether they held calls or puts, and on whether they were long or short.

Reputation or Bankruptcy Risk

Another fundamental risk occurs when an organization's reputation is damaged by events in its market. In 2017, Equifax (EFX) announced it had suffered a major data breach affecting more than 140 million people. Its stock price plummeted from $143 to $90 per share in only six days, before taking back some of the loss and settling at $107 per share. The change in share price is shown in Fig. 2.

The dramatic decline in the stock price came as a surprise not only to those holding shares of Equifax, but also to options traders with open positions. Although this level of surprise is rare, it does occur; and it points out the fact that fundamental issues (like the severity of the Equifax data breach) directly impact stock and option values.

Similar surprises have occurred in the past, including the news several years ago that Enron's financial statements had exaggerated profits and excluded liabilities. The news affected not only Enron but also its independent auditor, Arthur Andersen, Enron's independent auditing firm, was forced out of business as a consequence of its involvement in the deception of Enron stockholders.

When publicly traded companies go out of business, it is more severe as a market risk than many investors realize. A comparison between 1955 and 2016 reveals that only 12% of Fortune 500 companies as of 50 years ago were still in

Chart courtesy of StockCharts.com

Fig. 2 Equifax stock chart

business 50 years later. A similar level of turnover is seen among the companies in S&P 500 and in both cases, the rate of change is increasing over time.[13]

This analysis reveals that very little of the current market of "blue chip" corporations lasts indefinitely. This is only partly due to obsolescence of product or service. It is also caused by declining attention paid by management to the customer, to competition, and to the importance of keeping an edge throughout the markets served. A good example of this is Eastman Kodak, a company that refused to get into the digital camera market until much later than its competitors. Kodak held on to the idea that it was the leading film producer in the world, even long after most people had stopped using film camera technology. This is the same problem faced in the first decade of the twentieth century when automobiles were first introduced. The entire industry of blacksmithing, stables, and wagon manufacturing was changed and made obsolete in only a few years, but many refused to accept the change and ended up out of business. In 1890, there were over 13,000 wagon and carriage businesses in operation in the United States.[14]

Only a few years later, those that did not adapt were out of business. A few converted their business models from building and servicing wagons or manufacturing buggy whips, to one or more ways of working within the new automotive industry. So investors—like companies—failing to recognize change and what it means for the future, will not profit from long-term strategies in industries that become obsolete.

In the future, investors face the same risk. The Fortune 500 companies of today include companies that will not be in existence in the future, many in the near future. So the old-style buy-and-hold strategy could itself be high-risk, given the accelerating rate of change not only in the market, but in which companies will remain part of that market. Both stock investors and options traders will need to adjust risk-based thinking in order to ensure profitability in coming years. This is where hedging with options can provide protection for equity positions in the portfolio. The question every investor has to ask is: Will the companies in my portfolio today contain fundamental value next year or the year after?

Earnings Surprises

Companies come and go, at times unpredictably. A more common occurrence, though, is the quarterly earnings surprise. Even a small departure between expected earnings per share and the actual reported can cause a stock's price to spike upward with a positive outcome or downward with a negative one. In most cases, the spike is exaggerated and, over a series of days, will retreat back toward established trading range levels.

Earnings surprises help options traders to time their trades. Ignoring a coming earnings announcement can be an expensive mistake, because the difficulty is in knowing whether a surprise will be positive or negative, and whether it will be big or small. So holding an open options position the day of the announcement could be a windfall or a disaster. This is especially true for anyone holding an open short position. Those willing to speculate on prices moving in either direction can employ a variety of strategies based on the assumption that the price will move enough points to yield profits on one side of the trade or the other.

A more sensible strategic approach is to wait until the earnings results are announced, and then open an options trade based on the direction of the surprise—especially if the surprise is large and the resulting price movement is extreme. If the price reaction is extreme, the timing of the trade can be based on the contrarian approach, assuming that the degree of price movement is irrational and will be self-correcting in the short term. So after a negative surprise and a move of price gapping down, the contrarian trade would be to buy calls or sell puts, expecting a price rise in the immediate future. A positive surprise may also result in an exaggerated price spike above established levels. A contrarian swing trader would then buy puts or sell calls in the expectation of a correction to soon follow.

For example, on October 4, 2017, Monsanto (MON) announced earnings, which represented a positive surprise of 152.6% earnings per share above estimates. The price response, as expected, was also positive, as shown in Fig. 3.

The initial reaction was mild, but once it occurred, the stock price moved rapidly from the level of $117 per share up to $122. However, all of those

Fig. 3 Monsanto stock chart

gains were given back within one month. The long-term line of resistance drawn on the chart reveals that after the earnings surprise settled down, price levels continued on the long-established gradual rise in price levels.

Confirmation Bias Risk

A final variety of risk faced by options traders is not based on fundamental or technical indicators, but on perception. An analysis of *investor psychology* reveals some common pitfalls suffered by market participants. For example, stock purchasers may fall into the trap called *anchoring*, which is the belief that a beginning assumption continues to apply even after circumstances have changed. Belief that a particular company is a "good investment" might persist even when developments contradict those assumptions.

Another form of anchoring is based on a belief that the price paid when stock is first bought is a starting point, a "zero" line, and that prices will rise from that point onward. So if and when prices decline, it violates the initial assumption.

Investors are susceptible to many forms of *confirmation bias*, a tendency to accept facts confirming a belief, and to ignore or fail to even recognize facts that are contradictory. In technical analysis—for example, the study of price patterns on stock charts—confirmation bias is common, and a particular reversal signal might be accepted even when other signals point to divergent outcomes.

A related tendency is called *loss aversion*, a preference for avoiding losses over experiencing gains. In this behavior, personal reaction to a loss has a higher magnitude than a net gain. Consequently, investors may tend to take all steps to avoid losses, including holding positions open and watching small losses turn into big losses and even total losses. A sensible policy would be to cut losses and turn focus to other situations, but many investors and traders find themselves unable to take losses of any size without excessive focus. These tendencies affect outcomes in trading, as:

> biased inferences can lead to suboptimal investment behavior and anomalous market pricing. Academic finance is currently faced with the challenge of distinguishing between several potential explanations, both behavioral and rational, for a number of documented anomalies.[15]

Inferences can easily distort judgment among traders, even those who consider themselves as rational in decision-making. Another form of confirmation bias is less rational. Magical thinking is a belief or set of beliefs based on superstition or even on religion. A trader who wears a "lucky shirt" in the belief that it will lead to profitable trades is suffering from magical thinking, also termed "associative" thinking. A rational analysis reveals the obvious: there is no such thing as a "lucky shirt" or "lucky hat." But behavior often defies rational thought.

A more destructive form of magical thinking may be based on an underlying belief based on religious beliefs. If a trader believes, "I do not deserve to win," it might lead to intentional creation of high-risk trades more likely to result in losses than in profits.

The range of risks faced by every trader is extensive. Focusing only on the binary analysis of an options trade as potentially leading to a profit or a loss is only one part of the larger risk universe. However, a focus on this singular form of risk is common, and a broader view of other risks leads to more informed trade decisions.

Notes

1. Sill, K. (January–Febuary, 1997). The Economic Benefits and Risks of Derivative Securities. *The Business Review*, pp. 15–26.
2. Campbell, J. Y., Polk, C. & Vuolteenaho, T. (January 1, 2010). Growth or Glamour? Fundamentals and Systematic Risk in Stock Returns. *Review of Financial Studies*, Vol. 23, No. 1, pp. 305–344.
3. Ni, S. X., Pan, J. & Poteshman, A. M. (September 20, 2005). Volatility Information Trading in the Option Market. *The Journal of Finance*, Vol. LXIII, No. 3, pp. 1059–1091.
4. Duffie, D., Pan J. & Singleton K. (2000). Transform Analysis and Asset Pricing for Affine Jump Diffusions. *Econometrica*, Vol. 68, pp. 1343–1376.
5. Source: Chicago Board Options Exchange (CBOE).
6. Black, F. (1976). Studies of Stock Price Volatility Changes. Proceedings of the 1976 Meetings of the American Statistical Association, Business and Economic Statistics Section, pp. 177–181.
7. Feldstein, M. (December, 1980). Inflation and the Stock Market. *American Economic Review*, Vol. 70, pp. 839–847.
8. Source: Bureau of Labor Statistics (BLS), at https://www.bls.gov/cpi
9. Chaput, J. S. & Ederington, L. H. (January 1, 2003). Option Spread and Combination Trading. *Journal of Derivatives*, Vol. 10, No. 4, pp. 70–88.
10. Mitra, S. (2013). Operational Risk of Option Hedging. *Economic Modelling*, Vol. 33, pp. 194–203.
11. The basics of mutual fund investing. *The Motley Fool*. At www.fool.com/how-to-invest/the-basics-of-mutual-fund-investing.aspx, downloaded November 21, 2017.

12. Carlsson, C. & Fullér, R. (January 10, 2003). A Fuzzy Approach to Real Option Valuation. *Fuzzy Sets and Systems*, Vol. 139, No. 2, pp. 297–312.
13. Perry, M. J. (December 13, 2016). Fortune 500 firms 1955 v. 2016: Only 12% remain, thanks to the creative destruction that fuels economic prosperity. *AEIdeas*. http://www.aei.org/publication/fortune-500-firms-1955-v-2016-only-12-remain-thanks-to-the-creative-destruction-that-fuels-economic-prosperity, retrieved November 21, 2017.
14. Kinney, T. A. (2004). *The Carriage Trade: Making Horse-Drawn Vehicles in America*. Baltimore, MD: Johns Hopkins University Press, p. 263.
15. Ko, K. J. & Huang, Z. (January 3, 2012). Persistence of Beliefs in an Investment Experiment. *Quarterly Journal of Finance*, Vol. 2, No. 1, pp. 12–50.

Option Strategies

The sheer number of options strategies, when arranged alphabetically, presents ease of access but does not fully describe the varying levels of risk they entail. For that, it is necessary to track the payoff diagrams, examples, and amounts of capital required to put a strategy into place. In the following examples, actual stock prices and options premiums have been used. However, identification of a company or date of the options expirations is not necessary; the observations presented in this chapter apply in all cases, and examples are only a starting point for understanding the attributes of each strategy: long or short positions, risk levels, profit potential, and a range of possible actions that can be taken before expiration—rolling, closing, or exercising positions.

Examples exclude trading costs. Given the widespread use of online discount brokerage services in which fees are quite low, this is a minor factor. Assuming the average fee is $5 per contract, the net effect of transaction fees is not substantial. However, costs of entering and exiting positions should be taken into account in calculating potential profit. Examples generally are limited to single options. In practice, the use of multiple option contracts further reduces the transaction cost, another point to be factored in to the calculation of net outcome. Of much greater concern is the bid and ask prices and the bid/ask spread between the two values. The bid is what will be received upon the sale of an option (whether selling to open or to close), and the ask price is the price a trader pays when purchasing an option.

Tables for several of the following strategies are provided to demonstrate outcomes at various underlying price levels, assuming the full position is left open until the day of expiration for each option contract. To link to each table, go to the website at https://www.thomsettpublishing.com/option-strategies

M. C. Thomsett, *The Complete Options Trader*,
https://doi.org/10.1007/978-3-319-76505-1_4

(for the first half of the alphabet) or https://www.thomsettpublishing.com/option-strategies-n-z (for the first half of the alphabet), and from there, link to the strategy to find its table.

In practice, however, stock movement is far more likely to provide opportunities to close out part or all of a position at a profit, well before expiration date. The short side of a multiple-option strategy can be closed when time value evaporates, leaving only the long side. However, if a long side is closed due to substantial change in the price of the underlying, that may leave short positions open in uncovered status, greatly increasing risk; and also setting up a greater requirement for posting collateral in the margin account.

The majority of examples employ the least number of contracts possible. However, the use of multiple contracts may enhance profits as well as add greater risks. For example, in rolling forward to avoid exercise, replacing a single short option with two, three, or more later-expiring short contracts may produce a net credit while improving future profit potential. This is a practical consideration for writing covered calls if and when enough underlying stock is owned to provide coverage for a flexible rolling strategy. This point should be kept in mind for all strategies. The number of open contracts as well as ratio levels in combinations can be varied based on risk levels, the amount of underlying stock held, and available margin credit.

Alligator spread – any spread involving complex combinations of offsetting options, to the extent that the trading costs will potentially "eat up" any profits. It is possible to design a strategy to provide virtually no loss exposure with limited profit potential, as in the *butterfly* spread. However, if the number of offsetting positions is too great, the potential profits will not materialize on a net basis. Trading costs and broker commissions make the position impractical in many cases. Option traders also have to consider the possibility that in overly complex option spreads and combinations, they may face (a) collateral requirements, which tie up capital, and (b) unexpected tax consequences due to the *anti-straddle rules* that penalize traders entering two-sided transactions and realizing losses and profits in different years.

Bear call spread – a variation of the bear spread employing only calls and creating a net credit. The profit is maximized when the market value of the underlying stocks declines; however, risk is limited to the difference between long and short positions. The spread creates a limited maximum profit potential in exchange for a limited maximum loss. A loss occurs when the stock's price rises above both call strikes, and is limited to the point spread, minus the original credit received when the position was opened.

The breakeven on this position resides in between the two strike prices. Profit is equal to the amount of the net credit received (the bear call spread

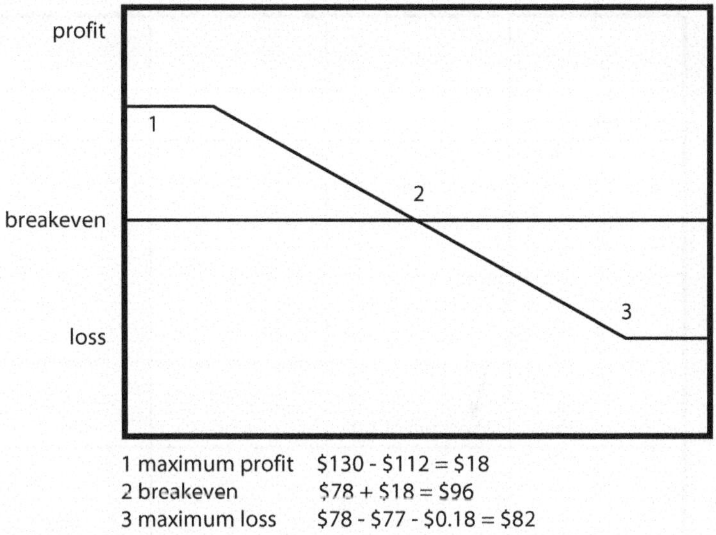

Fig. 1 Bear call spread

always creates a credit because current value of the lower short call will always exceed the value of the higher long call). The outcomes are illustrated in Fig. 1.

Example: The current underlying price is $78.14. A bear call spread is set up with the following trades:

Buy 13-day 79 call, ask 1.12
Sell 13-day 78 call, bid 1.30
  Net credit 0.18

Outcomes:

Maximum profit	*$130 – $112 = $18*
Breakeven	*$78 + $18 = $96*
Maximum loss	*$78 – $77 – $0.18 = $82*

To see a table showing outcomes at various price levels, link on **bear call spread** at the website https://thomsettsguide.com/options-strategies/

Bear put ladder – a strategy employing a long put spread and, in addition, a short put at a strike below the spread strikes. For example, a bear put ladder is set up by buying a 110 put at an ask price of 108.10 and selling a 105 put at a bid of 100. Maximum profit will be earned when the stock closes between the two short strikes by expiration. Profit would be the net of (a) the credit gained when the position was opened or, if a net debit, a negative; and (b) the

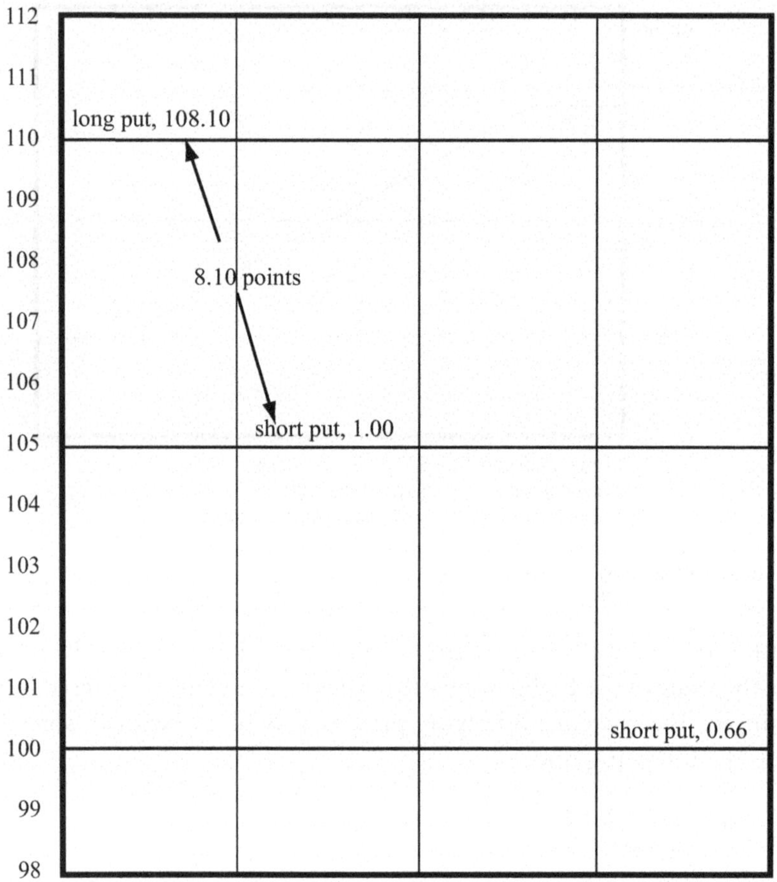

Fig. 2 Bear put ladder

point spread between the higher long and short positions. In this example, that would be five points, or $500 (110 minus 105). If the stock were to decline below the lower put's strike, exposure nets out to one uncovered put, minus the point spread described above. The structure of this position is summarized in Fig. 2.

Bear put spread – a debit spread entered into when a trader believes the underlying price is going to decline. Unlike the bear call spread which sets up a net credit, the bear put spread creates a net debit. It combines an ITM long put with an OTM short put. This sets up a limited maximum profit and loss. Breakeven is equal to the higher strike minus the net debit paid. Profit, breakeven, and loss are shown in the diagram in Fig. 3.

Example: The current underlying price is $130.01. A bear put spread is set up with the following trades:

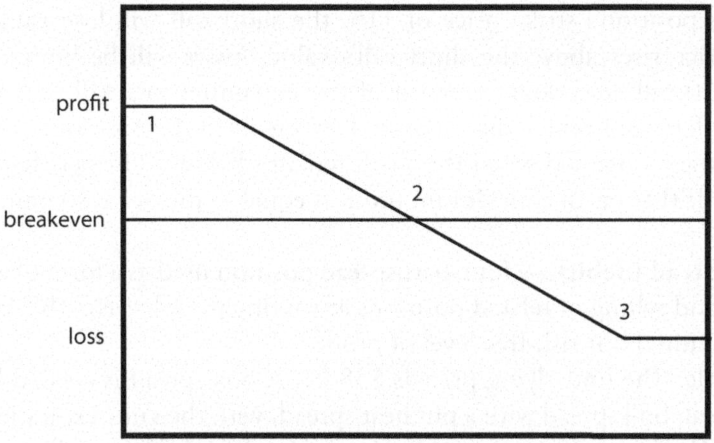

1 maximum profit $131 - $129 – 1.05 = $95
2 breakeven $131 - $1.05 = $129.95
3 maximum loss $105

Fig. 3 Bear put spread

Buy 20-day 131 put, ask 2.34
Sell 20-day 129 put, bid 1.29
Net debit 1.05

Outcomes:

Maximum profit	$131 – $129 – 1.05 = $95
Breakeven	$131 – $1.05 = $129.95
Maximum loss	$105

To see a table showing outcomes at various price levels, link on **bear put spread** at the website https://thomsettsguide.com/options-strategies/

Bear spread – any spread strategy in which the position will be profitable if the underlying stock's market value falls. The bear spread can be designed using either puts or calls.

Example of a bear spread using puts: A bear spread is created by selling a put with a lower strike and buying a put with a higher strike. This limits both profits and losses; however, profit occurs if and when the underlying stock's value falls. The previous example of a bear put spread illustrates this.

In a bear spread using calls, a higher short position is offset by a lower long position. For example, a bear spread created on an underlying trading at $108.10 is set up through buying a 120 call at 4.30 and selling a 115 call at 6.10 for a net credit of 1.80. As long as the underlying stock remains below the short position's strike price of 115, the short call will lose value; if the stock's price rises above the short call's value, losses will be limited by the higher 120 call, and dollar amount of the maximum loss will be $320 (five points difference in the strikes, minus 1.80 credit in the position). The greatest advantage is gained when the stock remains below $115 per share in this example. If that occurs, maximum profit is equal to the net 1.80 points in the position.

Box spread (debit) – a four-part spread position used as a form of arbitrage (buying and selling of related positions at varying price levels). This is used to create a limited but risk-free level of profit.

Example: The underlying price is $58.91. A box spread is created by combining a call bull spread with a put bear spread, with the same expiration for all options. The first half consists of buying a 55 call at 5.60 and selling a 60 call at 2.50. The second half consists of buying a 60 put at 2.75 and selling a 55 put at 1.20:

Buy 55 call, ask price	5.60	
Sell 60 call, bid price	2.50	
Net debit		3.10
Buy 60 put, ask price	2.75	
Sell 55 put, bid price	1.20	
Net debit		1.55
Box spread debit		4.65

This position locks in a profit of 5.00 ($500) while costing $465. Accordingly, risk has been eliminated in the position. This riskless feature can be tested at any price level:

$$\begin{aligned} \textit{Expiration Value of Box} &= \textit{Higher Strike Price} \\ &\quad - \textit{Lower Strike Price}\,(\$500) \end{aligned}$$

$$\textit{Risk} - \textit{free Profit} = \textit{Expiration Value of Box} - \textit{Net Premium Paid}\,(\$35)$$

If the stock closes above 60, the puts would both be worthless and the calls would net out at a value of 5 points, the difference between the spreads. If the stock were to close between 55 and 60, the OTM options (60 short call and 55 short put) would be worthless and the ITM options (55 long call and 60 long put) would net out with intrinsic value of 5. (No matter where expiration existed, the difference between strike prices and expiration price will always be 5.) For example, if the stock closed at 57.50, both options would be worth 2.50. If the stock closes below 55, the calls would expire worthless and the net value of the puts would be 5, the spread between the two strikes (see Fig. 4).

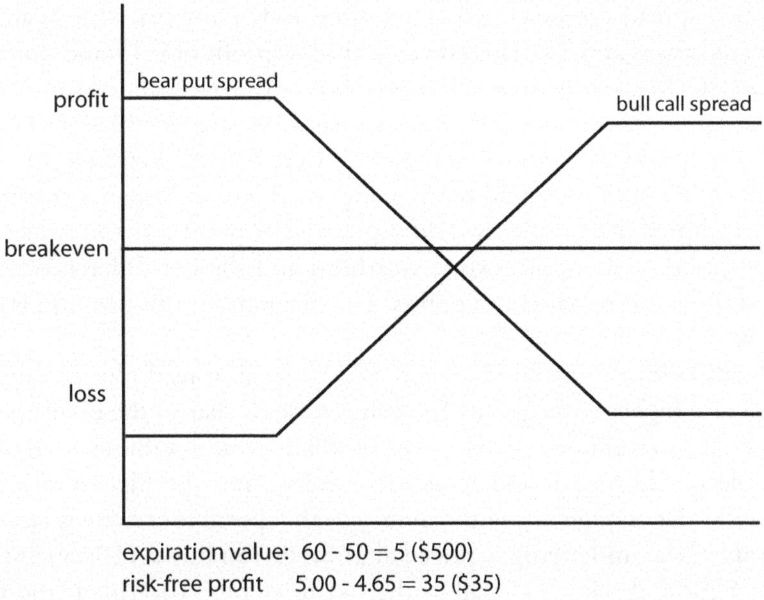

Fig. 4 Box spread (debit)

While this example ensures a breakeven at any price, the position can be used to create additional profits by exiting short positions upon decline in time value, and holding open call and put positions, converting to a simple long spread. The risk at that point consists of the original cost (5) minus profits from selling the short options. For example, if the short call and put were both closed for a net of 2, the remaining debit is 3. The position needs movement of 3 points or more, either above the long call strike of 55 or below the long put strike of 60. This narrow range requirement makes an additional small profit quite possible.

Box spread (credit) – similar to the debit spread described above, but working with a net credit instead of a debit. In this case, the trader sells the spread and creates a credit. The position can be closed (bought out) at any time at a fixed price.

Example: The underlying was worth $93.69 per share. A credit box spread is created by buying a 95 call at an ask of 4.90 and selling a 90 call at a bid of 7.94, and buying a 90 put at an ask of 3.40 and selling a 95 put at 5.50:

Buy 95 call, ask price	4.90	
Sell 90 call, bid price	7.94	
Net credit		−3.04
Buy 90 put, ask price	3.40	
Sell 95 put, bid price	5.50	
Net credit		−2.10
Box spread credit		−5.14

This box spread can be closed at any time and at any price for 5, although the net credit was at 5.14. This creates a riskless profit of 0.14 and potentially higher profits from early close of short positions due to declined time value. If the stock were to close above 95, the puts would expire worthless and the calls retain their spread of 5 points. If the stock were to close between 90 and 95, the long OTM options would both expire worthless and the net cost to close the remaining short options would remain at 5 points. If the stock closed below 90, both calls would expire worthless and the net difference between long and short put remains at 5 points. The diagram for this position is shown in Fig. 5.

Bull call ladder – the combination of a long call spread plus an additional *short* call at a higher strike price. The concept holds that in the event the stock price rises, the lowest (long) strike price call will increase in value enough to offset the mid-level (short) call and to satisfy exercise, and the highest strike price (short) call is far enough out of the money so that possible exercise is remote.

Example: The underlying is priced at 108.10. You buy a 110 call at the ask price of 8.30 and sell a 115 call at the bid price of 6.10. This is the typical spread pattern using calls. However, you also sell a 120 call for 4.30 at the same time, creating the ladder (the term "ladder" also is termed a "Christmas tree"). The net position is:

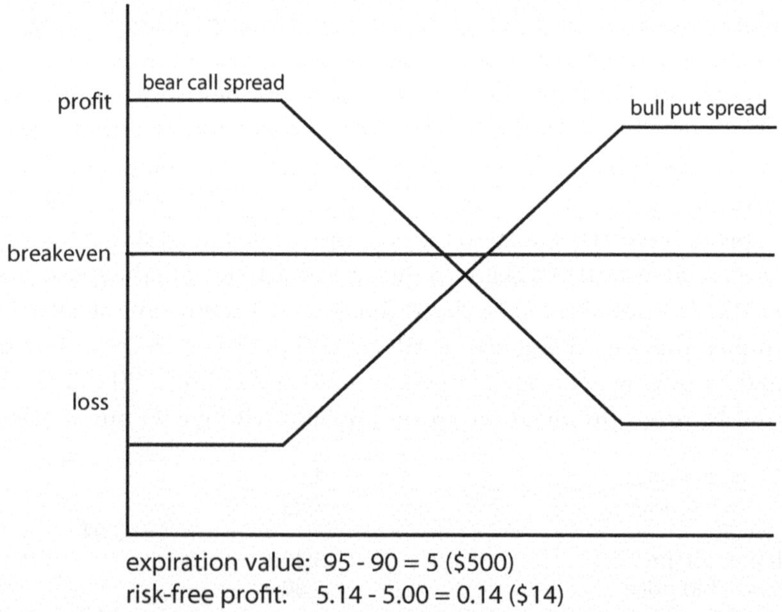

Fig. 5 Box spread (credit)

July 110 long call	−8.30
July 115 short call	6.10
July 120 short call	4.30
Net credit	2.10

If none of these positions are closed by expiration, the following profit or loss occurs:

Stock price 127 approximates a breakeven price. This consists of intrinsic value in the long call of 17 (127–110); less intrinsic value in the 115 short call of 12 and in the 120 short of 7; plus the original net credit of 2.10:

Long call profit	17.00
Short 115 call loss	−12.00
Short 120 call loss	−7.00
Original position credit	2.10
Net	0.10

Above 127, the net loss grows by two points for every point increase, due to the combination of two short positions and one long position, adjusted by a fixed 2.10 initial credit.

If the stock closes between the two short positions, profit consists of the 5-point spread between the lower short and the long, plus the initial credit of 2.10. The higher short of 120 expires worthless. For example, if the stock closes at 117:

Long call profit	7.00
Short 115 call loss	−2.00
Short 120 call expiration	0
Original position credit	2.10
Net	7.10

If the stock closes between 120 and 127, the profit declines by one dollar per point in the stock increase. For example, at 122, the 7.10 profit above falls to 5.10; and at 126, it falls to 1.10.

If the stock closes between the long and the lower short, profit consisted of long call intrinsic value plus the initial credit of 2.10. For example, if the stock closes at 112, profit would be 4.10:

Long call profit	2.00
Short 115 call expiration	0
Short 120 call expiration	0
Original position credit	2.10
Net	4.10

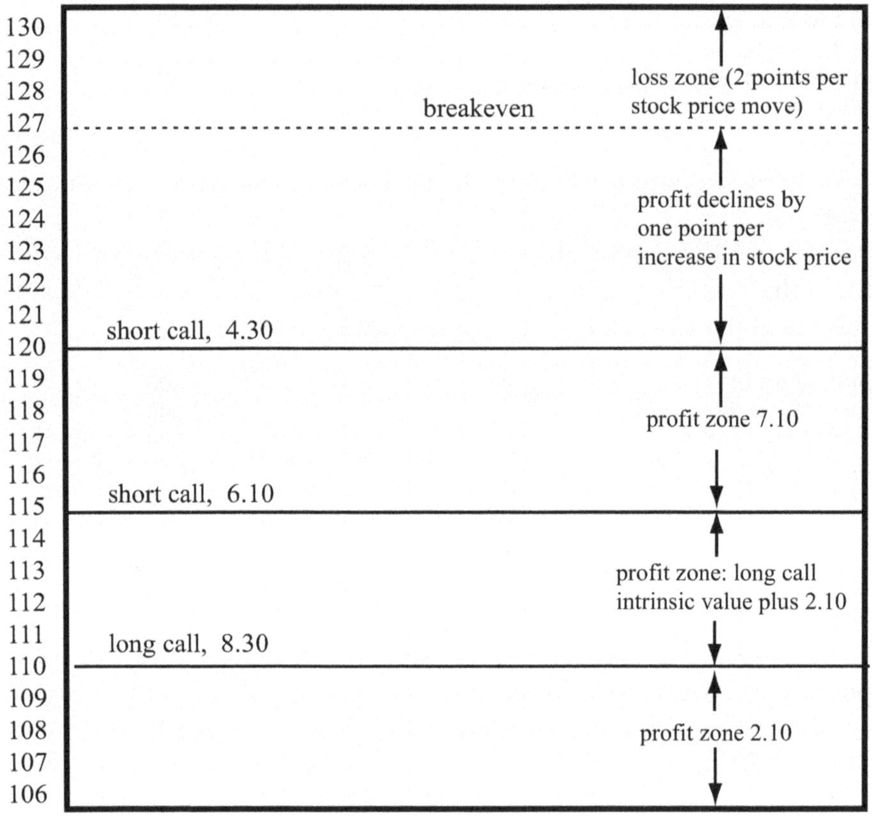

Fig. 6 Bull call ladder

If the stock closes below the long position, all options expire worthless and the initial credit of 2.10 is a fixed profit. The structure of the ladder is shown in Fig. 6.

Bull call spread – a variation of the vertical spread, designed to produce maximum profits when the underlying stock rises. This position involves a long call at one strike with a short call at a higher strike. If the same relative position is open but expiration is different for each side, it becomes a diagonal spread.

The bull call spread offers a combined limited profit and limited risk. Risk never exceeds the net cost to open the position, and the strategy is favored by many investors over a simple long call purchase because the cost is lower. Even so, the position always creates a net debit when both sides are opened at the same time, because the lower strike call trades at a higher price than those calls with higher strikes. An exception: If each side of the spread is opened at different times and based on stock price movement, an original long or short position is converted to a spread. In this case, it is possible to create a bull call spread with a net credit.

Net breakeven on this strategy resides between the two strike prices and is equal to the strike of the long call plus the net debit paid. A limited profit zone exists above the higher strike; this is always a fixed profit equal to the point difference between strikes, minus the cost to create the position. Maximum loss is realized if the underlying stock's price ends up at expiration below the lower strike. The maximum loss in the position is equal to the net debit involved in opening the position.

Example: You create a bull call spread on a stock valued at $93.69 per share. You buy a 90 call at the ask price of 4.70 and sell a 95 at the bid price of 1.45.

The payoff levels for the bull call spread are shown in Fig. 7.

To see a table showing outcomes at various price levels, link on **bull call spread** at the website https://thomsettsguide.com/options-strategies/

Bull put ladder – also called the short put ladder, this strategy combines unlimited profit potential with a limited risk. It is an effective strategy when volatility is expected to be high.

The bull put ladder consists of selling one in the money put, and buying a put at or close to the money, and buying another put out of the money. Profit will be limited if and when the stock price rises above the upper breakeven

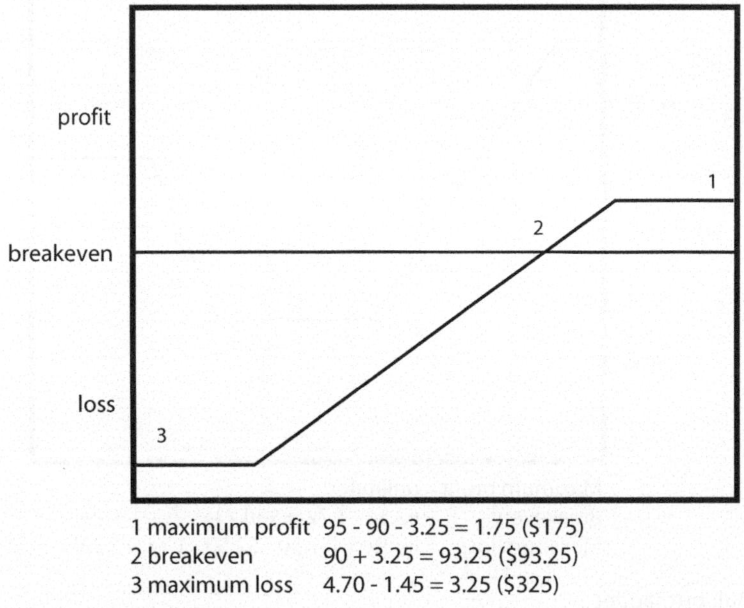

Fig. 7 Bull call spread

point; larger, potentially unlimited profits will occur if the stock price falls below the lower breakeven point. Losses will occur if the stock price closes between the strikes of the two long puts. The position has two breakeven points, one above the short put strike, and the other below the two long put strikes.

Example: The underlying is valued at $58.91. You sell a 62.50 put at the bid of 3.40; buy a 57.50 put at the ask of 1.30; and buy a 52.50 put at the ask of 0.33. The net credit you receive for this position is 1.77. The two breakeven points occur on the upside between 60 and 61 with a fixed net profit from that point upward; and on the downside between 49 and 50 per share with profit increasing dollar for dollar with decline in the stock from that point downward.

This strategy is also summarized at Fig. 8.

To see a table showing outcomes at various price levels, link on **bull put ladder** at the website https://thomsettsguide.com/options-strategies/

Bull put spread – a variation of spread using puts. This strategy combines a long put at one strike with a short put at a higher strike. The greatest potential profit is achieved when the stock price rises.

For example, the underlying is valued at 108.10. A bull put spread—to be used if you believe the stock price is going to rise—is constructed by buying a buying a 105 put at the ask of 2.95 and selling a 110 put at the bid of 5.00.

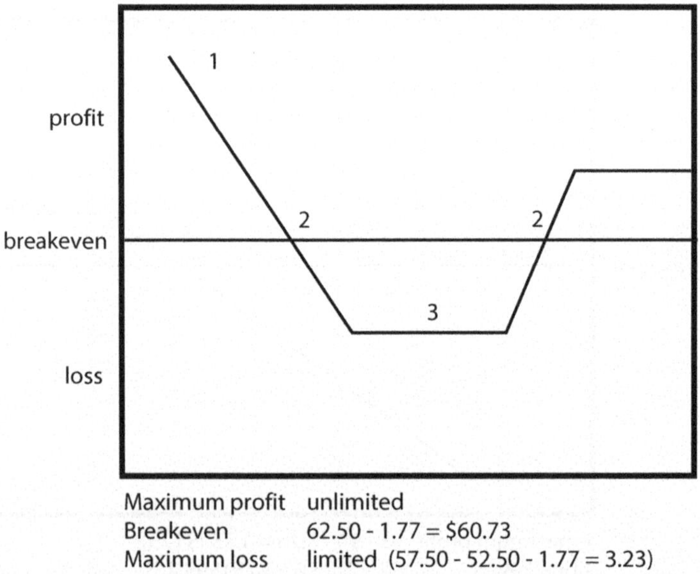

Fig. 8 Bull put ladder

The net credit in this example is 2.05. The spreads between the two strikes is five points. If the stock price rises above the higher (short) strike, the maximum profit of 2.05 ($205) will be earned since both puts will expire worthless. Risk is limited as well. If the stock closes between the two put strikes, profit or loss depends on the net credit received. If the stock price closes below the lower strike, the maximum loss of 2.95 will be realized, which is the difference between the five-point spread and the net cost of the position (5.00–2.05).

To see a table showing outcomes at various price levels, link on **bull put spread** at the website https://thomsettsguide.com/options-strategies/

The payoff diagram revealing profit, breakeven, and loss is shown in Fig. 9.

Bull spread – any spread that will produce profits when the underlying stock's market price rises. The strategy may involve either calls or puts. The trader accepts the potential of a limited profit in exchange for the limited risk.

A bull spread employing calls combines a long strike below a short strike. Because the long strike will have more ITM value if and when the underlying stock moves higher than the short call, profit is limited to the point spread between the strikes, minus the cost of creating the position.

A bull spread with puts is designed in a similar manner, and a limited profit will exist upon a rise in the underlying stock because the short put loses its premium value when out of the money. Risk is also limited because a higher long position put will offset the short put risk, plus the point spread.

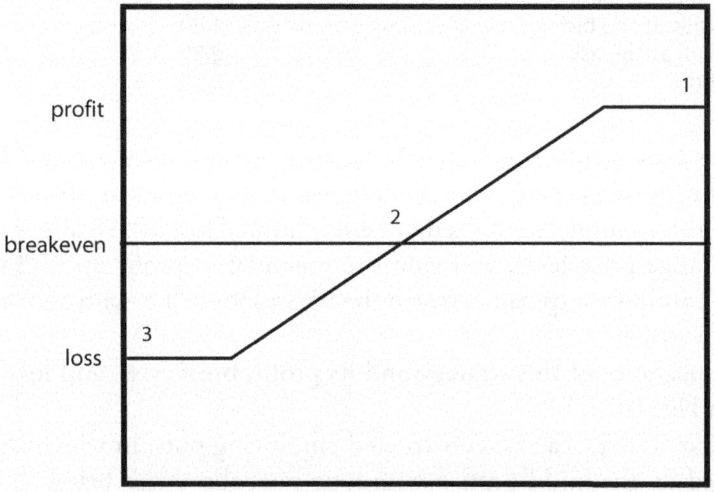

Maximum profit	5.00 - 2.95 = 2.05 ($205)
Breakeven	110 - 2.05 = 107.95 ($107.95)
Maximum loss	110 - 105 - 2.05 = 2.95 ($295)

Fig. 9 Bull put spread

Butterfly spread – a complex spread involving the simultaneous use of offsetting calls or puts. On one side, a range of strike prices are employed and offset by a range of either higher or lower strike price ranges at the same time. Traders may employ either calls or puts in the butterfly spread.

An example involving calls: The underlying is valued at $93.69. You construct a spread involving calls ranging between 85 and 95 strikes:

85 call	9.90
90 call	5.90
95 call	2.85

A butterfly spread combines two separate spreads in a single position: one a bull spread and the other a bear spread. For a relatively small cost, risk is limited. If you believe the stock will not experience much volatility between now and expiration, you may earn a limited profit from this position. However, two attributes have to be considered, given the severely limited profit potential of the butterfly. First is trading costs, which may absorb much of the maximum profit. Second is margin requirement, which expands with the number of outstanding option contracts. If the margin requirement stretches your portfolio resources, it may not be worth the exchange of limited risk and limited profit.

In the example, a butterfly is created by buying the high and low call strikes, and selling two of the middle strikes:

Buy 1 85 call at the ask	−9.90
Sell 2 90 calls at the bid	+11.80
Buy 1 95 call at the ask	−2.85
Net debit	−0.95

For less than $100, this butterfly is set up with limited risk on both the upside and the downside. The greatest risk in this position, in fact, is 0.95 ($95). In this example, for a fixed price and limited loss of $95 above or below the mid-range price level, you gain the potential of profit up to $405. The butterfly combines a spread between the 95 and 90 strike, with another at the 90 and 85 strike.

The appearance of this strategy and its profit, breakeven, and loss prices is shown in Fig. 10.

A similar strategy can be constructed employing puts, in which short puts are opened on the middle range with long puts above and below. In all butterfly spreads, the number of long and short positions is identical. (If and when a dissimilar number of options are employed, it becomes a variation of

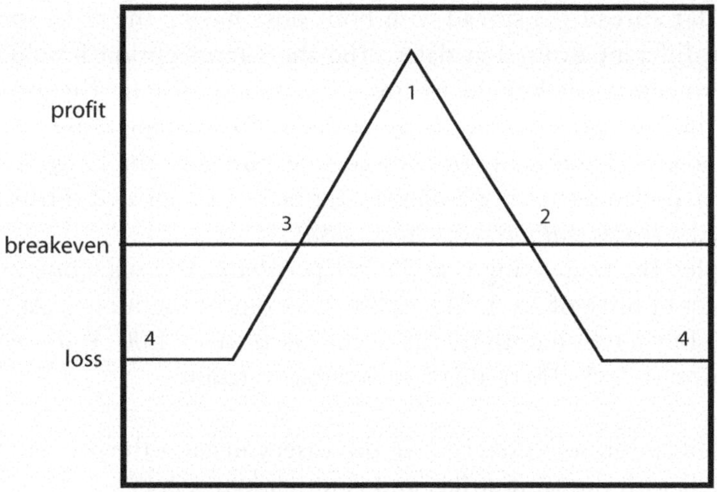

Maximum profit 90 - 85 - 0.95 = 4.05 ($405)
Breakeven, upper 95 - 0.95 = 94.05 ($94.05)
Breakeven, lower 85 + 0.95 = 85.95 ($85.95)
Maximum loss 0.95 ($95)

Fig. 10 Butterfly spread

a *ratio* on either long or short side, such as the ladder or the ratio *calendar combination spread.*)

Butterfly spreads can be reversed as well. Using calls, a high and low short position can be opened and offset with the purchase of two mid-range long calls. Using puts, a high and low short position would be opened and offset with mid-range long puts. However, in both of these instances, the likelihood of exercise would be greatly increased. The concept of the butterfly spread makes sense for most traders when short positions reside in between higher- and lower-strike price long positions.

The theory of the butterfly spread may be mathematically interesting, but in practice it is less practical. The creation of a strategy with initial breakeven or credit benefit limits potential profits, but trading costs in opening and closing positions are likely to eliminate or even exceed the limited profit levels, a situation known as an *alligator spread*—one in which any limited profits are "eaten up" by the trading costs.

To see a table showing outcomes at various price levels, link on **butterfly spread** at the website https://thomsettsguide.com/options-strategies/

Buy-write – alternative name for the covered call, with the two sides representing a buy (of stock) and a short sale of the right via a call.

Calendar spread – a spread with both sides having the same strike price but with different expiration dates. The short-term option is sold and the longer-term option is bought to cover the short position. The greater time value in the later position creates a net debit; the strategy assumes the short call can be closed profitably or allowed to expire, and the longer-term long position may benefit from a rising stock price and increased intrinsic value. Also called a *horizontal spread* or *time spread.*

Example: The underlying is at $58.91 per share. You sell a one-month 60 call at the bid price of 1.65. This call is 1.09 out of the money. At the same time, you buy a two-month 60 call at the ask price of 4.00. Your net cost for this position is 2.35. There are three possible outcomes:

1. The short position is exercised. In this case, you cover the position with the long call with the same strike, and your net loss is 2.35.
2. The short position expires worthless. You continue to hold the long two-month call, which you acquired for a net cost of 2.35, hoping for a profit. A variation of this theme is that the short position is closed at a small profit. For example, its value falls to 0.35, and you buy to close. Your basis in the two-month call is then adjusted to 2.70 (2.35 + 0.35).
3. The short position expires worthless and you close the two-month call at a loss. In this case, the loss on the two-month call is reduced by the profit on the one-month call, creating either a smaller loss or a minimal net profit.

In the example using calls, this variety is termed a bullish calendar spread. If puts are used with a longer-term long put, it is a bearish calendar spread. An example of the bullish (call-based) calendar spread outcomes is shown in Fig. 11

Calendar straddle – a strategy employing two separate straddles. The near-term straddle is sold and the farther-out straddle is bought. This strategy relies on rapid time decay, creating a net profit in the shorter-term short position.

It is a strategy designed to exploit volatility, and based on the assumption that it will be possible to close the short positions at a profit, and then experience potential gains in the longer-term long straddle position.

The payoff diagram is identical to that of the calendar spread shown in Fig. 11, but the design of this position is more complex because rather than involving two options, it combines two separate straddles. Overall, both profit and loss potential are limited in this position due to the nature of the straddle, with both sides opened at the same strike. Maximum gain is created when the underlying is trading exactly at the strike of the short options; both sides will thus expire worthless. However, even if this occurs, the longer-term long straddle, with its net debit, remains open. For this to develop into a profitable position, underlying price movement has to exceed the number of points equal to the net debit.

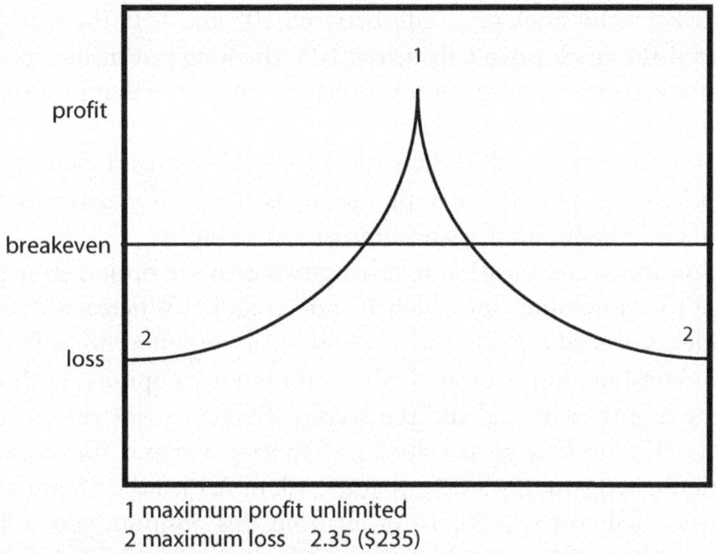

Fig. 11 Calendar spread

Maximum loss is equal to the overall debit paid for the calendar straddle. It occurs if and when the underlying moves many points above or below the strike of the short straddle. The risk is managed by using longer-term long positions to satisfy or offset losses on the nearer-term short positions.

Collar – a protective strategy combining a covered call and a long put, both slightly out of the money. This position is opened when an existing position is held in the underlying. The purpose to the collar is to provide low-cost or no-cost insurance in the event of a move to the downside.

For example, 100 shares of the underlying were bought at $95 per share, and the current value is $108.10. A collar may be used to protect 10 points of the paper profits by buying a 105 put at the ask price of 6.40 and selling a 110 covered call for the bid price of 8.30, both at the same expiration. The net credit on this collar is 1.90. If the stock's price rises and the covered call is exercised, profit will consist of the net credit of 1.90 ($190) plus the appreciated stock (strike of 110 minus original basis of 95, or 15 points ($1500)). If the stock's price remains below the 110 strike until expiration, the call position is entirely profit; and if the stock's price falls below the put strike of 105, the put offsets the loss below that level point for point.

With the current value of stock at $108.10, the credit on the collar of 1.90 reduces current basis value to 106.20 (looking at this another way, the original basis in stock to be reduced from 95 per share down to 93.10) (95 less 1.90). If the stock price rises, the short call will be exercised and stock called away at the 110 strike; if the stock price falls between 105 and 110, the net 1.90 is all profit; and if the stock price falls below 105, the long put insures profits and caps the market risk, picking up one dollar in intrinsic value for every dollar lost in market value of the stock.

Maximum profit is equal to the strike of the call minus the purchase price of the underlying, plus the net premium received. The maximum profit, breakeven, and maximum loss are summarized in Fig. 12.

Combination – any position involving two or more option strategies that are open at the same time, but which are not straddles. Whereas a straddle will contain identical strike price and expiration, a combination will vary. For example, a combination is created when you buy two options both expiring in the same month, with call and put having different strike prices.

Example: The underlying is valued at $58.91 per share. You create a long combination when you buy a 60 call at the ask of 2.40 and a 55 put at the ask of 1.10. The total cost is 3.50. To profit from this position, you will require movement in the stock's price, either 3.5 points above 60 or 3.5 points below 55 (strike prices of top and bottom option minus the net cost of the position).

A short combination requires selling of two positions rather than buying. For example, if instead of buying options on the underlying, they were sold,

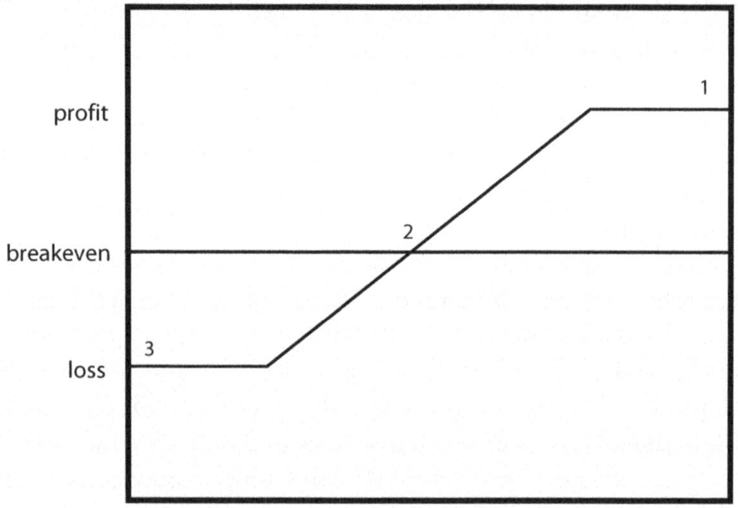

1 maximum profit 110 - 95 + 1.90 = 16.90 ($1,690), combining capital gain with covered call profit
2 breakeven 95 + 1.90 = 96.90 ($96.90)
3 maximum loss 108.10 - 105 - 1.90 = -1.20), excluding capital gain on stock of 105 - 95 = 20 ($2,000)

Fig. 12 Collar

it would create a credit combination. This would be achieved by selling a 60 call at the bid of 2.10 and selling a 55 put at the bid of 0.95. The net credit is 2.65. Now a profit is possible as long as the stock price remains between the two strikes, below the call strike of 60 and above the put strike of 55. Breakeven is 2.65 points above the call strike and 2.65 points below the put strike.

Profits in the short combination can be managed and created in one of two ways. First, as time value declines in either option, one or both sides can be closed at a profit. Second, as either side goes in the money, exercise can be avoided by closing the short position or by rolling forward to a later expiration. In the roll, either option can be kept at the same strike but a later expiration; or the call can be rolled forward and up; or the put can be rolled forward and down. By changing the strike, the chances of exercise are mitigated for the moment and in the event of later exercise, this creates additional exercise profit.

Condor – also called a flat-top butterfly, the condor combines a bull and a bear spread in a single, four-part position. The typical butterfly involves three different strikes. For example, you would hold two long calls, each with different strike prices, and sell two calls at the same strike in between the other two. A condor involves four separate strikes: two long and two short.

Example: The underlying is valued currently at $93.69. You construct a condor position using four calls with different strikes:

Buy 1 90 call at the ask	−10.10
Sell 1 95 call at the bid	+7.30
Sell 1 100 call at the bid	+5.00
Buy 1 105 call at the ask	−3.20
Net debit	−1.00

To see a table showing outcomes at various price levels, link on **condor** at the website https://thomsettsguide.com/options-strategies/

The condor expands the profitable middle range over a comparable three-strike butterfly. The outcome is summarized in Fig. 13.

Contingent buy – a calendar spread based on buying a long-term LEAPS call and paying for it will a series of short calls or puts. The theory behind the contingent buy is that the current price is attractive, but the trader either cannot afford to invest in shares today, or desires to wait out of concern for possible price decline.

The initial long call is paid for with a series of short-term short calls or short puts. The idea timing of the short side is one to two weeks. Selling positions on the Friday one week prior to expiration sets up maximum advantage because the typical option loses 34% of time value between Friday and Monday before expiration (on average). This occurs because the time from

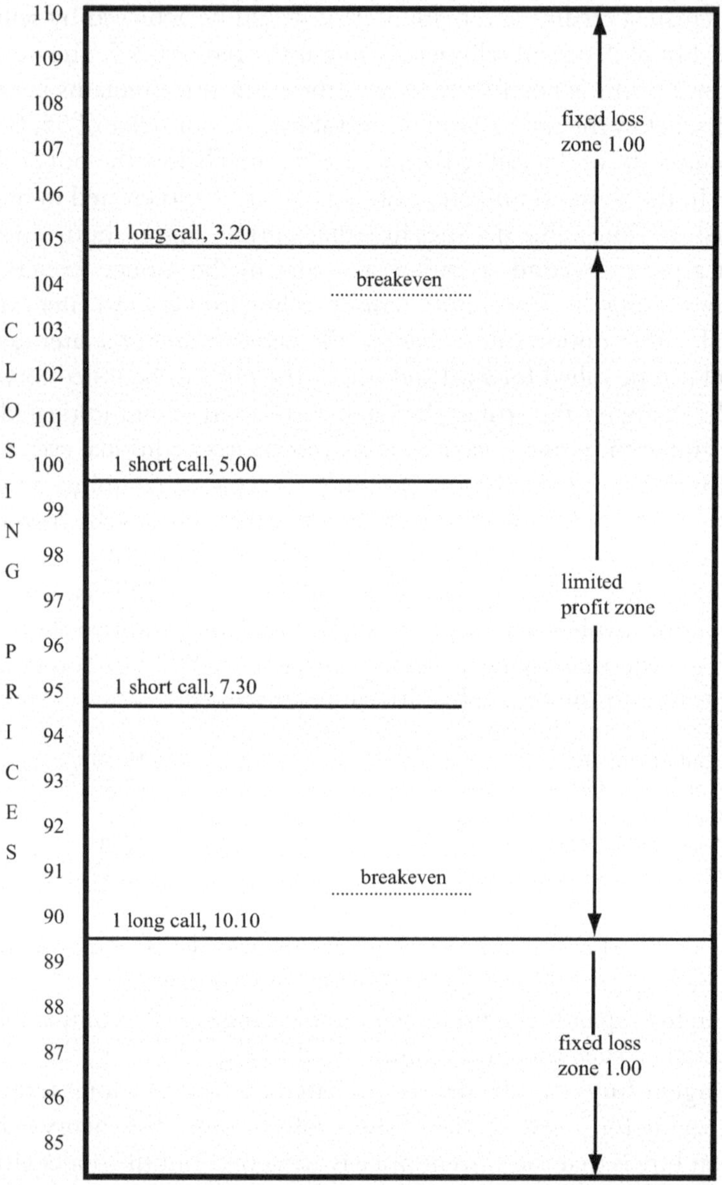

Fig. 13 Condor

Friday to Monday is three days, but only one trading day separates the two days. The risk of holding an uncovered short position over the weekend is that it cannot be known how much a price will change between the two sessions.

Selling short positions may be timed to exploit short-term price movement. A trader will sell short-term puts at the bottom of the swing, preferably at support or below Bollinger Bands' lower band; and sell short puts at the top of the swing, either at resistance ore at or above the upper Bollinger Band. The selection of uncovered calls contains considerable risk because the position has potential for large losses. In comparison, short puts are preferable because their market risk is identical to that of covered calls.

The long call can be closed at any time and if its intrinsic value increases, profits can be taken. However, closer to expiration, there are three choices. If the underlying value is below the call's strike, no action has to be taken. The call will expire worthless, but its value has declined to zero due to the series of sales in previous months. Second, the call can be sold to take profits. Third, if the underlying price is substantially higher than the call's strike, the call can be exercised and shares bought at the fixed strike.

Contingent sell – a strategy designed to hedge market risk in a long position. When a trader owns 100 shares of the underlying, opening an ATM LEAPS can freeze the market risk at the strike, minus the cost of the put. For example, a one-year 55 put opened at an ask price of 5.50 freezes market risk below $49.50 per share (55–4.50).

In the contingent sale, the long put is paid for in a series of short installments. Either short calls or short puts are sold to pay for the long put over time. The ideal timing for short positions is the Friday before expiration. Between Friday and Monday, the average option loses 34% of its remaining time value. By Monday, the position can be bought to close at a profit, assuming that the underlying has not moved significantly so that the short option's value has increased. By selling a series of short options over many months, the long put can be paid for, taking its net basis down to zero.

The long-term long LEAPS put can be closed at any time to take profits. This occurs if and when the underlying price declines below the strike. Closer to expiration, three outcomes are possible. If the underlying price is higher than the put's strike, no action is necessary and the put expires worthless. However, its net basis is zero since the series of short sales in preceding months pays for the put. Second, if the underlying price is lower than the strike, the put can be sold to take profits. Third, the put can be exercised and shares sold at the fixed strike, which will be greater than the current market value of shares. This demonstrates that the contingent sell strategy is effective in hedging market risk over the long term.

Conversion – a strategy combining three parts together: a long put, a short call, and 100 shares of the underlying. Both options have the same expiration and strike, and this position creates locked-in limited profit, as long as the position cost is lower than the option strike levels.

Example: The underlying is valued at $58.91. You buy 100 shares at that price. You also buy a 55 put at the ask of 1.10 and sell a 55 call at the bid of

5.70. Your credit for the option positions is 4.60. This reduces your net cost of stock to 5$4.31 per share ($58.91–$4.60). If the stock remains above the 55 strike, the call is exercised and stock is called away at 55, for a profit of 0.69 ($55.00–$54.31). If the stock price falls below 55, the entire call premium represents a profit and the put value offsets decline in the stock price point for point. The net position profit of 0.69 is the profit this position can earn in either event. This may be varied if the short position can be closed profitably prior to expiration, in which case the outstanding put provides continuing downside protection for the long stock.

The payoff diagram for a conversion is shown in Fig. 14.

Covered call – a strategy combining ownership of 100 shares of the underlying stock. One call is sold short against 100 shares, covering the risk of the short option. If you do not own 100 shares, the call is not covered, but is *naked* and risks are much greater.

For example, 100 shares of the underlying were purchased at $103 per share. In selecting an appropriate call for this strategy, you need to plan for the contingency of exercise. So if you were to sell a 100 call, the calculation of net return would have to allow for the loss of three points (current value of $103 less strike of $100). It makes sense to always write covered calls so that in the event of exercise, the combined stock and option outcome will create an overall net profit (from option premium and capital gain).

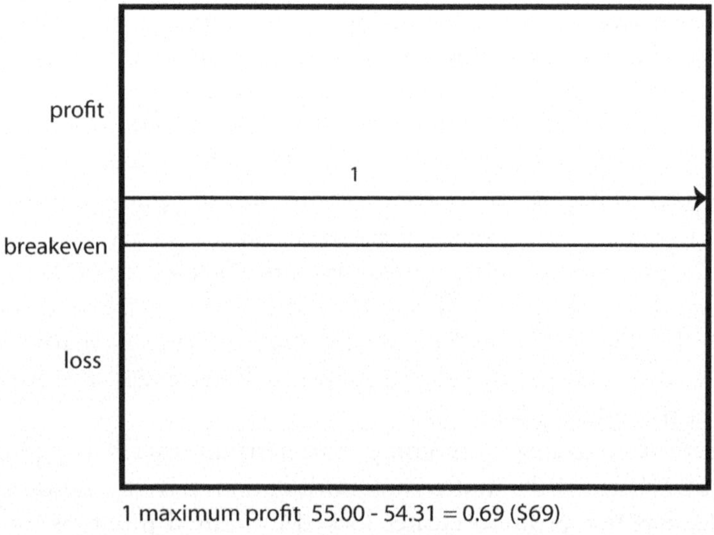

Fig. 14 Conversion

Downside protection: Covered calls discount the basis in stock, providing downside protection. In the above example, the basis is $103 per share; if you sell a call and receive 4.00 in premium, this reduces your net basis in the stock to $99 per share ($103–$4). The option premium you receive when you sell a covered call is credited to your account, pending one of several possible outcomes. In the example of acquiring 100 shares at $103 per share, assume that current value is $108.10. You may select a number of different calls based on strike price and time to expiration. These include among others:

105 call at bid of 4.90 (immediate income of $490 plus $310 in profit from stock if the short call is exercised). The call expires in three weeks.
110 call at bid of 2.15 (immediate income of $215 plus $700 in profit from stock if the short call is exercised). The call expires in three weeks.
105 call at bid of 6.30 ($630 + $200 profit on stock) with nearly two months until exercise.
110 call at bid of 3.63 ($363 + $700 profit on stock) with nearly two months until exercise.

The above examples are all short-term covered calls. The two 105 calls are more than three points in the money, meaning chances for exercise are strong; however, the richer premium may justify this strategy if you are willing to sell the stock. The 110 calls are out of the money and offer less option premium but potentially higher capital gains if the short call is exercised.

Return calculations: In calculating the return from a covered call strategy, consider all possible outcomes:

(a) stock value falls, time value declines, and the call can be bought to close at a profit, freeing you to repeat the strategy with a different call.
(b) stock remains at or below the option's strike and expires worthless; all of the option premium is profit and you are free to repeat the strategy.
(c) stock price rises and you accept exercise.
(d) stock price rises above strike and you roll forward (or forward and up) to avoid exercise.

To accurately compare outcomes from various covered call selections, dividends continue to be earned even when the short call is opened, and remain earned until the call is exercised or stock is sold. Comparisons should be annualized as well, so that they are accurate. To annualize, divide the projected return by the number of days until expiration, and multiply the result by 365 (days) to approximate the return you would earn over an entire year.

Return calculations may include option premium only, or by compared with dividend and capital gain for total return if and when exercised.

Appropriate use: Covered calls are appropriate to use when exercise is an acceptable outcomes, and when you want to discount your basis to either force an exercise sale or later avoid exercise and repeat the covered call strategy several times. It is one of many ways to take paper profits without selling stock, or to use as part of a combined strategy involving various combinations of other calls or calls and puts.

Conservative strategy: The covered calls defines the extent of a conservative option strategy, since all outcomes are going to be profitable if the strategy is properly timed, no matter what the outcome. The only negatives to the covered call occur when a stock's market price rises dramatically and stock is called away when the short call is exercised, creating a realized lost opportunity; or when the underlying value declines below net basis, setting up a paper loss. For most covered call enthusiasts, this is a risk worth accepting, considering the consistency or returns and safety in the strategy.

Tax considerations: Tax law affects capital gains based on the type of covered call selected. A *qualified* covered call allows you to claim long-term gains on stock profits after exercise, but an *unqualified* covered call may toll the 12-month count or start it over. This type of call is deemed too far in the money at the time the covered call is opened. Thus, traders selecting deep ITM calls should be aware of the potential for loss of favorable capital gains treatment due to this important tax rule. An unqualified covered call may be created unintentionally when a current position is bought to close and rolled to a later expiration, when the stock price has increased enough to exceed the boundaries for a qualified covered call.

In the example of stock purchased at $103 and currently valued at $108.10, a three-week covered call at the strike of 110 creates potential profit of $915 (option premium of $215 and capital gain if and when exercised of $700). Excluding dividends earned, this position includes option premium with capital gains.

To see a table showing outcomes at various price levels, link on **covered call** at the website https://thomsettsguide.com/options-strategies/

The payoff diagram for a covered call is shown in Fig. 15.

Covered combination – a strategy with three parts: ownership of 100 shares of stock, a short call, and a short put. The options have the same expiration but different strike prices. The call is covered, and the put is uncovered. In the event the put is exercised, the trader acquires an additional 100 shares at the strike. In the event the call is exercised, the 100 shares of stock are called away and only the short put remains.

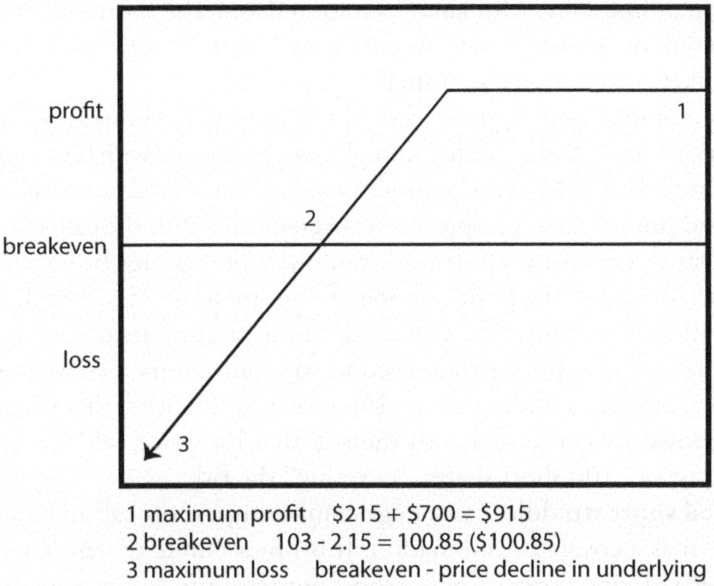

Fig. 15 Covered call

Example: You own 100 shares originally acquired at $55 per share. The current price is $58.91. You open a covered combination by selling a 55 call at the bid of 4.90 and selling a 60 put at the bid of 2.20. Your total credit for this combination is 7.10 ($710). Although both options are in the money, the 7.10-point range extends the breakeven point between 48 and 67 (seven points below the call strike and seven points above the put price). If either option is exercised within this zone, the position is profitable. For example, if the stock falls to $52 per share, the put is exercised and you purchase an additional 100 shares at $60 (a loss of eight points). However, with an additional 100 shares, subsequent option positions can be opened to offset the loss of 0.90 ($90). This loss is the difference between the eight points and the 7.10 premium received. If the stock rises and is called away at $55, you keep the $710 received for the position and you break even on the stock (basis was $55 per share and strike of the call is 55).

The most likely outcome of a short-term covered combination is rapid decline in time value, resulting in one of the two positions expiring worthless, and the other being closed at a profit or rolled forward to avoid exercise. In the example above, although both options are in the money, time value is considerable. The call contains 0.99 of time value (premium 4.90 less intrinsic value of 3.91) and the put contains 1.11 in time value (premium 2.20 less intrinsic value of 1.09). The strategy's most likely outcome will be to close one or both positions when time value declines occurs, or to roll forward to take advantage of additional time value with later expiration dates. The shorter the timeframe until expiration, the better the chance of profitable results, since one or both sides are likely to be closed for a smaller premium.

In this example, both options were in the money. In comparison, a covered combination (also called a covered strangle) can be opened with both options out of the money. This reduces the premium income but also reduces exercise risk.

Covered put – a strategy opposite a covered call. With the call, owning 100 shares of stock covers the short position, but a put cannot be covered in the same way. To "cover" the position, one of two situations is required. First, the trader maintains adequate cash in an account or combined with margin to pay for exercise at a put's strike. Second, the put covers a short position in stock. For example, a trader is short 100 shares in the belief that the price will decline. However, concerned with the risk that the price will rise, the trader sells one put per 100 short shares, "covering" the risk.

Covered short straddle – a strategy combining a short call and a short put, also known as a covered combination. It is not accurate to describe the position as covered, since exercise of the short put results in shares being put to the trader.

Covered strangle – also called a covered combination, a position with three parts: 100 shares of the underlying, a short call (covered) and a short put (uncovered). Both options should be out of the money.

For example, a covered strangle is created for 100 shares of stock originally purchased for $87 per share. Current value is $90. You sell a 95 call at the bid of 2.00 and an 85 put at the bid of 1.80. Total premium income is 3.80 ($380).

Maximum profit is equal to the strike of the short call minus the purchase price of the underlying, plus premium received: *95 – 87 – 3.80 = 11.80 ($1180)*

Breakeven price is the combined purchase price of the underlying and strike of the short put, less the net premium received; with the net sum divided by 2: *(87 + 85 – 3.80) ÷ 2 = 84.10 ($84.10 per share)*

Maximum loss is equal to the price of the underlying plus the strike of the short put, less the sum of twice the underlying, and minus the maximum profit: *90 + 85 – (90 × 2) = 11.80 = 16.80 ($1680)*

The payoff diagram for the covered strangle is shown in Fig. 16.

Credit spread – any spread in which the net receipt from short positions exceeds the net cost of long positions, with the net deposited in the trader's account. The credit is used as part of the calculated breakeven, profit or loss pricing. The larger the credit, the more likely a profit in any spread.

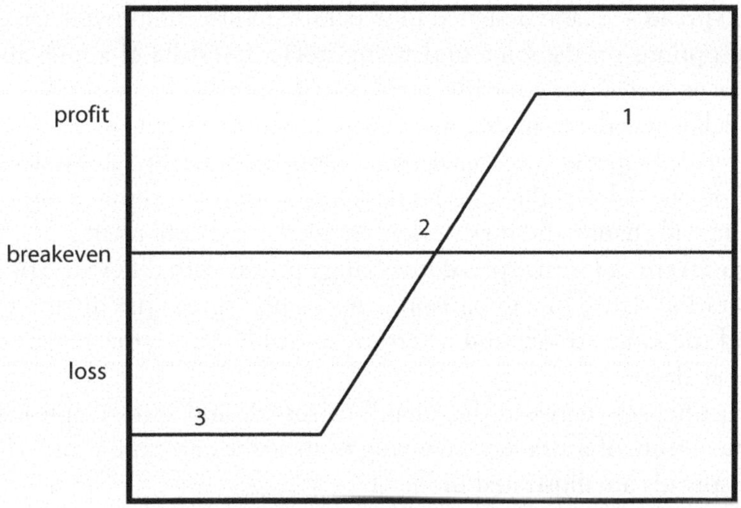

1 maximum profit 95 - 89 + 3.80 = 11.80 ($1,180)
2 breakeven (87 + 85 - 3.80) ÷ 2 = 84.10 ($84.10 per share)
3 maximum loss 90 + 85 - (90 * 2) - 11.80 = 16.80 ($1,680)

Fig. 16 Covered strangle

Debit spread – a spread in which the net cost of long positions is higher than the net receipt from short positions, with that net to be paid by the trader. The debit is used to adjust calculated breakeven, profit, and loss pricing. The larger the debit, the less likely a profit in any spread.

Delta hedge – a strategy based on option price change (measured by delta) compared with price change in the underlying. When the option's price movement is dissimilar to the point movement in the underlying, the delta quantifies this difference. Delta for options always ranges between 0.00 and 1.00 (for calls) and between 0.00 and −1.00 (for puts). For example, if the stock rises one point but the option rises only one-half point, its delta is 0.50. When the underlying and option premium move exactly the same number of points, delta is 1.00.

The delta hedge takes advantage of the adjustments in price movement. For example, OTM calls tend to have very low delta factors. A delta hedge strategy can be devised assuming that with less responsive price movement, some positions (especially short positions) are likely to be more profitable than ITM options, whose delta is closer to 1.00. Options with higher ratios may be better trades for long positions because of the delta, meaning that less time value erosion and closer intrinsic value tracking can be anticipated.

Delta spread – a ratio designed to maximize returns from two separate delta values of options on the same underlying stock. The delta of a long and short option are opened at the same time, with likelihood that the short side will erode more quickly and the long side will hold value or increase in value to a greater extent. The delta spread (also called a ratio spread because the value is determined by dividing one delta by the other) is designed to anticipate how changes in each side's delta will change and how option premium levels will react.

Diagonal spread – any spread involving options with different strike prices and expiration dates. In comparison, a horizontal spread has different expirations and the same strikes; and a vertical spread has the same expirations but different strikes.

The distinctions between diagonal, horizontal, and vertical spreads determines the nature of a strategy involving both strike and expiration. The three types of spreads are illustrated in Fig. 17.

Gut strangle (long) – a *gut strangle (long)* is a neutral strategy combining the purchase of an ITM call and an ITM put with the same expiration date.

The usual form of a strangle combines OTM positions, and the gut strangle is the opposite. It offers unlimited profit potential, two breakeven price points, and limited risk. Because the net debit paid for ITM positions is likely to be far higher than OTM trades, the long gut strangle requires considerable price movement in order to become profitable.

Profit is achieved when the price of the underlying higher than the strike of the long call, plus the net premium paid; or when the underlying price is lower than the strike of the long put less premium paid.

There are two price points for breakeven. The upper breakeven is net premium paid (for both options) plus the long call strike. The lower breakeven is the strike of the long put minus net premium paid.

Maximum loss occurs when the underlying is located between the two strikes. It is equal to the net premium paid plus the long put strike, minus the long call strike.

For example, the underlying is trading at $60 per share. You enter a long gut strangle by buying a 62.50 put at the ask price of 4 ($400) and you buy a 57.50 call at the ask price of 3.75 ($375). The total debit is 7.75 points ($775).

The underlying has to move at least 7.75 points to achieve a profit. For example, if the underlying advances to $71 per share, the profit on the long gut is $325 (*71 – 60 – 7.75 = 3.25, or $325*). If the underlying declines to $52 per share, profit is $25 (*60 – 52 – 7.75 – 0.25, or $25*).

Breakeven occurs at two prices, upper and lower. Upper breakeven is $65.25 (*57.50 + 7.75 = 65.25, or $65.25*). Lower breakeven is $54.75 (*62.50 – 7.75 = 54.75, or $54.75*).

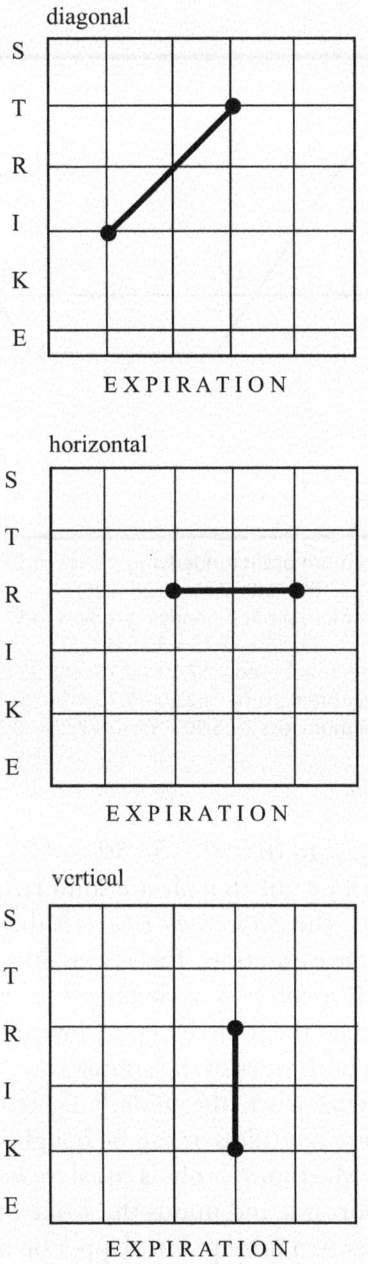

Fig. 17 Types of spreads

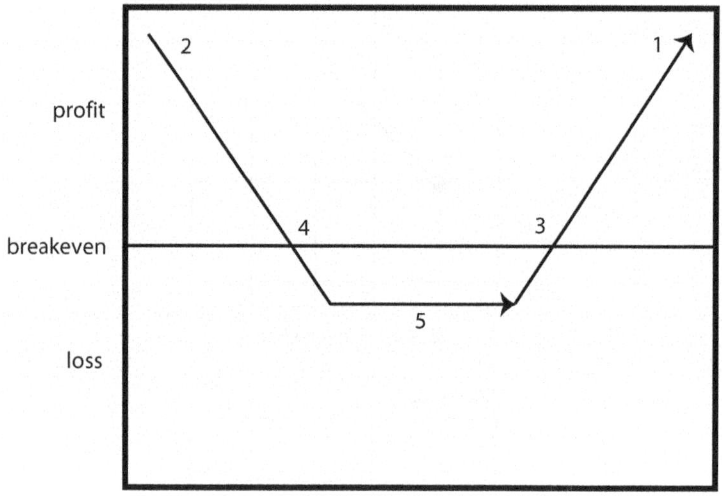

1 maximum profit (underlying moves to $72)
60 – 52 – 7.75 – 0.25 ($25)
2 maximum profit (underlying moves to $71)
71 – 60 – 7.75 = 3.25 ($325)
3 upper breakeven 57.50 + 7.75 = 65.25 ($65.25)
4 lower breakeven 62.50 – 7.75 = 54.75 ($54.75)
3 maximum loss 65.50 – 57.50 – 7.75 = 0.25 ($25)

Fig. 18 Gut strangle (long)

The limited loss is equal to (*65.50 – 57.50 – 7.75 = 0.25 or $25*).

The outcomes of the long gut strangle are summarized in Fig. 18

Gut strangle (short) – the *gut strangle (short)* is the sale of an ITM call and an ITM put with the same expiration. This is a credit spread, but because both sides are in the money, it involves considerable risk. It is designed to produce a limited profit if and when the underlying has low volatility; however, potential loss is unlimited on both sides of the strategy.

Maximum profit occurs when the underlying remains between the two strikes, so both will expire worthless or can be bought to close at a profit, due to declining time value. Maximum profit is equal to the net premium received, plus the strike of the short put and minus the strike of the short call.

Breakeven is located at two price points. Upper breakeven is the sum of net premium received, plus the strike of the short call. Lower breakeven is the strike of the short put, minus the net premium received.

Loss is unlimited in the short gut strangle. It occurs if and when the price moves substantially above or below the range of the strikes, adjusted by the net premium received. If the price of the underlying is lower than the net of short put strike minus premium received, a loss results. If the price of the underlying is greater than the sum of the short call strike plus net premium received, a loss results.

For example, the underlying is valued at $30 per share. A short gut is opened by selling a 28 call at the bid of 3.50 ($350) and selling a 32 put at the bid of 5 ($500). The total credit received is 8.50 ($850).

Maximum profit is the net premium received, plus the difference in the two strikes: (*8.5 + 32 – 30 = 10.50 ($10.50)*).

Upper breakeven is the underlying price equal to the net received plus the strike of the short call: (8.5 + 28 = 36.5, or $36.50). Lower breakeven is the underlying price equal to the short put strike minus the net premium received: (*32 – 8.5 = 23.50, or $23.50*).

Maximum loss depends on the degree of underlying price movement. If the underlying advances to $41 per share, the loss is that price minus the strike of the short call, minus the net received: (*41 – 28 – 8.5 = 4.5, or $450*). If the underlying declines to $21 per share, loss is equal to the strike of the short put less the price of the underlying and minus the net received: (*32 – 21 – 8.5 = 2.50, or $250*).

The outcome for a short gut strangle is shown in Fig. 19.

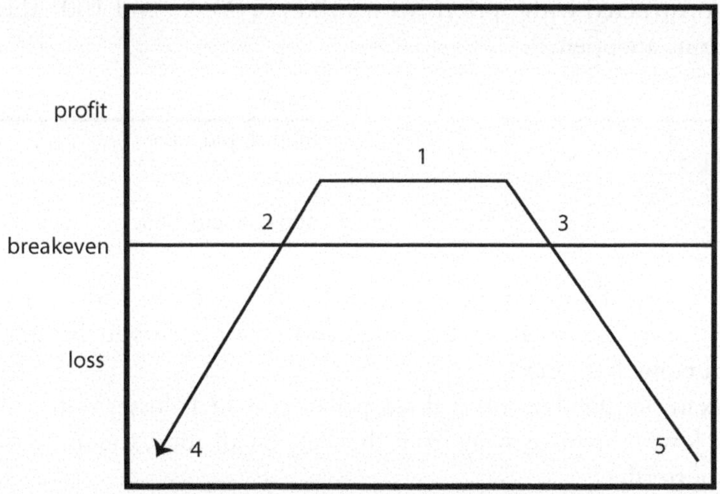

1 maximum profit 8.5 + 32 – 30 = 10.50 ($10.50)
2 lower breakeven 32 – 8.5 = 23.50 ($23.50)
3 upper breakeven 8.5 + 28 = 36.5 ($36.50)
4 maximum loss (underlying declines to $21)
32 – 21 – 8.5 = 2.50 ($250)
3 maximum loss (underling advances to $41)
41 – 28 – 8.5 = 4.5 ($450)

Fig. 19 Gut strangle (short)

Hedge - a strategy set up to offset one position with another, usually resulting in combining limited profits with limited risk, often set up to limit losses in one position. For example, the owner of stock may buy a put to protect paper profits. In the event the stocks' price fell below the put strike, the decline will be match point-for-point in intrinsic value of the put. In this instance, the put hedges the risk of loss in the stock.

Hedge ratio – the delta of a ratio, a comparison between the delta of two offsetting options. The purpose of the ratio is to identify the point where a neutral hedge exists, so that offsetting positions approximate zero risk.

Horizontal spread – a spread consisting of options with the same strikes but different expirations.

Iron butterfly (long) – a combined straddle and combination (compared with the simple butterfly, which is two spreads), providing limited profit potential with limited risk. A long iron butterfly consists of four options (compared with three in the standard butterfly). Profit occurs when the stock's price ends up below the lowest strike or above the highest strike in the position (in a short iron butterfly, profit occurs between the strike ranges). The net may be either a debit or a credit, depending on the combined pricing of the options selected.

Example: The underlying is valued at $93.69 per share. The long iron butterfly is constructed with options with strikes of 90, 95 and 100. The following positions are opened:

Long	Short
	90 put, bid 1.85
95 put, ask 2.50	
95 call, ask 1.45	
	100 call, bid 1.05

The net cost of this position is 1.05 (2.50 + 1.45 – 1.85 – 1.05). The breakeven range occurs in a mid-range and profit occurs if the stock closes above or below that range.

This example involves only three prices at which losses will result. The higher or lower the price away from this very small zone, the more profitable the iron butterfly.

Maximum profit for the long iron butterfly is equal to the strike of the short call, less the strike of the strike of the long call, less the premium paid: (*100 – 95 – 1.05 = 3.95, or $395*).

Lower breakeven is the sum of the middle strike less the premium paid: (*95 – 1.05 = 93.95, or $93.95*). Upper breakeven is found by adding the net paid to the middle strike: (*95 + 1.05 = 96.05, or $96.05*).

Maximum loss is the strike of the short call less the strike of the long call, minus maximum profit: (*100 – 95 – 3.95 = 1.05, or $105*).

These outcomes are illustrated in Fig. 20.

To see a table showing outcomes at various price levels, link on **iron butterfly (long)** at the website https://thomsettsguide.com/options-strategies/

Iron butterfly (short) – a combined straddle and combination (compared with the simple butterfly, which is two spreads), providing limited profit potential with limited risk. A short iron butterfly consists of four options (compared with three in the standard butterfly). Profit occurs when the stock's price ends up between the strike ranges (in a long iron butterfly, profit occurs below the lowest strike or above the highest strike). The net may be either a debit or a credit, depending on the combined pricing of the options selected.

Example: The underlying was worth $93.69. The short iron butterfly is constructed with options with 90, 95 and 100 just like the long iron butterfly, but in reverse (long positions become short and vice versa). The following positions are opened, with all options expiring in February:

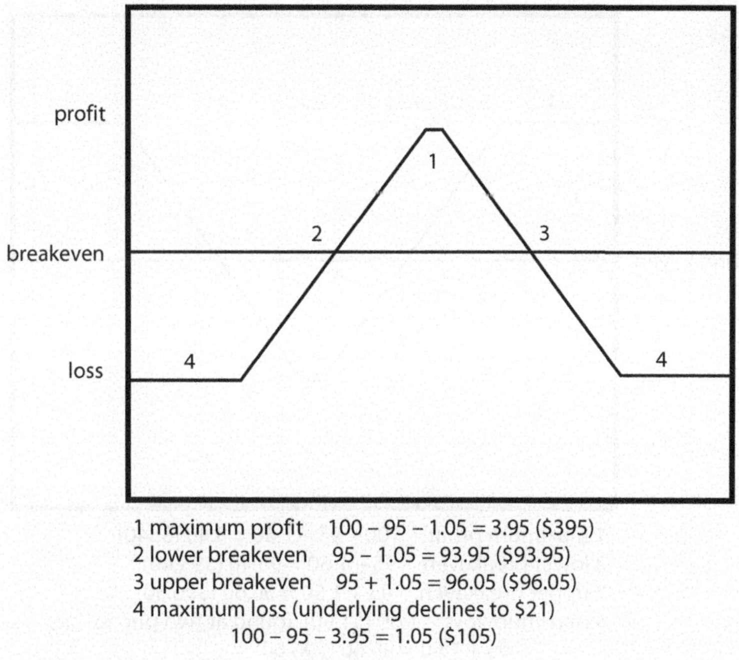

Fig. 20 Iron butterfly (long)

Long	Short
	90 put, bid 1.70
95 put, ask 2.65	
95 call, ask 1.60	
	100 call, bid 0.95

The net debit of this position is 1.60 (2.65 + 1.60 – 1.70 – 0.95).

Although the potential profit and loss levels are easily recognized, it is likely that short positions would be closed early or rolled forward, either to take profits or avoid exercise. Matching the long and short sides makes sense if and when early closing of positions occurs.

Maximum profit if held to the last trading day is equal to the strike of the short call, less strike of the long call, less the net premium: (*100 – 95 – 1.60 = 3.40, or $340*). Breakeven is equal to the middle strike plus net premium (*95 + 1.60 = 96.60, or $96.60*); or middle strike less net premium (*95 – 1.60 = 93.40, or $93.40*).

Maximum loss is the net debit of $160.

These outcomes are illustrated in Fig. 21.

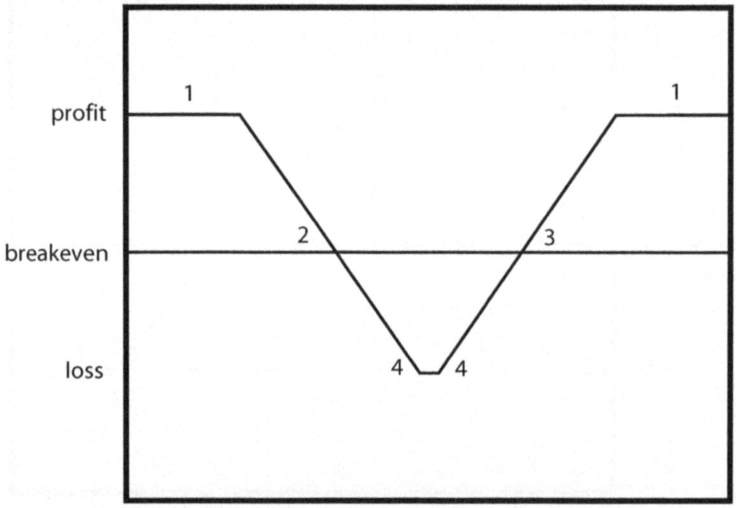

1 maximum profit 100 – 95 – 1.60 = 3.40 ($340)
2 lower breakeven 95 – 1.60 = 93.40 ($93.40)
3 upper breakeven 95 + 1.60 = 96.60 ($96.60)
4 maximum loss 1.60 ($1.60), found at two prices:
95 + 1.60 = 96.60 ($96.60)
95 - 1.60 = 93.40 ($93.40)

Fig. 21 Iron butterfly (short)

To see a table showing outcomes at various price levels, link on **iron butterfly (short)** at the website https://thomsettsguide.com/options-strategies/

Leg in/leg out – a leg consists of the parts in a combination option strategy. Simple straddles and spreads have two legs, consisting of long and short options or of option type (calls or puts). A combination is created when one side exists and the trader enters a subsequent transaction that creates a straddle or spread (leg in). Similarly, when a combination already exists, a trader may close one side to take partial profits, converting a combination to a single long or short position (leg out).

Long call – an option granting its owner the right to buy 100 shares of the underlying stock, at the fixed strike price, and on or before the expiration date. In comparison, a long put gives its owner the right to sell 100 shares of the underlying; and a short call is an open contract in which the call rights are granted to someone else in exchange for receipt of the option premium.

Long calls are employed by traders in numerous ways:

1. *Swing trading.* If you own shares of stock as a long-term investment, you will not always want to sell when prices move. However, when prices dip, buying calls is one way to swing trade on the temporary price movement.
2. *Simple speculation.* The most popular form of long call trading is to earn short-term profits. Even though 75% of all long options held until expiration will expire worthless or lose money, this remains a popular activity.
3. *To tie in a future price.* If you plan to buy shares in the future, buying a call today provides leverage and locks in the price for future purchase.
4. *To cover a short position.* The long call is used by short sellers of stock to insure against the contingency of loss in the event the stock's price rises. The open long call offsets each point lost with an increase of one point in intrinsic value.
5. *As part of a straddle or spread.* The combination strategies involving two or more sides require the use of offsetting positions. Long calls offset short calls or long puts.
6. *To balance time, cost, and proximity of leverage.* The selection of a long call is a balance between time and cost. The sooner expiration occurs, the cheaper the call; and the longer the time to expiration, the higher the premium cost. The closer the strike to the current price of the underlying, the more responsive premium movement will be to movement of the underlying. For each of these considerations, the long call is a fixed-cost form of leverage, and selection is a balance between time, cost, and proximity (moneyness) of the call.

Example: The underlying stock price is $124.71 per share. Available calls at the closest strike of 125 are a 6-day contract at the ask of 0.79; a 13-day weekly contract with an ask of 1.23; and a 20-day call with an ask of 1.55. Considering the prices of these three calls, you decide to purchase the 13-day option at the ask price of 0.79 ($79).

Profit is unlimited, and occurs when the price of the underlying exceeds the sum of the strike plus the cost of the call, adjusted for that price level. For example, if the underlying price rises to $128, profit is 2.21 ($221): *128 – 125 – 0.79 = 2.21 ($221)*.

Breakeven is set at the sum of the strike plus cost of the call: *125 + 0.79 = 125.79 ($125.79)*.

Maximum loss is equal to the cost of the long call, or 0.79 ($79).

These outcomes are illustrated in Fig. 22.

To see a table showing outcomes at various price levels, link on **long call** at the website https://thomsettsguide.com/options-strategies/

Long call butterfly – a butterfly position combining a bull spread and a bear spread together, using calls. It is designed to produce profits when the underlying stock price remains within the boundaries of high and low strikes. This position includes four trades and three strikes with the same expiration. One call is purchased at the high and at the low strikes, and two calls are sold at a strike in between. This strategy limits both profit and risk.

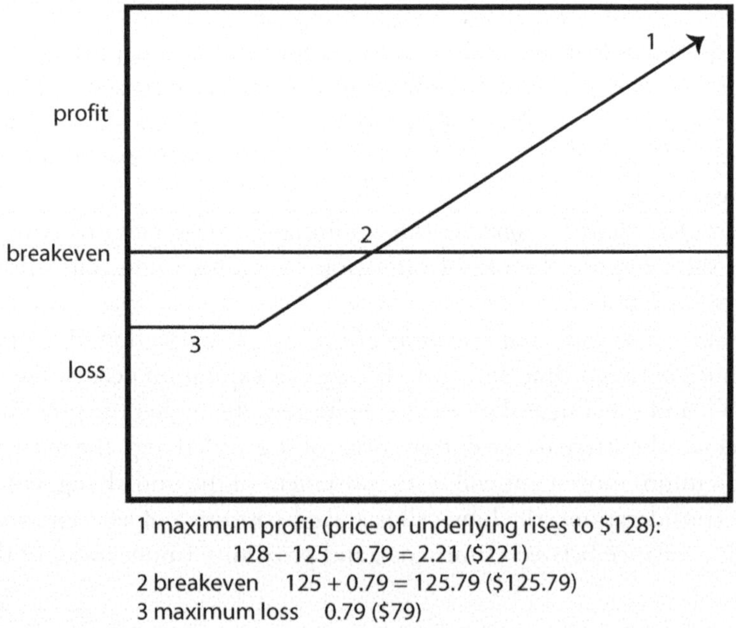

Fig. 22 Long call

Example: The underlying is priced at the ask of $58.91. You construct a long call butterfly with calls and at strikes of 55, 60 and 65. You buy one 55 at 7.60 and one 65 call at 1.90; and sell two 60 calls at 4.00 each. Your net debit is 1.50.

Both maximum profit and loss are limited. Profit occurs if and when underlying price remains in a middle zone. Maximum loss is fixed and occurs if price moves above or below that middle zone. Breakeven occurs at two price points, both marking the crossover above or below the middle zone.

To see a table showing outcomes at various price levels, link on **long call butterfly** at the website https://thomsettsguide.com/options-strategies/

Long call condor – a strategy similar to the butterfly and using long and short calls, with the distinction that the two middle calls are opened with different strikes. Thus, four different strikes are used instead of three (the butterfly involves doubling up the middle strike with twice as many options, but the condor employs the same number of calls at all strike prices with the two middle positions offsetting the higher and lower). This expands the potential profit price range beyond that of the butterfly.

Example: You open, the underlying is priced at $108.10 per share. You open a condor by selling two middle-strike calls, and protecting that position with one higher-strike and one lower-strike long call. The short positions are the 105 strike at the bid of 11.00 and the 110 strike at the bid of 8.30; the long positions are 100 at the ask of 15.80 and 115 at the ask of 6.10. Your net debit is 2.60.

Both profit and loss are limited with this strategy. Maximum profit occurs when the underlying is priced between the two short strikes located in the middle, by the point of expiration. It is equal to the lower short strike less the lower long strike, less the net premium paid: (*105 – 100 – 2.60 = 2.40 ($240)*).

This position has two breakeven points. The upper breakeven is equal to the strike of the higher long call less net premium paid: (*115 – 2.60 = 112.40, or $112.40*). The lower breakeven is at the strike of the lowest long call plus net premium paid: (*100 + 2.60 = 102.60, or $102.60*).

The maximum loss is equal to the net debit paid, or 2.60 ($260). This occurs when the underlying price ends up above the highest strike or below the lowest strike.

The profit, breakeven, and loss levels for the long call condor are illustrated in Fig. 23.

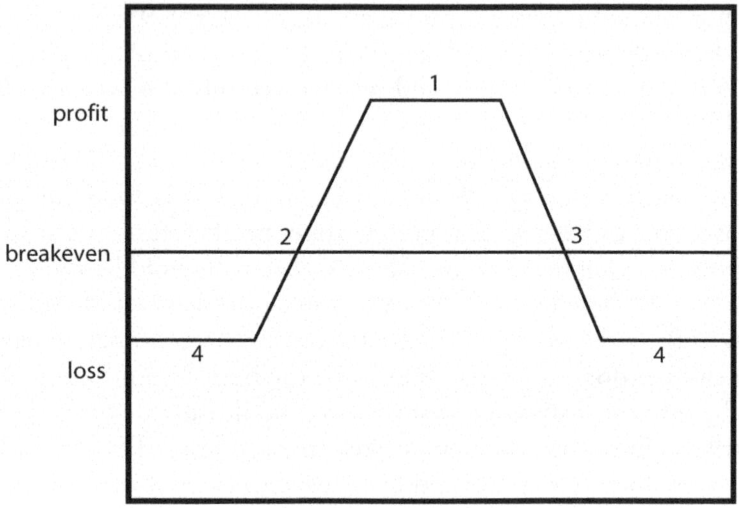

1 maximum profit (105 – 100 – 2.60 = 2.40 ($240)
2 lower breakeven (100 + 2.60 = 102.60, or $102.60)
3 upper breakeven (115 – 2.60 = 112.40, or $112.40)
4 maximum loss 2.60 ($260)

Fig. 23 Long call condor

To see a table showing outcomes at various price levels, link on **long call condor** at the website https://thomsettsguide.com/options-strategies/

Long combination – a strategy involving long options, including:

1. Synthetic long stock, involving a long call and a short put at the same strike.
2. Any grouping that is designed to minimize risk, often in exchange for a limited potential profit.
3. Straddles or spreads using long positions rather than short positions.

Long iron butterfly – a butterfly employing both calls and puts. The middle strike consists of one short call and one short put with the same strike; the higher and lower strikes are long: a call at the higher strike and a put at the lower strike. All options have the same expiration unless it is constructed as a diagonal position; in that case, the short options are usually shorter-term. In the traditional butterfly strategy, either calls or puts are used exclusively; the long iron butterfly used both types of options. Losses are limited at both top and bottom; maximum profit is equal to the credit on the position.

Example: You construct a long iron butterfly on an underlying priced at \$93.69 per share. The short options include a 95 call at the bid of 2.85 and a 95 put at the bid of 4.00. The long options are a 100 call at the ask of 1.05 and a 90 put at the ask of 1.85. The net credit on this position is 3.95.

Both profit and loss are limited in the long iron butterfly. Profit is at maximum when the underlying is at the strike of the short options at the point of expiration, so that all options expire worthless and the profit is equal to the net credit of 3.95 (\$395)

Breakeven is located at two price points for the underlying. The upper breakeven is equal to the price of the short call plus premium received: (*95 + 3.95 = 98.95, or \$98.95*). Lower breakeven is equal to the price of the short put minus net premium received: (*95 – 3.95 = 91.05*).

Maximum loss occurs when the underlying ends at expiration above the strike of the long call minus the short call, or below the strike of the long put; both are adjusted for the credit resulting from opening the position. Higher maximum loss: (*100 – 95 – 3.95 = 1.05, or \$105*). Lower maximum loss is identical but calculated on the basis of the net difference between the two put strikes, minus the met credit: (*95 – 90 – 3.95 = 1.05, or \$105*).

The appearance of the profit, breakeven, and loss for the long iron butterfly is shown in Fig. 24.

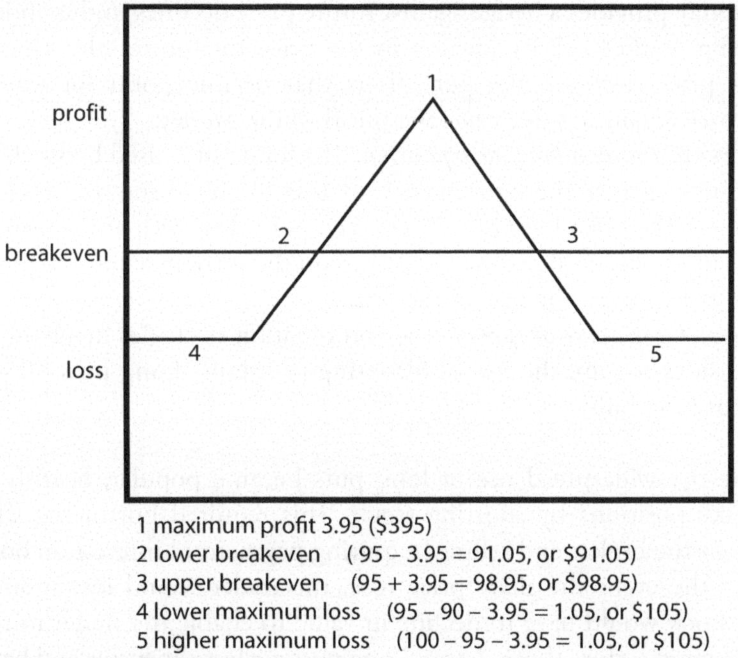

Fig. 24 Long iron butterfly

To see a table showing outcomes at various price levels, link on **long iron butterfly** at the website https://www.thomsettpublishing.com/option-strategies.

Long put – an open option contract providing its owner the contractual right to *sell* 100 shares of the underlying stock, at the fixed strike price, and on or before the expiration date. In comparison, a long call gives its owner the right to *buy* 100 shares of the underlying; and a short put is an open contract in which the put rights are granted to someone else in exchange for receipt of the option premium.

Long puts are employed by traders in numerous ways:

1. *Swing trading.* If you own shares of stock as a long-term investment, you will not want to sell when prices rise or fall. However, when prices rise, buying puts is one method for swing trading on the price movement, and on the expectation that prices will next move downward.
2. *Simple speculation.* One of the most popular forms of long put trading is to earn short-term profits. Even though 75% of all long options held until expiration will expire worthless, this remains a popular activity. A majority of long puts are closed before expiration, so the 75% statistics does not apply to all puts.
3. *To tie in a future sale price.* If you plan to sell shares in the future, buying a put today provides a hedge against future price declines in the underlying, freezing market risk by locking in the price for future sale. Thus, if the stock price declines, the put offsets that decline point for point with increased intrinsic value once the put is in the money.
4. *To cover or insure a long stock position.* The long put is used by stock owners to insure against the contingency of loss in the event the stock's price declines. The open long put offsets each point lost with an increase of one point in intrinsic value. The breakeven on the insurance put is equal to the put's strike minus the cost of the put.
5. *As part of a straddle or spread.* The combination strategies involving two or more sides require the use of offsetting positions. Long puts offset short puts or long calls.

Before the widespread use of long puts became popular, bearish traders could take positions by shorting stock. This required borrowing shares of stock from the broker and selling, requiring payment of interest on borrowed stock. In the event the share price rose, the trader would lose money. The shorted stock would have to decline in value to enable the trader to realize a profit, buying to close those shares. Long puts are less expensive and have risks limited to the price of the put. In comparison, shorting stock has unlimited risks. The put, however, has a limited lifetime in comparison to shorting shares of stock.

Example: The current price per share of the underlying is $961.35. A long put with a 960 strike is opened at the ask price of 8.20. The potential level of profit is limited only in the sense that the underlying price cannot fall below zero. In the example of a 960 strike bought for 8.20, if the underlying price fell to 943, profit would be: (*960 – 943 – 8.20 = 8.80, or $880*).

The breakeven price is equal to the long put's strike less premium paid: (*960 – 8.20 = 951.80, or $951.80*).

Maximum loss is limited to the price of the long put: 8.20, or $820.

The outcome and levels of profit, breakeven, and loss are summarized in Fig. 25.

To see a table showing outcomes at various price levels, link on **long put** at the website https://thomsettsguide.com/options-strategies/

Long put butterfly – a butterfly position combining a bull spread and a bear spread together and using puts. It is designed to produce profits when the underlying stock price remains within the boundaries of high and low strikes. This position includes four trades for three strikes with the same expiration. The highest and lowest strikes are long puts, and two short puts are sold at the middle strike. This strategy limits both profit and risk.

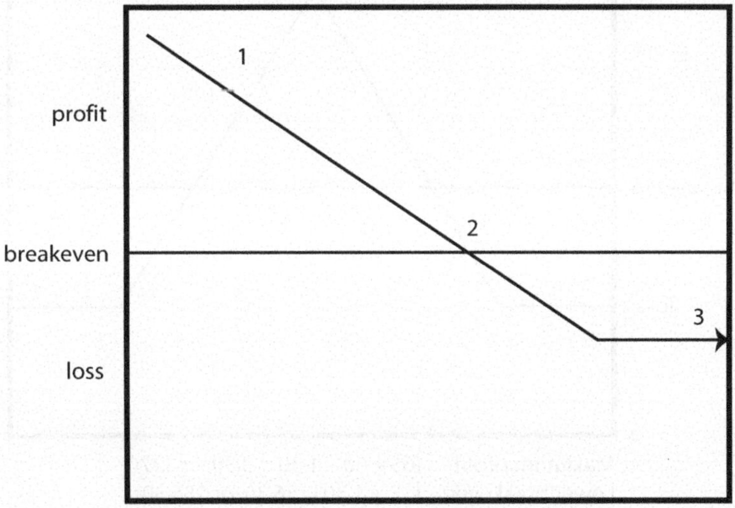

1 maximum profit (underling decline to $943):
(960 – 943 – 8.20 = 8.80, or $880)
2 breakeven (960 – 8.20 = 951.80, or $951.80)
3 maximum loss 8.20, or $820

Fig. 25 Long put

Example: You construct a long put butterfly on the underlying valued at $58.91 per share. The position combines a long 65 put at the ask of 6.60, two short 60 puts at the bid 3.70 each (7.40 total), and one long 55 put at the ask of 2.10. Net debit is 1.30, which is also the maximum loss on this strategy.

Maximum profit is limited and is realized when the underling price equals the difference between the high long strike and the short strike, less the net debit: (*65 – 60 – 1.30 = 3.70, or $370*).

Breakeven occurs at two price points. Lower breakeven is at the lower long put strike plus premium paid: (*55 + 1.30 = 56.30, or $56.30*). Upper breakeven is located at the highest long strike less premium paid: (*65 – 1.30 = 63.70, or $63.70*).

Maximum loss is also limited to the net cost of the position: 1.30, or $130. It is located either above or below the middle-range profit.

These outcomes are illustrated in Fig. 26.

To see a table showing outcomes at various price levels, link on **long put butterfly** at the website https://thomsettsguide.com/options-strategies/

Long put condor – an expansion on the long put butterfly, consisting of spreading the two middle puts between two different strikes. This expands the

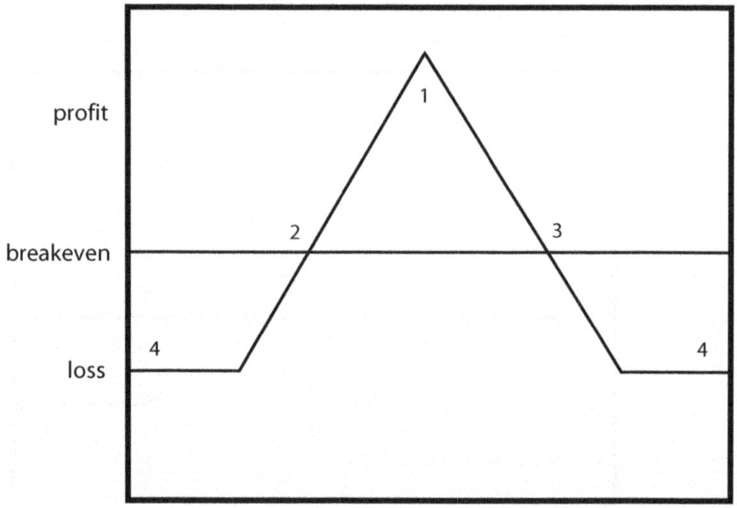

Maximum profit	(65 – 60 – 1.30 = 3.70, or $370)
Lower breakeven	(55 + 1.30 = 56.30, or $56.30)
Upper breakeven	(65 – 1.30 = 63.70, or $63.70)
Maximum loss	1.30, or $130

Fig. 26 Long put butterfly

total range into four different strikes, with the two long positions at highest and lowest, and the two short puts in the two middle-range strikes.

Example: Referring to example of a long put butterfly opened with the stock price at $58.91, it is modified by expanding to include four strikes, all with the same expiration. This consists of a long 65 put at the ask of 6.60, a short 62.50 put at the bid of 4.90, a short 60 put at the bid of 3.70, and a long 55 put at the ask of 2.10. Net debit is 0.10. In this strategy, maximum loss on the upside is limited to the net cost of 0.10. On the downside, that loss is expanded to 2.60 maximum (cost of 0.10 plus addition of 2.5 points for the expanded short positions in the middle) (62.50 – 60.00).

Maximum profit is equal to the higher long strike minus the higher short strike, plus the net debit: (*65 – 62.50 + 0.10 = 2.60, or $2.60*).

There are two breakeven prices. Lower breakeven is at the underlying price equal to the lower short strike minus net profit: (*60 – 2.60 = 57.40, or $57.40*). Upper breakeven is equal to the underlying price of the higher long strike less premium paid: (*65 – 0.10 = 64.90, or $64.90*).

Maximum loss is equal to the net debit paid: 0.10, or $10.

These outcomes are illustrated in Fig. 27.

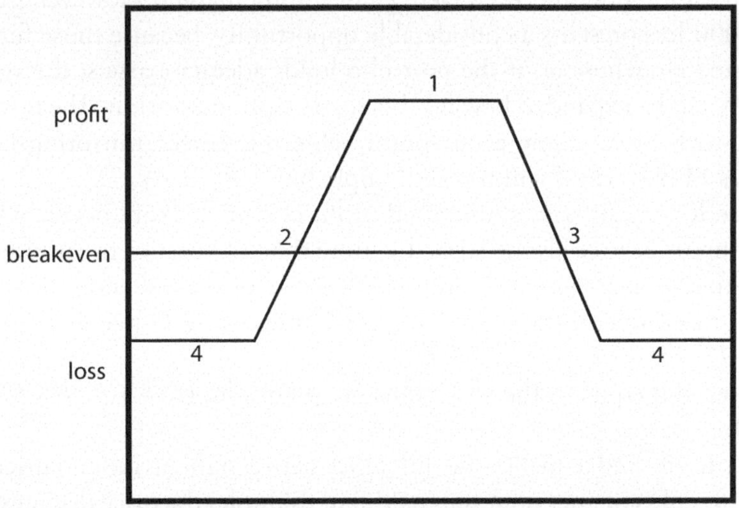

1 maximum profit (65 – 62.50 + 0.10 = 2.60, or $2.60)
2 lower breakeven (60 – 2.60 = 57.40, or $57.40)
3 upper breakeven (65 - 0.10 = 64.90, or $64.90)
4 maximum loss 0.10, or $10

Fig. 27 Long put condor

To see a table showing outcomes at various price levels, link on **long put condor** at the website https://thomsettsguide.com/options-strategies/

Long stock (synthetic) – an option position that mirrors price performance of stock, whether rising or falling. The synthetic position enables you to take a position in the stock for less money than it would require to purchase shares. This is accomplished by entering into a long call and a short put with identical strike and expiration. If the stock's price rises, the short put becomes worthless and the long call gains value. If the stock remains at or slightly above the strike, the position expires without creating either profit or loss. If the stock price falls, the call becomes worthless and the put is exercised, resulting in acquisition of 100 shares at the strike. Alternatively, the short can be closed or rolled forward to avoid exercise.

Example: You create a long stock synthetic position on an underlying valued at $93.69. This combines the purchase of a 95 call at the ask of 7.30 and selling a 95 put at the bid of 7.00. The net cost is 0.30 ($30). As the cost of this position is small, the leverage advantage is considerable. Buying 100 shares would cost $9369, and for $30, you achieve the same market advantage with a long synthetic position. The primary risk—having 100 shares put to you after a decline—is identical to the risk of purchasing 100 shares close to the strike of the put, and then facing a declining market. However, investing over $9000 less presents a considerable opportunity, because those funds can be invested elsewhere or, if the portfolio holds adequate assets, the synthetic approach can be expanded beyond this single-option position. The position at various stock prices show a one-point value movement mirroring how the stock would perform if you were to simply buy 100 shares.

Synthetic long stock has unlimited profit potential. Profit occurs when the underlying price exceeds the strike by more than the cost of the position, and is equal to the underlying price minus the strike of the call and minus the net debit. For example, if the underlying price moves to $99 per share, profit is: (*$99 – 95 – 0.30 = 3.70, or $370*).

Breakeven if equal to the strike plus net premium: (*$95 + 0.30 = 95.30, or $95.30*).

Loss is unlimited, equal to the difference between the strike and price of the underlying, plus the net premium paid. For example, the price declines to $89 per share. Loss at that price level is: (*95 – 89 + 0.30 = 6.30, or $630*).

The outcome is illustrated in Fig. 28.

To see a table showing outcomes at various price levels, link on **long stock (synthetic)** at the website https://thomsettsguide.com/options-strategies/

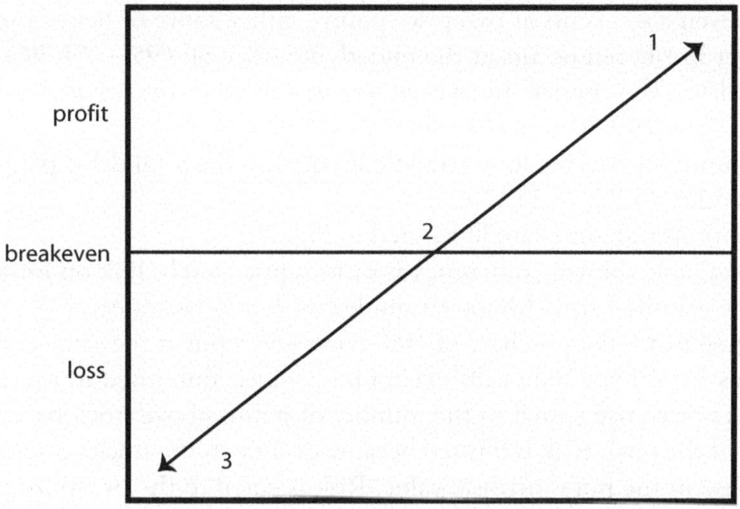

1 maximum profit (price of underlying rises to $99):
($99 – 95 – 0.30 = 3.70, or $370)
2 breakeven ($95 + 0.30 = 95.30, or $95.30)
3 maximum loss (price of underlying declines to $89):
(95 – 89 + 0.30 = 6.30, or $630)

Fig. 28 Long stock (synthetic)

Long straddle – the simultaneous purchase of a call and a put on the same underlying, with the same strike, and with the same expiration. This strategy becomes profitable only if the stock's price exceeds the total cost of the position on either the upside or the downside.

For example, the long stock (synthetic) position involves a long call and a short put. Using the same underlying priced at $93.69, a long straddle at a 95 strike would involve a long call at the ask of 7.30 and a long put at the ask of 7.40. Your debit is 14.70, so to make a profit, the underlying price has to move more than 14.70 points, either above or below the strike of 95. This strategy would be worthwhile only if you anticipate exceptional volatility in either direction from the strikes.

Profit is unlimited and will occur if the underlying moves substantially in either direction. It must exceed the total cost of the position, however. For example, based on the strike of 95 and total cost of the long straddle of 14.70 points, maximum profit is achieved with a substantial price movement. If the underlying moves down to $78 per share, the lower maximum profit is: (*95 – 78 – 14.70 = 2.3, or $230*). If the underlying advances to $116 per share, the upper maximum profit is: (*116 – 95 – 14.70 = –6.30, or $630*).

Breakeven also occurs at two price points, either above or below the strike. The lower breakeven occurs at the underlying price of: (*95 – 14.70 = 80.30, or $80.30*). The upper breakeven occurs at the underlying price of: (*95 + 14.70 = 109.70, or $109.70*).

Maximum loss on the long straddle is equal to the total debit paid for the long straddle: 14.70, or $1470.

The various outcomes are illustrated in Fig. 29.

To see a table showing outcomes at various price levels, link on **long straddle** at the website https://thomsettsguide.com/options-strategies/

Married put – the purchase of 100 shares and a put at the same time. Also known as a synthetic long call, maximum profit is unlimited in the event of the stock's price rise (equal to the number of points above stock basis, minus the cost of the put). Risk is limited because decline in the stock's price is offset by increase in the put's intrinsic value. Risk is equal to the premium paid for the put plus any distance between the basis in stock and the put's strike.

For example, you buy 100 shares of the underlying at $108.10 per share. You purchase a 105 put at the ask of 4.55. The maximum underlying risk is

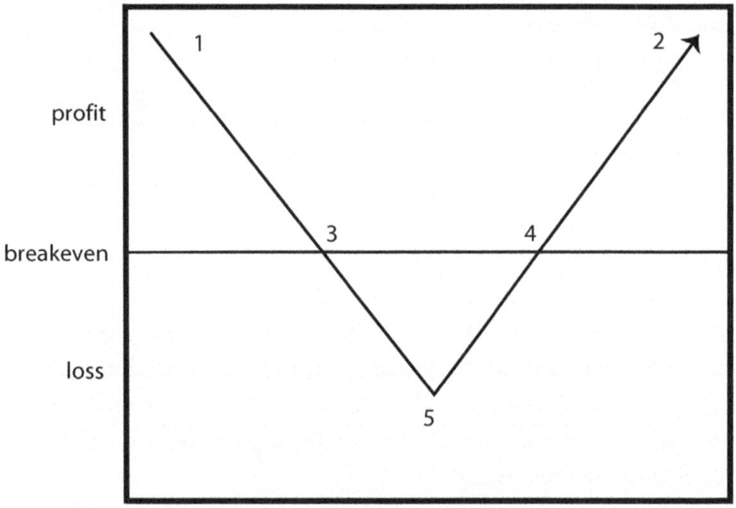

1 maximum profit (lower) (price declines to $78 per share:)
(95 – 78 – 14.70 = 2.3, or $230)
2 maximum profit (upper) (price advances to $116 per share):
(116 – 95 – 14.70 =- 6.30, or $630)
3 breakeven (lower) (95 – 14.70 = 80.30, or $80.30)
4 breakeven (upper) (95 + 14.70 = 109.70, or $109.70)
5 maximum loss 14.70, or $1,470

Fig. 29 Long straddle

3.10 points (108.10–105.00) and the put risk is the premium of 4.55. The breakeven on the position is 112.65 on the upside (basis of 108.10 + put premium of 4.55). On the downside, fixed loss risk maximum is 7.65 (gap between stock basis and put strike, plus put premium, or 108.10 – 105.00 + 4.55). So in exchange for unlimited profit potential above breakeven, you would be willing to fix the maximum potential loss.

Profit is unlimited. It is the price of the underlying less basis, less premium paid for the put. For example, if the underlying price rose to $116, profit would be: (*116 – 108.10 – 4.55 = 3.35, or $335*).

Breakeven is the purchase price of the underlying plus the cost of the put: (*108.10 + 4.55* = 112.65, or $112.65).

Maximum loss is limited and equals the net of the premium paid: 4.55 or $455.

The outcomes for this strategy are illustrated in Fig. 30.

To see a table showing outcomes at various price levels, link on **married put** at the website https://thomsettsguide.com/options-strategies/

Money spread *see* **Vertical spread.**

Naked option – a short position not hedged or covered by an offsetting long position. A call is naked (uncovered) when it is written without (a) owning

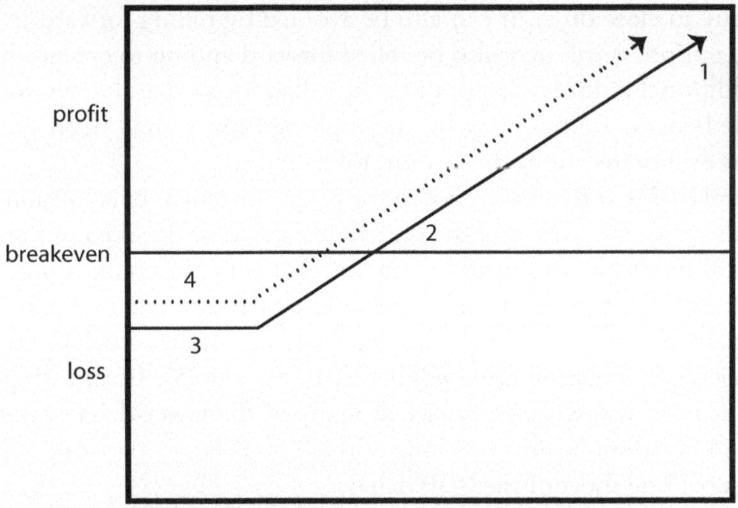

1 maximum profit (price of underlying rises to $116):
(116 – 108.10 – 4.55 = 3.35, or $335)
2 breakeven (108.10 + 4.55 = 112.65, or $112.65)
3 maximum loss, option 4.55, or $455
4 maximum loss, stock 108.10 - 105 = 3.10, or $310

Fig. 30 Married put

100 shares of the underlying, (b) owning a call that provides complete or partial hedging in a straddle or spread position, or (c) also holding an uncovered put, in which case the combined premium from selling both naked options provides a point spread of profit or reduced gain.

A put is uncovered whenever the position is sold without being offset by (a) a short stock position (thus, if the stock price rises, the loss in intrinsic value of the put offsets all or some of the loss on the short stock), (b) owning a put that offsets the short position in a straddle or spread position, or (c) holding a short call that provides a degree of protection against loss due to the combined short premium income of both options.

A naked call has unlimited risk, in theory, because a stock's price may rise indefinitely. On a practical level, the real market risk is limited to the *likely* maximum price increase, minus premium received from selling the call. A naked put does not have unlimited risk because a stock's price can fall only so far. This analysis usually refers to a zero value as the maximum risk, but in realistic terms, the risk faced when holding a naked put is the difference between strike price and the stock's tangible book value, minus the premium received from selling the put.

Naked calls and puts will not be exercised as long as they remain at the money or out of the money. Exercise can be avoided by closing the position with a buy to close order. It can also be avoided by rolling forward to a later-expiring option. A call may also be rolled forward and up to extend the strike to an additional point level; a put may be rolled forward and down to achieve the same benefit. Rolling may be accomplished for a small debit or, if time value has evaporated from the option, for a credit.

Neutral hedge ratio – reference to the price movement of an option in relation to the price movement of the underlying stock, or the delta of the option.

Neutral position – a spread or straddle that is neither bullish nor bearish. With the delta calculated, a trader will adjust each side of a two-part strategy to approximate neutrality. For example, if one option has a delta of 0.25 and another is 0.50, a neutral ratio will be 2:1 (0.50 ÷ 0.25). In adjusting a position to neutral, you will open twice as many of the lower-delta options (two short 0.25 positions against one long of the 0.50 delta, or two long 0.25 positions against one short of the 0.50 delta).

Put diagonal spread (bear) – a spread using puts and entered in the belief that the price of the underlying will decline in the near future. It involves buying a higher-strike, ITM put and selling a lower-strike OTM put expiring sooner.

Example: A put diagonal spread (bear) is set up on an underlying priced at $58.91. This combines a long 60 put at the ask of 3.70 that expires in one month, and a short 55 put at the bid of 1.10 that expires in two weeks. The net debit is 2.60. If the underlying price remains at or above 55 until the earlier expiration, the short put expires worthless; if the stock subsequently remains below the 60 strike, the long put can be closed for its intrinsic value before expiration. Timing is crucial for this position. Movement above or below each strike determines whether the position will be profitable or not. For a net debit of 2.60, you gain control over the longer-term put, assuming that the shorter-term put either expires worthless or loses time value by expiration (it was out of the money at sale, so the entire premium represented time value). The stock would need to fall to 53.90 to create breakeven on the short position (55 strike less premium of 1.10). Given the current price of 58.91, that is a five-point drop. If that were to occur, the long 60 strike put would contain 6.10 in intrinsic value, while the short put's offsetting intrinsic status would be 1.10, or a net advantage of five points.

Because two separate options, expiration dates and strikes are involved, the levels of profit, breakeven, and loss rely on the timing of each contract. The ideal price movement involves the underlying remaining unchanged or above the initial short option strike until expiration; and then declining below the long option strike before expiration of the long option. Another consideration is what to do when the short position expires or is closed. The trader can then sell another short put expiring before the long put and repeat this process indefinitely. This is especially applicable when the long option expires many months later, and the position is set up so that a series of short installments eventually pay for the long option.

Put diagonal spread (bull) – a diagonal spread using puts, based on the belief the price of the underlying will rise in the near future. It involves selling a higher-strike OTM put and buying a lower-strike, ITM put that expires later.

This is the opposite of the bearish put diagonal spread. Because it combines two separate strikes and expiration dates, the potential profit or loss has to be evaluated separately. The ideal price movement combines short expiration with later price movement to set up profits in the long put.

Put ratio backspread – also called a reverse put ratio spread, a position in which one or more puts are sold and a higher number of puts are bought with the same expiration but at a lower strike. This strategy features limited risk (limited only to the difference between long put strikes and zero) with unlimited profits. The strategy is worthwhile when you believe the underlying stock's price will decline before long put expiration.

Example: The underlying is valued at $108.10 per share. You believe that by mid-year this price will fall, so you open a 2:1 put ratio backspread. You sell one 110 put at the bid of 7.70 and buy two 105 puts at the ask of 6.40 each, for a total of 12.80. Your net debit is 5.10. The advantage in this position is that for zero net cost, you create significant profit potential in the event of a price decline. Because the ratio is 2:1, an ITM price decline will result in profits of two points in the long put side of this position, for each point lost in the short put. The major drawback is that it may require a considerable point drop in the underlying to create a profitable outcome. The outcomes are illustrated in Fig. 31

Ratio backspread (call) – also called a reverse call ratio spread, a strategy in which more calls are bought than sold. The long positions are bought at a higher strike but with the same expiration, and are greater in number to the extent of the ratio (e.g., in a 2:1 ratio, there will be two long calls and one short call).

Example: You open a 2:1 ratio backspread (call) when the underlying was at $93.69 per share. You buy two 95 calls at the ask of 7.30 each, for a total of 14.60; and sell one 90 call at the bid of 10.10. Your net debit is 4.50. If the stock price rises, the two long positions offset the one short position by two points to one at each rise in the underlying stock. If the stock price ends up at expiration between the two strikes, the maximum loss equals the debit plus the intrinsic value of the short position. If the stock's price falls below both strikes, the maximum loss is fixed at the debit of 4.50.

The range of outcomes for this strategy is summarized in Fig. 32.

Ratio backspread (put) – also known as the reverse put ratio spread, a strategy combining short puts with a larger number of long puts. All share the same expiration date; however, the long puts are at a lower strike. This position creates limited risk on the upside with theoretically unlimited profits if the underlying declines. The ratio is defined by the number of short and long positions; if there are two long and one short puts, it is a 2:1 ratio backspread.

Example: You open a 2:1 ratio backspread when the underlying was valued at $58.91 per share. This combined one short 60 put at the bid of 3.70 and two long 55 puts at the ask of 2.10, for a total of 4.20. Your net debit is 0.50. The advantage in this position is that as the underlying price falls below 50, you gain one point for each point of decline in the stock; and if the price rises above 60, the loss is fixed at 0.50. The major disadvantage is the extended middle loss range.

The outcomes for this strategy are summarized in Fig. 33.

Ratio calendar combination spread – a position coupling two ratio calendar spreads, one using calls and the other using puts. The call strike prices are higher than the put strike prices. This strategy is complex and profits limited, but if a high amount of time value is involved in the short positions, it can also be a profitable strategy with limited risk.

Example: The underlying is valued at 108.10. You initiate a ratio calendar combination spread with the following positions expiring in the months of January and February:

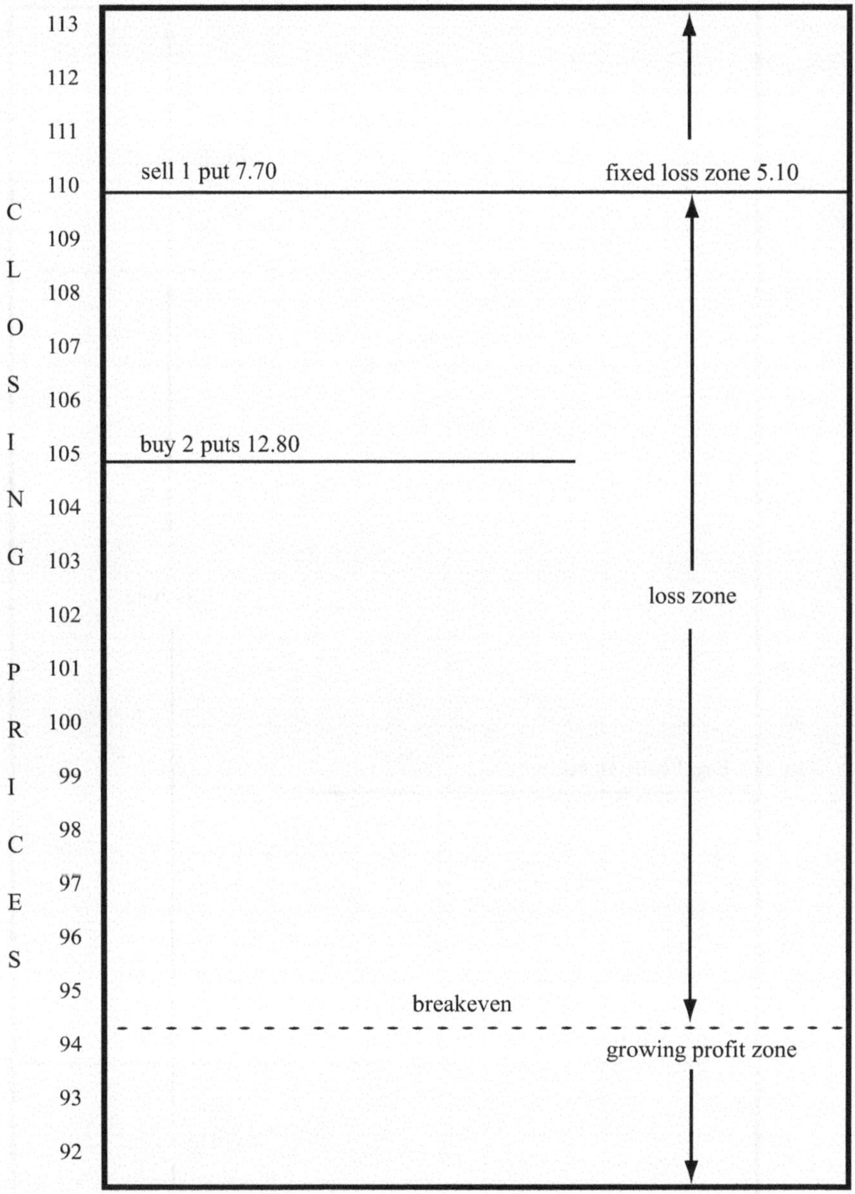

Fig. 31 Put ratio backspread

Sell January 105 put at the bid	1.70
Sell January 110 call at the bid	2.15
Credit	3.85
Buy February 105 put at the ask	2.95
Buy February 110 call at the ask	3.63
Debit	6.58
Total net debit	2.73

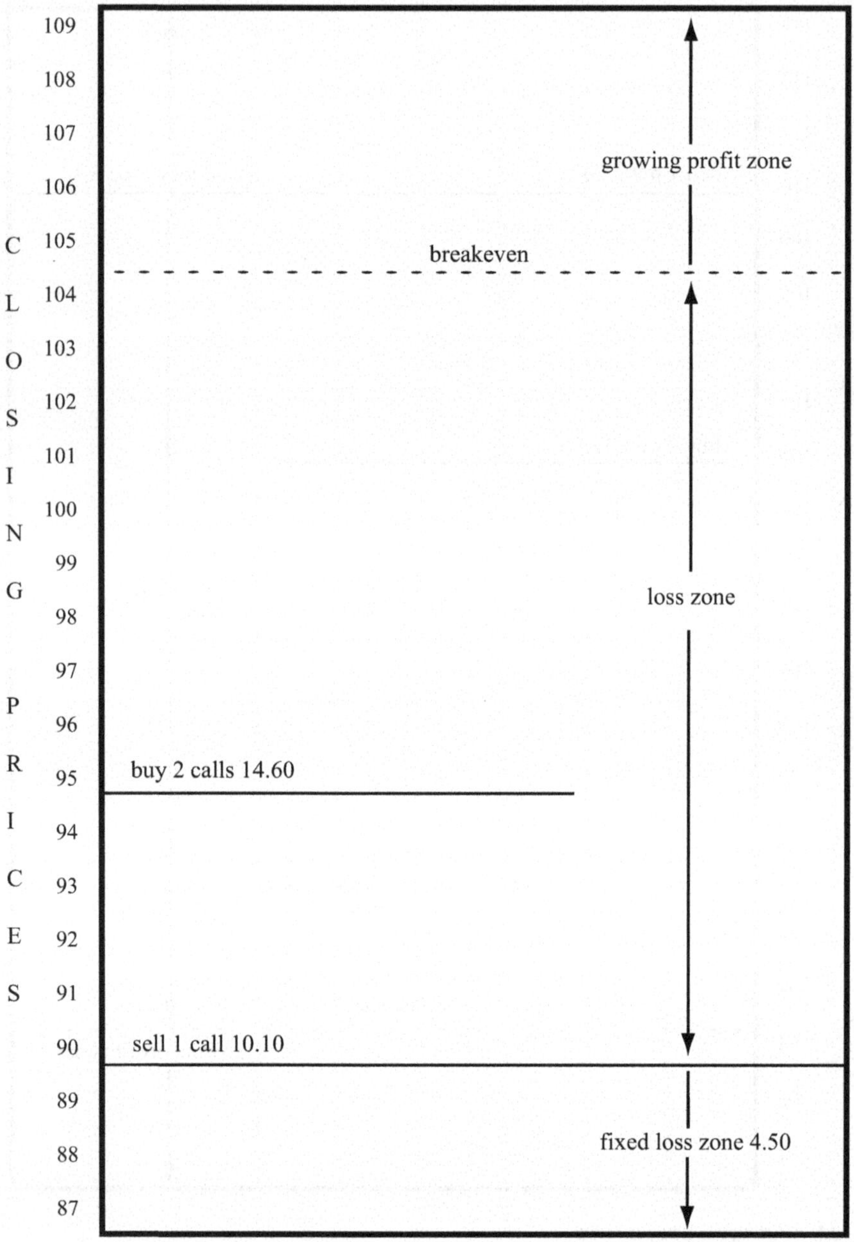

Fig. 32 Ratio backspread (call)

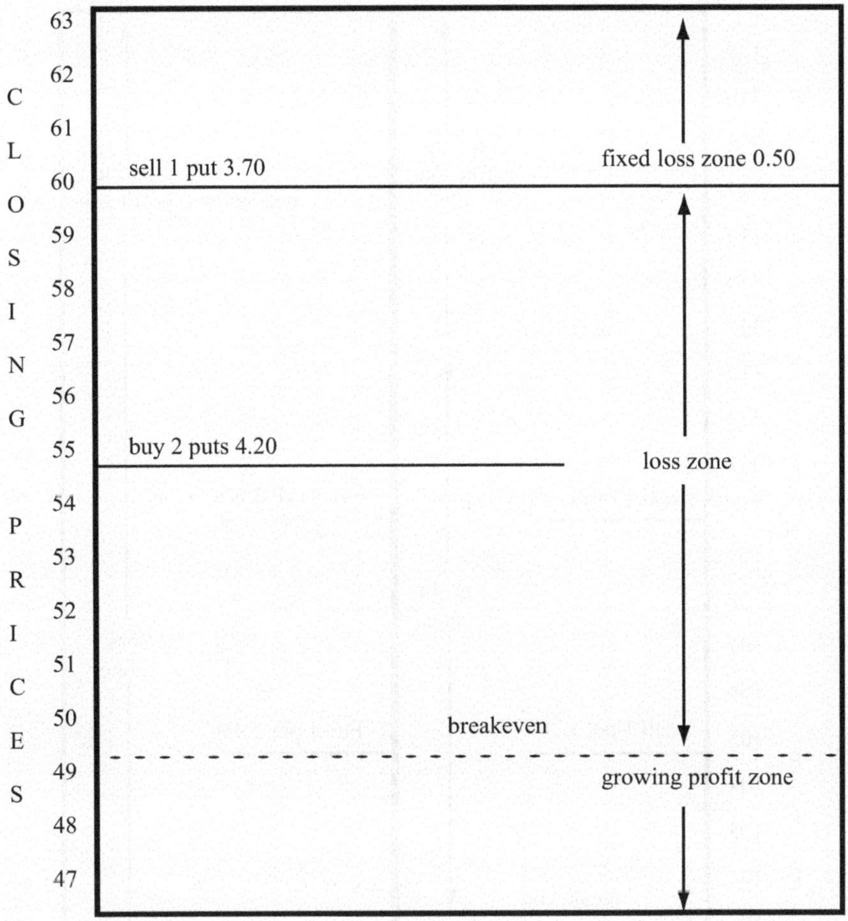

Fig. 33 Ratio backspread (put)

The advantage to this combination is maximized when the underlying stock price remains in the middle range until the earlier short options expirations, and then moves above or below that middle range. In this way, the short positions expire worthless or at a profit, leaving the potential for profits from the longer-term long positions.

The outcomes for this example are summarized in Fig. 34.

To see a table showing outcomes at various price levels, link on **ratio calendar combination spread** at the website https://thomsettsguide.com/options-strategies/

Ratio calendar spread (call) – a form of calendar spread in which more calls are sold than bought. For example, a 2:1 ratio would consist of selling two calls and buying one call. The short calls expire earlier than the long call. The narrower

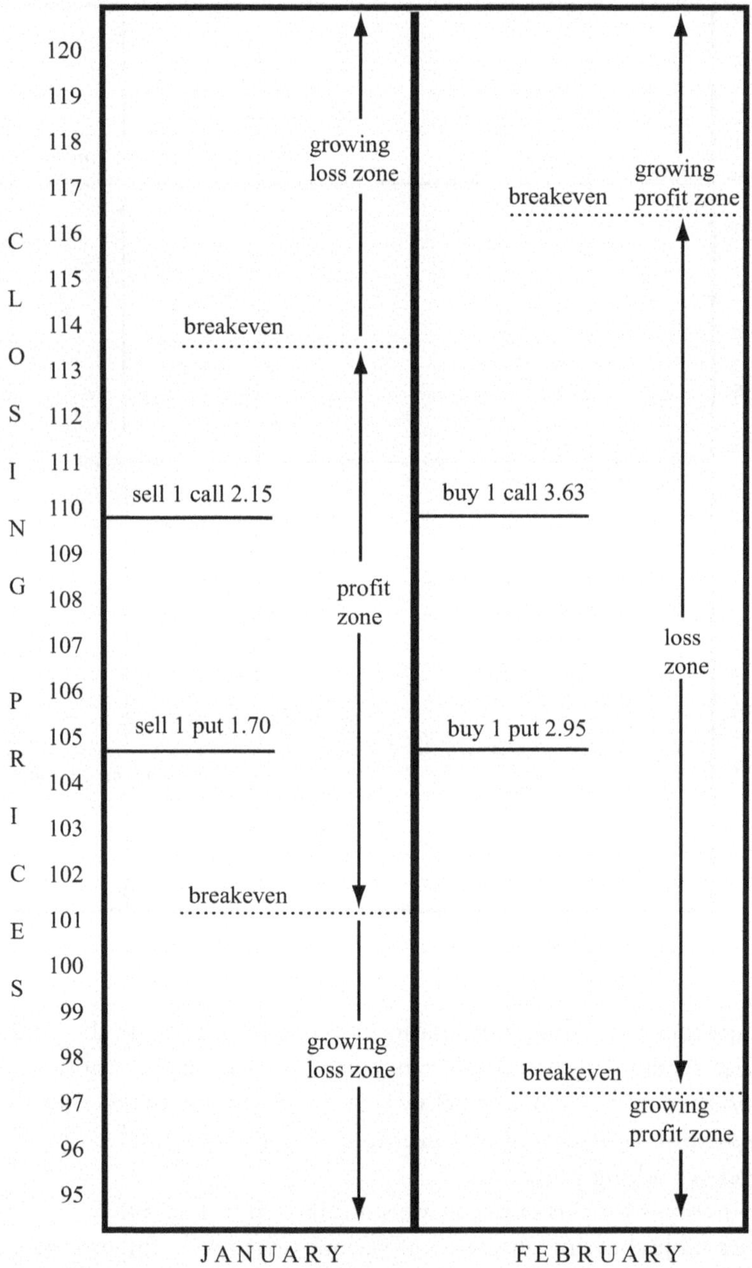

Fig. 34 Ratio calendar combination spread

the ratio, the less risk; for example, a 3:2 is less risky than a 2:1 because the uncovered portion of the strategy is reduced.

Example: You set up a 3:2 ratio calendar spread (call) when the underlying is valued at $93.69. You sell three July 90 calls at the bid of 10.10 each (30.30 total) and you buy two January 90 calls at the ask of 13.40 each (total 26.80). Your net credit is 3.50. In this case, you have a five-month span between the short and long positions, creating significant profit potential if the shorter-term, short calls expire worthless or can be closed at a profit. Because expiration is different for the short and long positions, the usual comparison is not made easily, as many variables can occur between the strikes. However, if the shorts can be closed profitably, the long positions will appreciate if and when the underlying price rises after short expiration.

The outcomes based on this example are shown in Fig. 35.

To see a table showing outcomes at various price levels, link on **ratio calendar spread (call)** at the website https://thomsettsguide.com/options-strategies/

Ratio calendar spread (put) – a strategy with both short puts and long puts. The short puts expire before the long puts, and all positions are opened with the same strike price. More short positions are opened, and the relationship between short-term short puts and longer-term long puts is expressed as a ratio. Selling two puts for every one bought creates a 2:1 ratio. Because short positions are partially uncovered, the closer the ratio, the less risk. A 3:2 ratio calendar spread contains less risk than a 2:1 with the same contracts.

Example: You create a 3:2 ratio calendar spread (put) on the underlying priced at closed at $58.91. You sell three March 60 puts at 2.85 each for a total credit of 8.55. You buy two June 60 puts at 3.70 each, for a total debit of 7.40. Your net credit is 1.15. Because expiration months are not the same, a side-by-side comparison is not complete. The best possible outcome is for the underlying to remain above the 60 strike until the March expiration, and to then fall below the 60 strike by the June expirations.

The outcomes based on this example are shown in Fig. 36.

To see a table showing outcomes at various price levels, link on **ratio calendar spread (put)** at the website https://thomsettsguide.com/options-strategies/

Ratio call spread – a neutral strategy combining long calls at one strike with a higher number of short calls at another strike, all with the same expiration. The ratio refers to the relationship between the short and long positions. For example, if you open two short calls and one long call, it creates a 2:1 ratio.

Example: You open a 2:1 ratio call spread on an underlying valued at $108.10 per share. Buying one 105 call at the ask of 8.90 and selling two 110

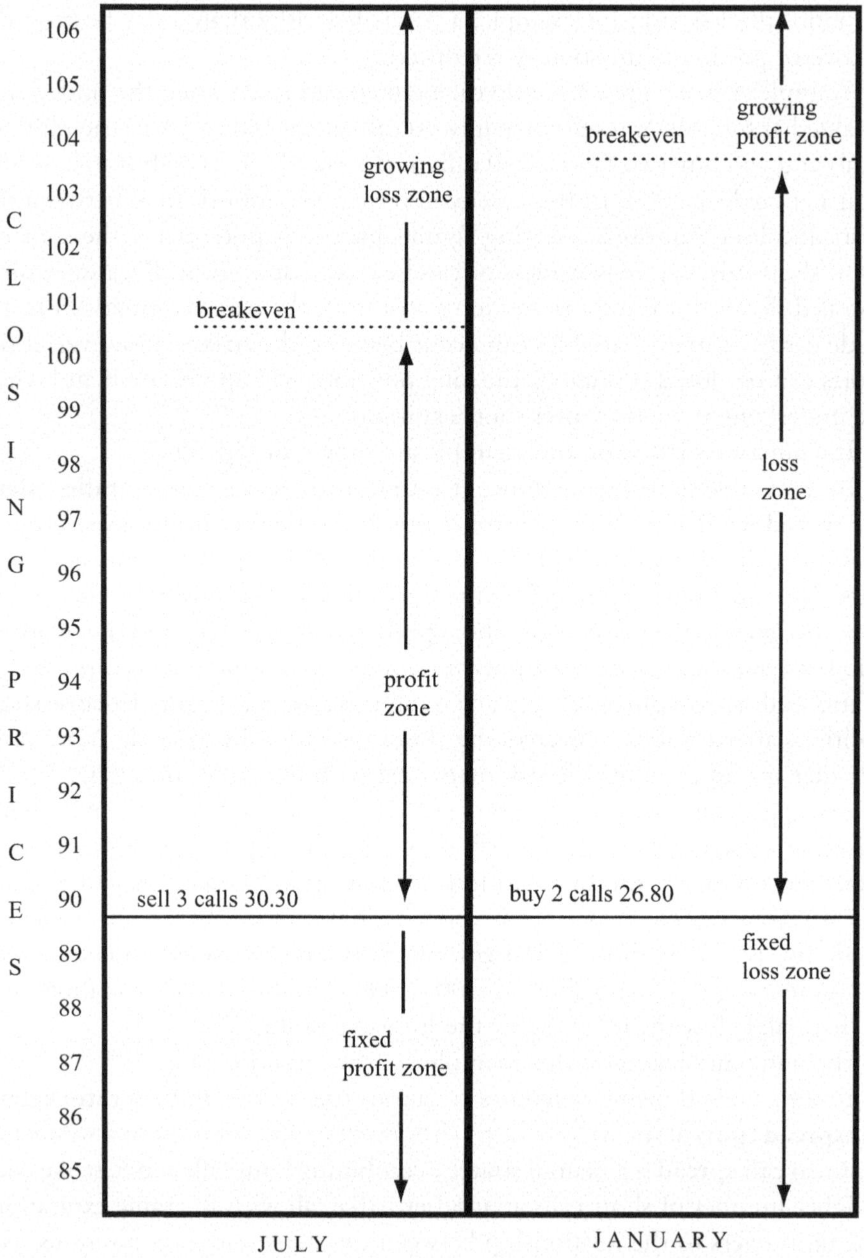

Fig. 35 Ratio calendar spread (call)

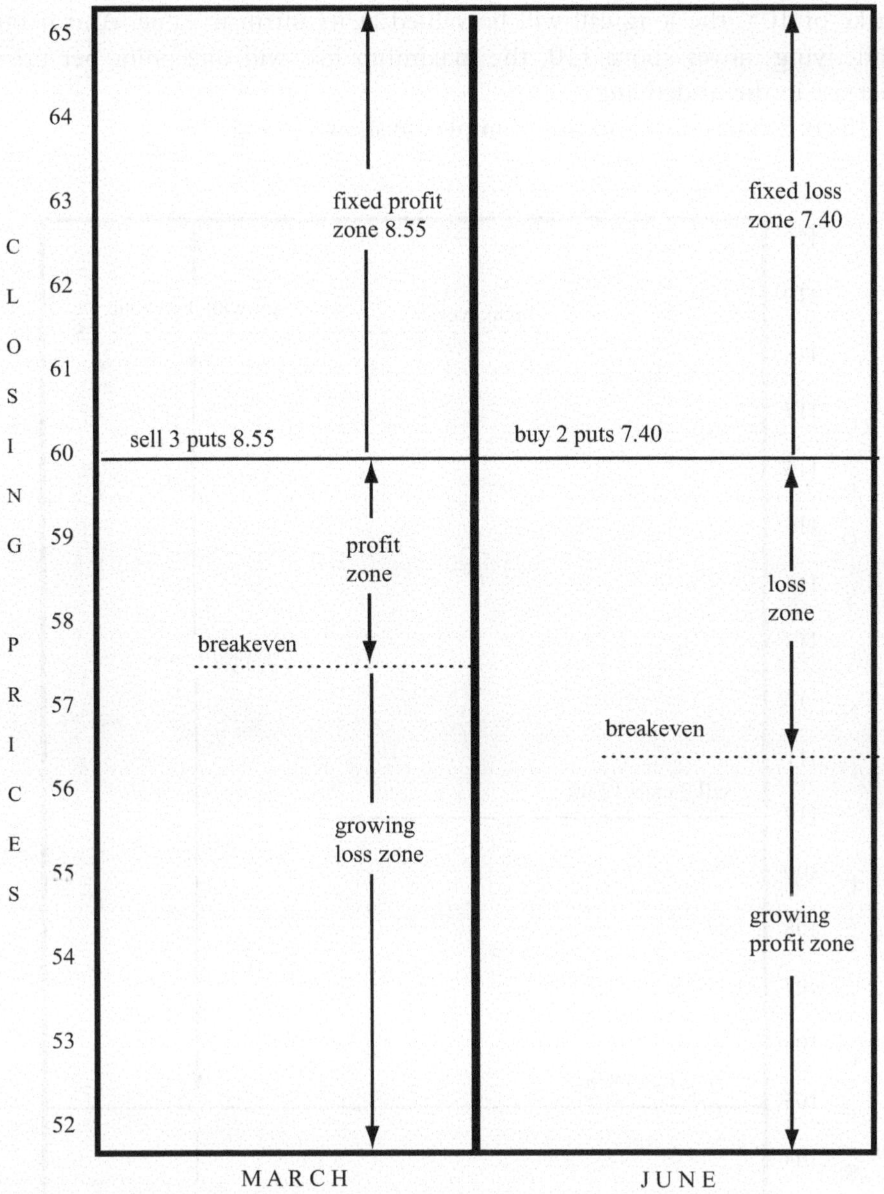

Fig. 36 Ratio calendar spread (put)

calls at the bid of 6.00 each, for a total of 12.00. Your net credit is 3.10. If the underlying remains below the short call strike of 110, the short calls expire worthless. Maximum loss will increase point for point with the underlying above the 118.10 level (115 + 3.10 credit). If the price rises above the long strike of 105, the long call will be valued at its intrinsic value. And if the underlying moves above 110, the maximum loss will one point per price increase in the underlying.

The outcomes based on this example are shown in Fig. 37.

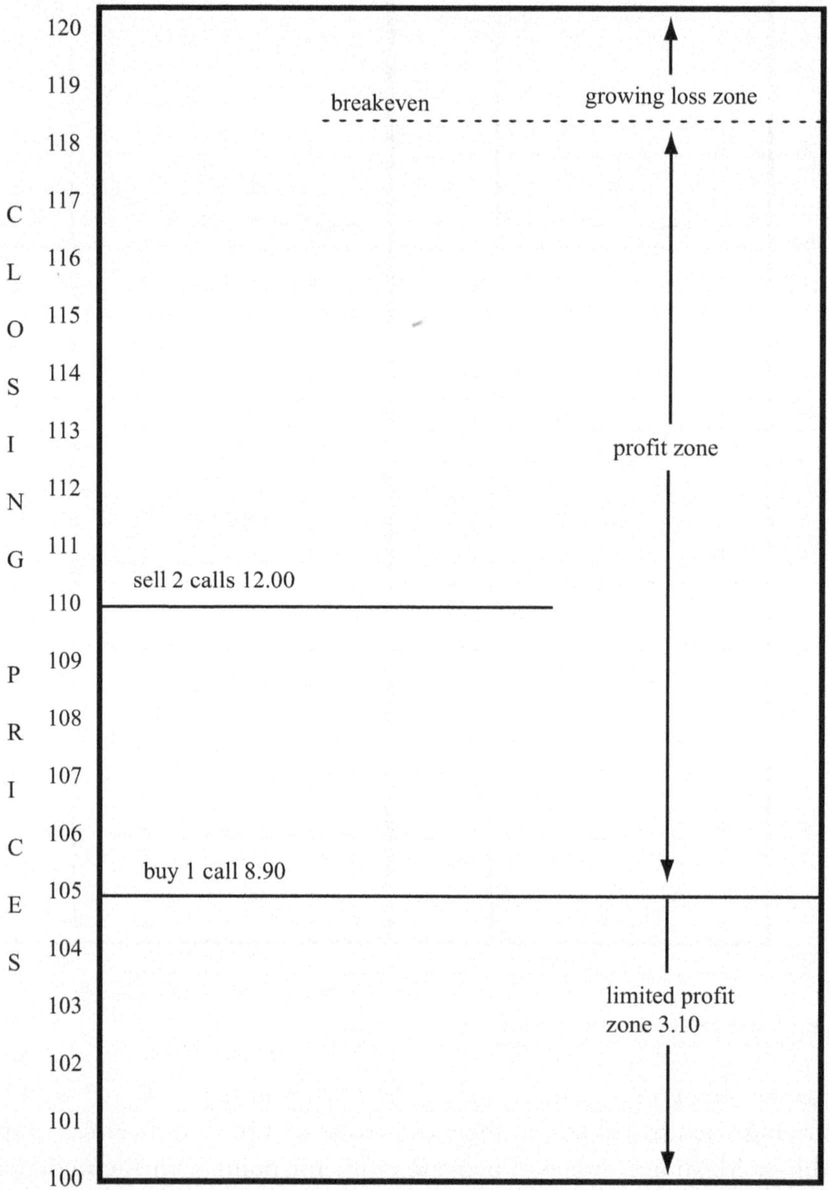

Fig. 37 Ratio call spread

To see a table showing outcomes at various price levels, link on **ratio call spread** at the website https://thomsettsguide.com/options-strategies/

Ratio put spread – a strategy with a dissimilar number of long and short puts. More puts are sold at a lower strike price than are bought at the higher strike. The downside risk can be significant, and the upside profit potential is limited. The ratio is defined by the relative numbers of puts on each side. If you sell two puts and buy one at a higher strike, you have created a 2:1 ratio put spread.

Example: You create a 2:1 ratio put on a stock valued at $108.10. You buy one 110 put at the ask of 6.90 and sell two 100 puts at the bid of 3.20 each, for a total of 6.40. Your net debit on this position is 0.50. This represents the maximum loss on the upside. There is a broad profit range in the middle, but an increasing loss potential on the downside.

The outcomes based on this example are shown in Fig. 38.

To see a table showing outcomes at various price levels, link on **ratio put spread** at the website https://thomsettsguide.com/options-strategies/

Ratio spread – a spread using either calls or puts, when a larger quantity of short positions are opened than long positions. Typically, the short positions are out of the money. All options in the ratio spread have the same expiration.

Ratio write – a variation of the covered call, in which a greater number of calls are written than are covered by long stock. The position consists of a series of covered calls plus one or more uncovered positions. However, it is more accurately viewed as the ratio of coverage. Because short positions can be closed to avoid losses, especially when time value declines, the risks of the ratio write are far less than for writing naked calls.

A popular ratio write is a 2:1, in which two calls are written against 100 shares of stock (e.g., or four calls against 200 shares). Risks are reduced, though, when the ratio is narrowed. So a 3:2 ratio write is less risky than a 2:1 ratio write.

Example: You create a 3:2 ratio write on an underlying valued at $58.91 per share. You bought 200 shares at $58.91 per share; you sold three 60 calls at the bid of 1.55 each, for a total of 4.65. The profit potential is immediate and considerable. The risk is that if the underlying price rises above 60, the 3:2 ratio works against the position. But it will require considerable movement to offset profits. The gain in the underlying has to be brought into the equation. Profit of 1.09 per share will occur at the strike. The 4.65 credit for the short calls also provides downside protection in the stock position. Thus, a loss in the underlying of 4.65, down to $54.26, represents a breakeven based on the price paid for shares, minus premium received from the short calls. It would require a rise in the underlying stock price of eight points to convert this into a loss position, or a decline of three points.

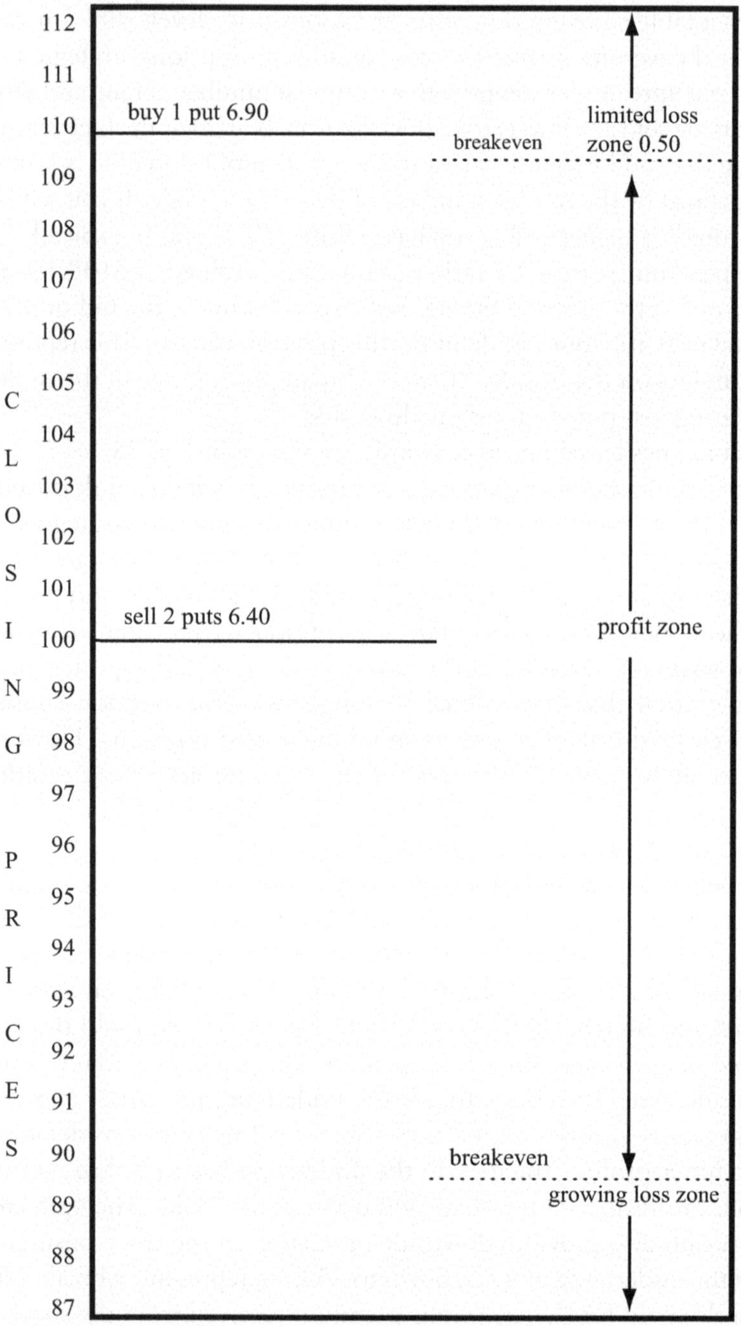

Fig. 38 Ratio put spread

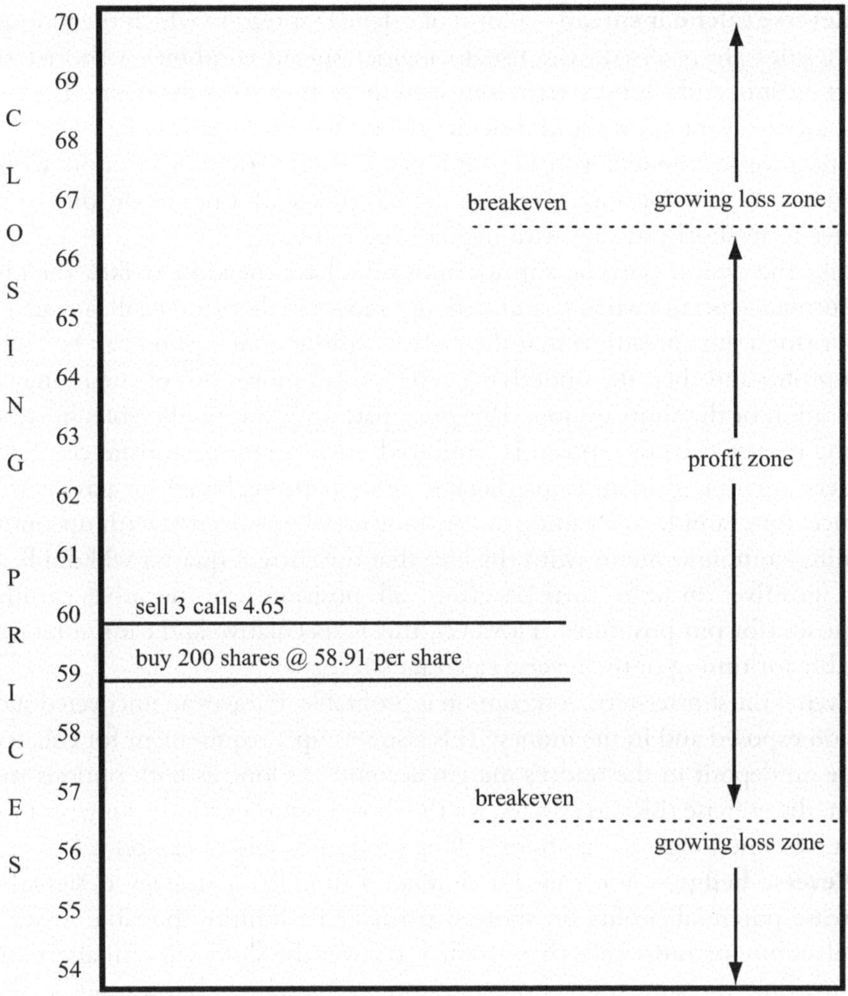

Fig. 39 Ratio write

The outcomes based on this example are shown in Fig. 39.

Reversal – a strategy combining three parts together: a short put, a long call, and short stock. For example, you shorted 100 shares at the price of $58.91. You create a reversal by selling a 60 put for 2.85 and buying a 60 call for 2.40. Your net credit is 0.45. This is the locked-in profit. If the stock price rises above the 60 strike, the call matches the rise point for point, offsetting the loss on the short stock. If the price falls below the 60 strike, the loss on the short put is offset by profit in the short stock.

Reverse calendar spread – a form of calendar spread in which the long and short sides are reversed. The usual calendar spread combines a short-term, short option, and a longer-term long option, setting up as net debit. The concept takes advantage of rapid time decay in the earlier expiration.

The reverse calendar spread combines a short-term long option with a longer-term short option. It creates the advantage of a net credit due to the longer-term short position with higher time value.

Like the typical calendar spread, both sides have the same strike. The ideal performance occurs when the underlying moves higher (for a call spreads) or lower (for a put spread) so that the earlier-expiring long option can be closed at a profit; and then the underlying reverses and moves out of the money by expiration of the short option. This price pattern is not predictable, however, so the reverse calendar spread is employed only in rare circumstances. Some traders attempt to identify predictable price patterns based on past performance; for example, the timing of the trade may be associated with upcoming earnings announcements, with the idea that the current quarter will duplicate past positive earnings surprises (for call positions) or negative earnings surprises (for put positions). However, this is speculative and cannot be used reliably for timing of the reverse calendar strategy.

Even if the shorter-term long option is profitable, it leaves an uncovered short option exposed and in the money. This also sets up a requirement for collateral to be on deposit in the trader's margin account. As long as both options were open, the exercise risk was covered for the short position with the long position. That offset no longer exists after the long position is sold or expires.

Reverse hedge – also called a simulated straddle, a strategy designed to increase potential profits on shorted stock while limiting possible losses. It involves buying more calls than needed to cover the short sale. An alternative to providing the same protection and profit potential is to buy a straddle; with both a long call and a long put open, the same protection and advantages can be achieved.

Example: The underlying is valued at $93.69 and you shorted 100 shares of the stock at that price. You believe the stock will decline substantially, but you also recognize that it could rise. So you want to open a reverse hedge to limit losses and to increase potential profits. If the stock price does decline, the shorted stock will become profitable. But if the price rises, you will experience a loss. The purchase of one call would offset the rise in price; the purchase of two or more calls creates a reverse hedge. In the event the stock's price rises, the calls will increase two points for every point of loss in the stock. With this in mind, you buy two 95 calls at the ask of 2.85 each, for a total debit of 5.70. To recapture the cost, you need the stock to decline beyond 5.7 points. If the stock's price rises 5.7 points or more, the reverse hedge produces profits.

Maximum profit is unlimited on both sides of the trade. The downside profit occurs when the underlying price and options moves farther than the net cost of the calls. For example, on the downside, if the stock price declines to $84 per share, the shorted stock is profitable by 9.69 points. The calls cost 5.70, so the net profit at this price is:

(*93.69 – 84 – 5.70 = 3.99, or $399*). As the stock price continues to decline, the short position picks up an additional point of profit, and the net cost of the two calls remains unchanged.

On the upside, the stock loses one point for each point of added value. However, the two options gain two points at each price level. For example, if the underlying price rises to $106 per share, the loss on short stock is 12.31 points. The 95 calls gain two points per gain in the stock price, so the overall net profit is: (((*106 – 95*) × *2*) – *5.70 – 12.31 = 3.99, or $399*).

Breakeven occurs at two price levels. The downside breakeven is equal to the initial stock price minus the cost of calls: (*93.69 – 5.70 = 87.99, or $87.99*). The upside breakeven occurs when the loss in the underlying is equal to the gain in the options. This is located in the example at $102 per share. The stock loss is: (*102 – 93.69 = 8.31, or $831*). At this point, the two calls have gained twice the points that the stock lost: (((*102 – 95*) × *2*) – *5.70 = 8 .30, or $830*).

Maximum loss for the options is the debit paid for the position (5.70, or $570). For the stock, maximum loss not offset by the options occurs at the strike of 95: (*95 – 93.69 = 1.31*). Once the underlying moves below the original basis of $93.69, the short position becomes profitable. Once the underlying prices moves above the strike, the options offset the stock loss by two points for each point the stock price moves.

The outcomes based on this example are shown in Fig. 40.

To see a table showing outcomes at various price levels, link on **reverse hedge** at the website https://thomsettsguide.com/options-strategies/

Rolling – a technique used to avoid exercise on short option positions. As the short option moves in the money, you can roll forward to a later expiration to avoid exercise. The added time value offsets the cost of closing one position for another in addition to deferring or escaping exercise. In theory, rolling can be performed indefinitely to perpetually avoid exercise. However, any time a short option is in the money, it can be exercised; but the most frequent occurrence is on the last trading day.

Traders may roll short positions as often as desired, but two disadvantages should be kept in mind. As long as the roll moves forward to a later expiration, it keeps the short position open and risk-exposed for a longer period of time. Second, the combined cost of trading between options and debits on a

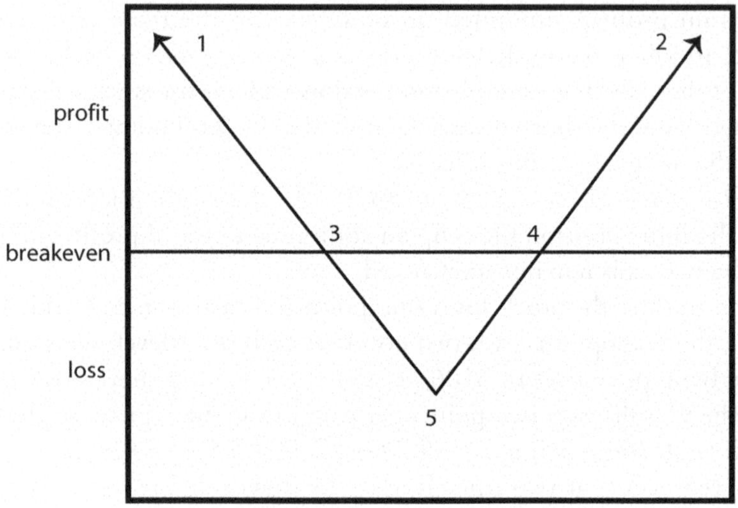

1 maximum profit (lower) (price declines to $84 per share:)
93.69 – 84 – 5.70 = 3.99, or $399
2 maximum profit (upper) (price advances to $106 per share):
((106 – 95) * 2) – 5.70 – 12.31 = 3.99, or $399
3 breakeven (lower) 93.69 – 5.70 = 87.99, or $87.99
4 breakeven (upper) (stock loss):
102 – 93.69 = 8.31, or $831
4 breakeven (upper) (option gain):
((102 – 95) * 2) – 5.70 = 8.30, or $830
5 maximum loss, options: 5.70, or $570
5 maximum non-offset loss, stock: 95 – 93.69 = 1.31, Or $131

Fig. 40 Reverse hedge

roll itself, may ultimately erode future profits, especially if the underlying stock's trend will be likely to keep these short positions moving in the money by future expiration dates. Rolling is potentially a profitable exercise avoidance strategy, but it should be used cautiously.

Four possible forms of rolling are:

1. *Rolling forward with the same strike.* The horizontal roll simply replaces the current strike with a later one. If time value is high enough, this roll creates a net credit between the buy to close and the new sell to open trades. The roll forward is applied to either short calls or short puts. The theory in support of the forward roll relies on two aspects to option trading. First, later expiration creates greater time value, which is an advantage to the seller. Second, the majority of exercise occurs at or near expiration, so rolling forward avoids exercise in most situations.

2. *Rolling forward with a higher strike.* This diagonal roll is applied to short calls. It replaces the current ITM strike with a later-expiring, OTM strike. This is possible to achieve with a small debit or, in some cases, with a net credit on the roll. The advantage is that it takes the short position out of the money, and sets up the potential for later exercise at a higher strike.
3. *Rolling forward with a lower strike.* This diagonal roll is applied to short puts. It replaces an ITM put with a later-expiring OTM put. In the event of exercise, the strike is lowered, creating a lower cost for future stock. It may be accomplished for little or no debit and possibly for a small credit on the exchange of positions.
4. *Rolling from one strike to another with the same expiration.* In some instances, it is advantageous to replace the strike but leave the expiration the same, through a vertical roll. When the difference in premium is lower than the distance between strikes, and exercise is certain (as in the case of a deep ITM short position), the loss on either call or put is reduced by that difference. For example, a covered call with a strike of 100 is valued at 9.10. The stock was worth $108.10 per share, so exercise is virtually certain by expiration. A vertical roll to the 105 strike, valued at the bid of 4.90, sets up two advantages. First, the net cost is 4.20 (9.10–4.90). If the short call is exercised, it will occur at a strike five points higher, so a net gain of 0.80 results (stock will be called away at 105 instead of 100, of $500 higher, but the cost of the vertical roll is only 4.20). The second advantage is in the possibility that the underlying will move below the strike, and the short position will then expire worthless. At the higher strike, the underlying is only 3.10 points in the money. A small downward move before expiration is possible, whereas a move of 8.10 points (required to move the 100 strike out of the money) is far less likely in only three weeks.

Short call – an open option contract in which the right to buy 100 shares of the underlying stock has been sold. An uncovered short call is a high-risk position, and a covered short call is very conservative (because you own the 100 shares that can be used to satisfy assignment). In comparison, a long call is one in which the holder owns the right to buy 100 shares of the underlying; and a short put grants the right to someone else to put 100 shares of stock to the trader at the fixed strike price.

Short calls are employed by traders in numerous ways:

1. *Swing trading.* If you own shares of stock as a long-term investment, you will not want to sell when prices rise or fall. However, when prices rise, selling covered calls is one way to swing trade on the temporary price movement. Once the price retreats, the short call can be closed at a profit.

2. *Simple speculation.* Short calls can be used to earn short-term profits. If these are covered calls, risk is minimal because 100 shares are owned. If uncovered, short calls are quite risky. This risk can be mitigated with the use of a ratio write. For example, you own 200 shares and you sell three calls.
3. *To insure a long stock position.* The short call is used by stock investors as one form of insurance against the stock's price decline. The open short call premium reduces potential losses if and when the price declines.
4. *As part of a straddle or spread.* The combination strategies involving two or more sides require the use of offsetting positions. Short calls offset short puts or long calls.

Short call butterfly – a neutral strategy used in anticipation of higher than average volatility in the underlying. It combines a bull spread with a bear spread like the long call butterfly, and provides limited profit with limited risk. However, while the long call butterfly contains two short positions in between a high and a low strike, the short call butterfly is the opposite: It includes a high and low strike short, with two long positions at a strike in between, all with the same expiration.

Example: You construct a short call butterfly on an underlying priced at $58.91. It includes June strikes of 55, 60 and 65. You sell one 55 call at the bid of 7.60 and one 65 call at the bid of 1.90. You buy two 60 calls at the ask of 4.00 each, for a total of 8.00. Your net credit is 1.50. The position results in a fixed profit equal to this credit on the high and low sides, with a limited loss zone in between.

Maximum profit is realized when the underlying price is higher than the highest strike or lower than the lowest strike. It is equal to the net credit: 1.50, or $150.

Breakeven is located on the lower side by adding the lowest strike of the short call to the net premium received: (*55 + 1.50 = 56.50, or $56.50*). Upper breakeven is equal to the strike of the highest short call minus the net premium received: (*65 – 1.50 = 63.50, or $63.50*).

Maximum loss occurs when the price of the underlying is equal to the strike of the short calls. It is calculated by subtracting the lower call strike from the higher call strike, and subtracting the net credit: (*60 – 55 – 1.50 = 3.50 or $350*).

The outcomes based on this example are shown in Fig. 41.

To see a table showing outcomes at various price levels, link on **short call butterfly** at the website https://thomsettsguide.com/options-strategies/

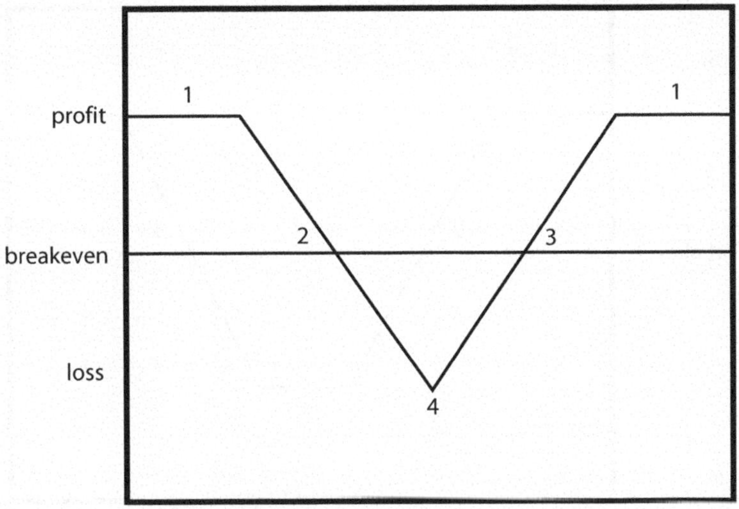

1 maximum profit 1.50, or $150
2 lower breakeven 55 + 1.50 = 56.50, or $56.50
3 upper breakeven 65 – 1.50 = 63.50, or $63.50
4 maximum loss 60 – 55 – 1.50 = 3.50, or $350

Fig. 41 Short call butterfly

Short call condor – a neutral strategy that, like the short call butterfly, combines limited profit with limited risk. Profit results from price movement in the underlying in either direction beyond the middle price zone. The two middle calls have different strikes, whereas the butterfly is confined to one. The result is that the short call condor involves four separate strikes with the same expiration. The high and low consist of short calls and the two middle strikes consist of long calls.

Example: You open a condor on an underlying priced at $108.10 by buying two middle-strike calls, and offsetting that position with one higher-strike and one lower-strike short call. The long positions are 105 at the ask of 11.00 and 110 at the ask of 8.30, and the short positions are 100 at the bid of 15.80 and 115 at the bid of 6.10. Your net credit is 2.60.

Maximum profit is equal to the amount of the net credit: 2.60, or $260.

Breakeven is found at two price points. Lower breakeven is equal to the strike of the lowest short call plus the net credit: (*100 + 2.60 = 102.60, or $102.60*). Upper breakeven is at the strike of the highest short call minus the net credit: (*115 – 2.60 = 112.40, or $112.4*).

Maximum loss occurs when the underlying ends up in between the two middle strikes. It is the net of the lower strike long call, minus the lower strike short put, minus the net credit: (*110 – 105 – 2.60 = 2.40, or $240*).

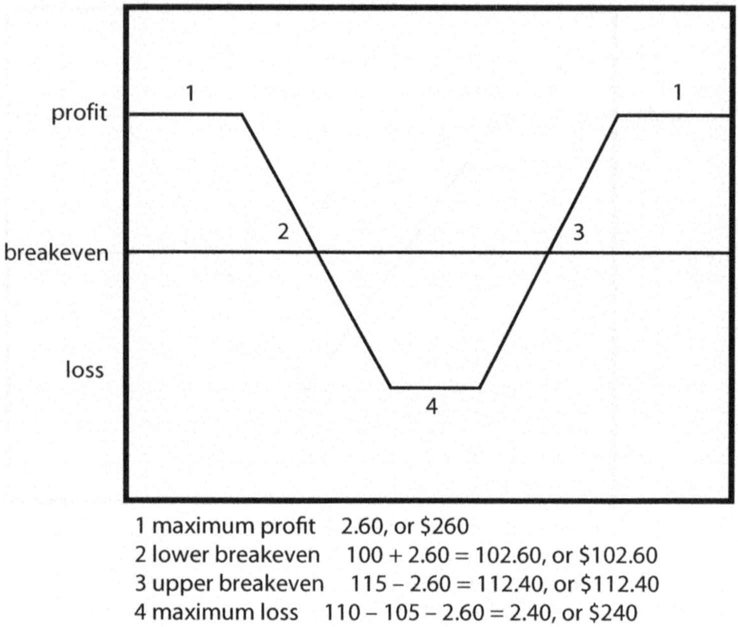

Fig. 42 Short call condor

The outcomes based on this example are shown in Fig. 42.

To see a table showing outcomes at various price levels, link on **short call condor** at the website https://thomsettsguide.com/options-strategies/

Short combo – a strategy based on short options, including:

1. Synthetic short stock comprised of a short call and a long put with the same strike.
2. Any grouping that is designed to minimize risk employing short options with offsetting protective positions (those may consist of open stock holdings, or of other long or short options that hedge the short position) .
3. Straddles or spreads using short positions rather than long positions.

Short iron butterfly – also called reverse iron butterfly, this strategy limits profits and risks and is designed to be profitable when the underlying moves significantly above or below a mid-range price. It involves both calls and puts, with the middle strike containing one long call and one long put with the same strike; and the higher and lower strikes are short. The higher strike has a short call and the lower strike is a short put. All options have the same expiration unless the strategy is constructed as a diagonal.

Example: You construct a short iron butterfly on an underlying priced at \$93.69. The long positions include a 95 call at the ask of 2.85 and a 95 put at the ask of 4.00. The short positions are a 100 call at the bid of 1.05 and a 90 put at the bid of 1.85. The net debit on this position is 3.95. The profit zone is narrow in this strategy. However, with the analysis constructed assuming all parts are left open until expiration, the strategy may become more profitable if and when short legs are closed early.

Maximum profit is limited and occurs when the underlying is below the short put strike or above the short call strike. Maximum is equal to the difference between strikes of long and short on each side, minus the net paid. Lower profit: (*95 – 90 – 3.95 = 1.05, or \$105*). Upper profit: (*100 – 95 – 3.95 = 1.05, or \$105*).

Breakeven is located on the lower side by subtracting the net paid from the strike of the long put: (*95 – 3.95 = 91.05, or \$91.05*). On the upper side, breakeven is equal to the strike of the long call plus the net paid: (*95 + 3.95 = 98.95, or \$98.95*).

Maximum loss is limited to the amount paid to open the position: 3.95, or \$395.

The outcomes based on this example are shown in Fig. 43.

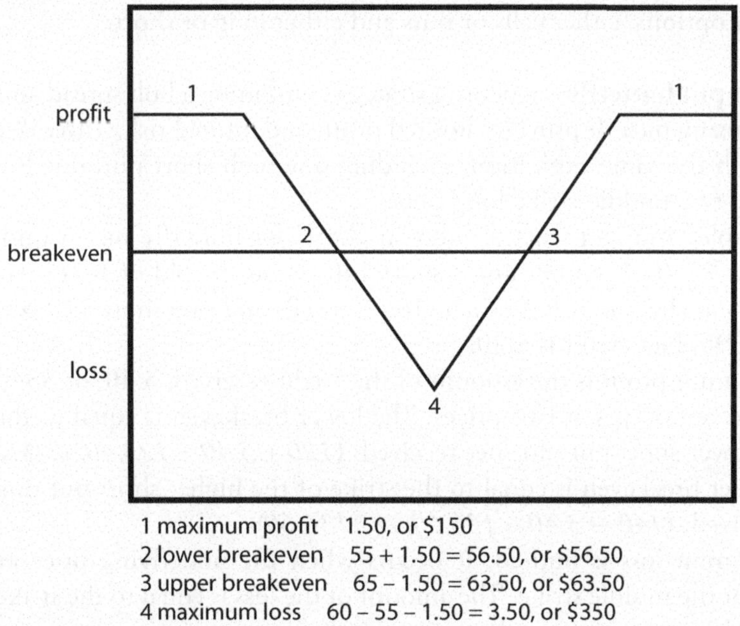

Fig. 43 Short iron butterfly

To see a table showing outcomes at various price levels, link on **short iron butterfly** at the website https://thomsettsguide.com/options-strategies/

Short put – any put option sold and in an open position. The put seller grants the buyer the right to put 100 shares to the seller at a fixed strike price. If the underlying price falls below the strike price, the put is exercised. The short put holder agrees to pay the strike even though the current market value of the underlying is lower at the time.

The short put risk is limited. Unlike the short call, which can theoretically include unlimited risk (because the underlying value could rise indefinitely), the short put risk is finite. The maximum loss is between strike price and zero; however, a more realistic risk is between strike price and tangible book value per share (or, liquidation value). It would be unlikely for the market value of the underlying to decline below this level.

Short puts may be used in many strategic varieties, including:

1. Speculation on the change in the underlying market value.
2. As part of a swing trading strategy, when the underlying price has dropped and the trader anticipates a short-term bounce.
3. As a form of contingent purchase when the trader is willing to acquire shares at the strike price.
4. Within a spread or straddle employing short puts in conjunction with other options, either calls or puts and either long or short.

Short put butterfly – a neutral strategy combining a bull spread and a bear spread, using puts. It provides limited profit and limited risk. Three strikes are used with the same expiration, including one high short put, one low short put, and two middle-strike long puts.

Example: You construct a one-year short put butterfly on an underlying priced at $130.01, combining a short 140 put at the bid of 14.15, two long 130 puts at the ask of 8.35 each (16.70 total), and one short 120 put at the bid of 5.95. Net credit is 3.40.

Maximum profit is the amount of the credit received: 3.40, or $340.

Breakeven occurs at two prices. The lower breakeven is equal to the strike of the lower short put plus net received: (*120 + 3.40 = 123.40, or $123.40*). The upper breakeven is equal to the strike of the higher short put minus the net received: (*140 – 3.40 = 136.60, or $136.60*).

Maximum loss is limited. It occurs when the underlying price ends up exactly at the middle strike. The amount of the loss is equal to the strike of the higher short put, minus the strike of the long put, minus net received: (*140 – 130 – 3.40 = 6.60, or $660*).

The outcomes based on this example are shown in Fig. 44.

To see a table showing outcomes at various price levels, link on **short put butterfly** at the website https://www.thomsettpublishing.com/option-strategies-n-z.

Short put condor – an expansion of the short put butterfly in which the middle puts are spread between two strikes rather than one. As a result, there are four strikes in the position instead of three, with the two short positions at highest and lowest and the two long positions in the two middle-range strikes.

Example: You construct a short put condor on the underlying at $58.91, with four strikes, all with the same expiration. This consists of a short 65 put at the bid of 6.60, a long 62.50 put at the ask of 4.90, a long 60 put at the ask of 3.70, and a short 57.50 put at the bid of 2.10. Net credit is 0.10.

Maximum profit is the amount of the credit: 0.10, or $10.

Breakeven occurs at two prices. Lower breakeven is equal to the strike of the lower short put, plus the net credit: (*57.50 + 0.10 = 57.60, or $57.60*). Upper breakeven is equal to the strike of the higher short put, minus the net credit: (*65 – 0.10 = 64.90, or $64.90*).

Maximum loss is limited to the higher short strike less the higher long strike, less the net credit: (*65 – 62.50 – 0.10 = 2.40, or $240*).

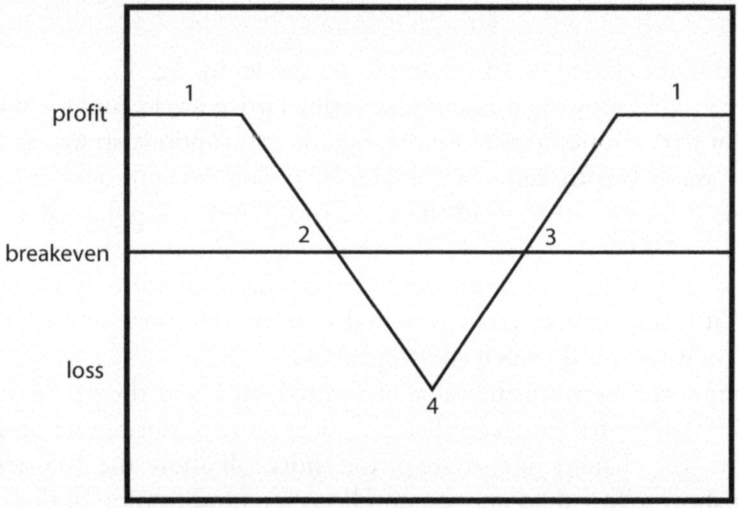

1 maximum profit 3.40, or $340
2 lower breakeven 120 + 3.40 = 123.40, or $123.40
3 upper breakeven 140 – 3.40 = 136.60, or $136.60
4 maximum loss 140 – 130 – 3.40 = 6,60, or $660

Fig. 44 Short put butterfly

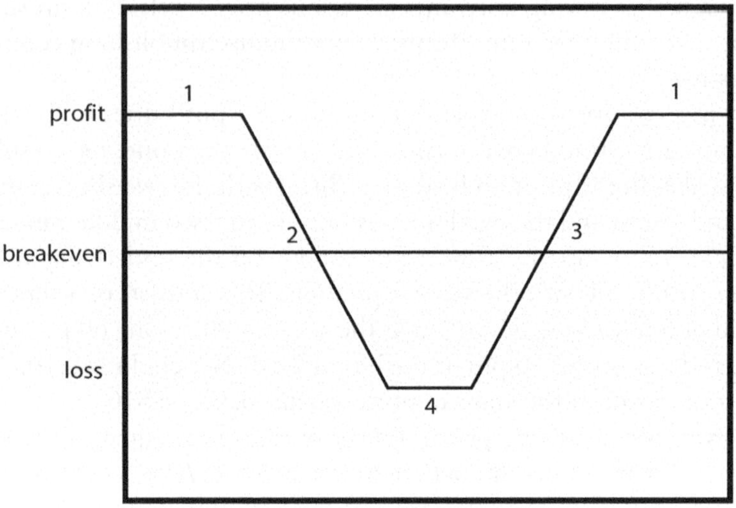

1 maximum profit 0.10, or $10
2 lower breakeven 57.50 + 0.10 = 57.60, or $57.60
3 upper breakeven 65 – 0.10 = 64.90, or $64.90
4 maximum loss 65 – 62.50 – 0.10 = 2.40, or $240

Fig. 45 Short put condor

The outcomes based on this example are shown in Fig. 45.

To see a table showing outcomes at various price levels, link on **short put condor** at the website https://thomsettsguide.com/options-strategies/

Short stock (synthetic) – a position involving two options—a long put and short call—set up to yield the same profit and risk potential as that of short selling 100 shares of stock. The options have the same strike and expiration. The risk is less and profit potential greater than with simply shorting stock. With the synthetic strategy, you do not need to borrow stock and pay interest on it, as you do when shorting stock.

A comparison between the value of shorted stock and the net value of the synthetic strategy demonstrates that the prices remain constant on upside and downside. The chances of exercise of the short call above the 105 strike add risk that short selling does not contain; however, modification of this strategy by covering the call mitigates this risk. The short call can be covered by owning 100 shares of stock. In this case, the synthetic strategy provides downside protection for the long position, and provides coverage for the call in the event of exercise.

Example: You set up a short stock (synthetic) position on an underlying priced at \$130.00. You sell a 130 call at the bid of 1.00 and buy a 130 put at the ask of 1.27. Your net debit is 0.27. If the stock falls below the strike of 130, the long put gains value. The position mirrors closely what will occur if stock were shorted (assuming underlying is valued at \$130 at the time a short is opened).

Maximum profit is accomplished when the underlying price declines. It is equal to the strike of the long put minus the current underlying price, minus the net debit. If the underlying price declines to \$125 per share, profit is: (*130 – 125 – 0.27 = 4.73, or \$473*).

Breakeven is equal to the long put strike plus net premium paid: (*130 + 0.27 = 130.27, or \$130.27*).

Maximum loss occurs if and when the underlying moves upward. It is equal to the underlying price, minus the cost per share, plus premium paid. For example, if the underlying price rises to \$134 per share, loss is: (*134 – 130 + 0.27 = 4.27, or \$427*).

The outcomes based on this example are shown in Fig. 46.

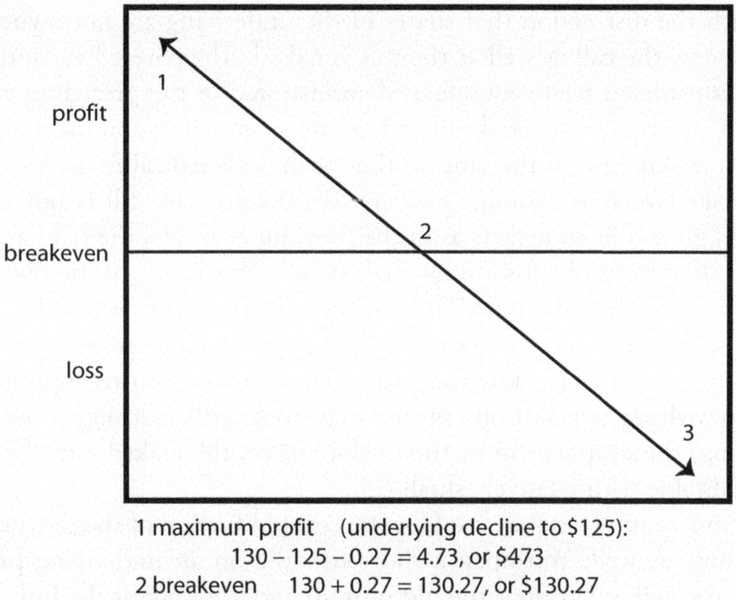

1 maximum profit (underlying decline to \$125):
130 – 125 – 0.27 = 4.73, or \$473
2 breakeven 130 + 0.27 = 130.27, or \$130.27
3 maximum loss (underlying rises to \$134):
134 – 130 + 0.27 = 4.27, or \$427

Fig. 46 Short stock (synthetic)

To see a table showing outcomes at various price levels, link on **short stock (synthetic)** at the website https://thomsettsguide.com/options-strategies/

Short straddle (covered) – the combined ownership of 100 shares of the underlying, with a short straddle (selling a call and selling a put). This strategy combines a covered call with an uncovered put. Because both options are short, either can be closed before expiration of the position, in which case you end up with either a straight covered call, or a naked put. It is likely that the OTM side would be closed first, leaving a short option in the money. However, this does not necessarily lead to exercise; a decline in time value of both option positions may allow you to close both sides profitably.

Example: You open a short straddle on an underlying priced at $93.69. You sell a 95 call at the bid of 4.90 and a 95 put at the bid of 5.50. Your total credit is 10.40, a "buffer" range of over 20 points: 10.4 points above *and* below the strike of 95.

Because this position combines two separate calls with 100 shares of long stock, the overall profitability has to take both stock and option outcomes into consideration. The outcome for the options portion of this strategy is summarized in Fig. 47.

Short straddle (naked) – a straddle very similar to the short straddle (covered) with the distinction that shares of the underlying are not owned. As a consequence, the call as well as the put is naked. The covered version of this may be considered relatively safe as demonstrated in the preceding explanation, as it combines a covered call with an uncovered put; and the market risk for the uncovered put is the same as that of the covered call.

The naked version contains greater risks because the call is not covered. However, given the same facts as in the previous example, the risks are not as severe as they would be for a single naked call. This is due to the two-option credit received when the position is opened. In the example for the covered version of this strategy, you gain a 20-point profit range resulting from the 10.4 points above and below the strike. The fact that you receive an overall credit by writing two options means that even with a strong move in the underlying, the evaporation of time value makes this naked straddle potentially profitable with relatively small risk.

The same example as that used for the covered version of the short straddle is used here as well: You open a short straddle on an underlying priced at $93.69. You sell a 95 call at the bid of 4.90 and a 95 put at the bid of 5.50. Your total credit is 10.40, a "buffer" range of over 20 points: 10.4 points above *and* below the strike of 95.

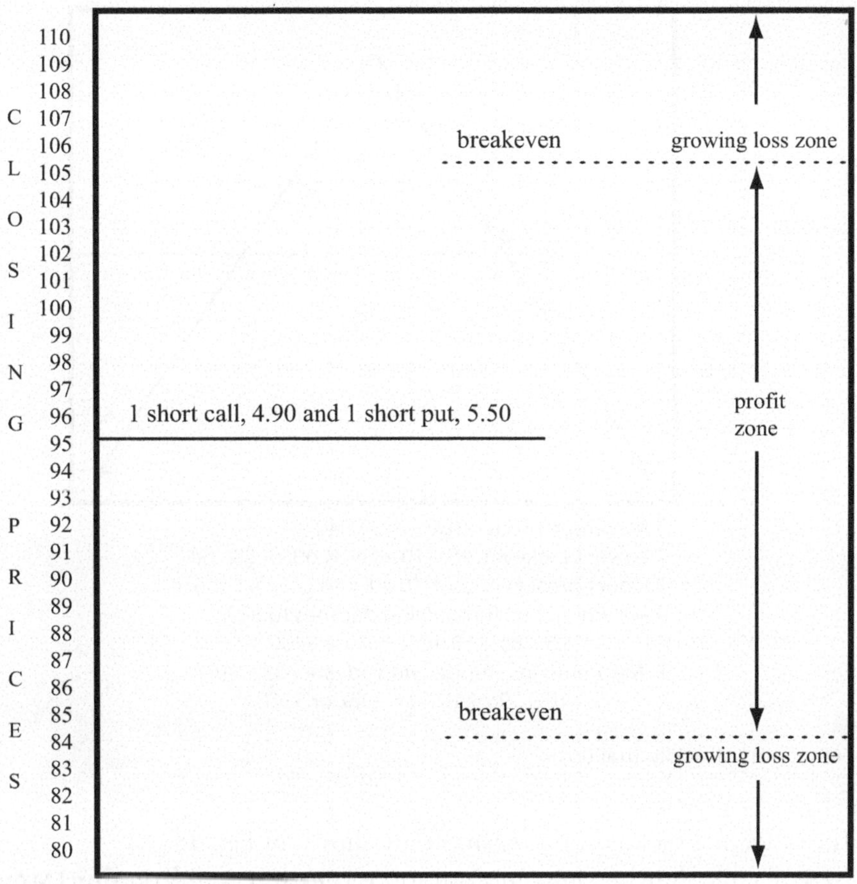

Fig. 47 Short straddle (covered)

Maximum profit is limited to the price of the two options. As the price moves away from this point, the profit declines within the buffer zone: 10.40, or $1040.

Two breakeven prices apply. On the lower side, breakeven is equal to the strike of the short put, minus net premium received: (*95 – 10.40 = 84.60, or $84.60*). Upper breakeven is located at the short call strike plus net received: (*95 + 10.40 = 105.40, or $105.40*).

Maximum loss is limited only by the degree of movement in the underlying. It occurs at two points, one below and one above. On the lower side, for example, if the underlying declines to $80 per share, maximum loss is the strike less the underlying price, less premium received: (*95 – 80 – 10.40 = 4.60, or $460*). On the upper side, if the underlying price rises to $107 per share, maximum loss is underlying price minus the strike, minus net premium received: (*107 – 95 – 10.40 = 1.60, or $160*).

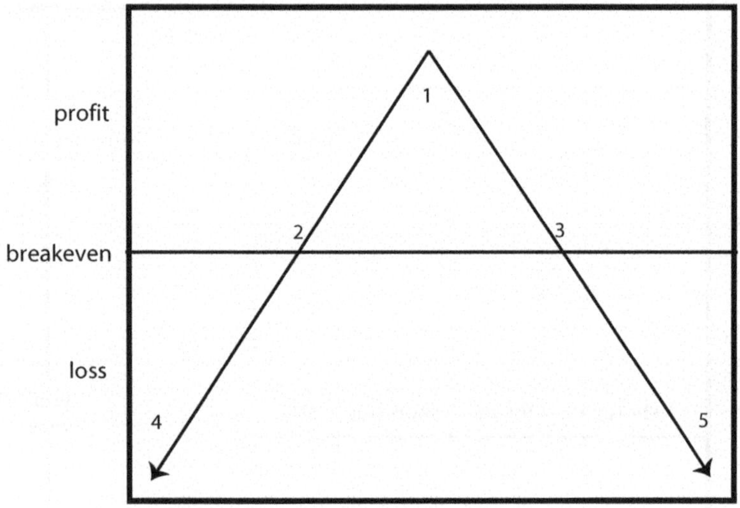

1 Maximum profit 10.40, or $1,040
2 Lower breakeven 95 – 10.40 = 84.60, or $84.60
3 Upper breakeven 95 + 10.40 = 105.40, or $105.40
4 Maximum loss (underlying declines to $80:
95 – 80 – 10.40 = 4.60, or $460
5 Maximum loss (underlying advanced to $107):
107 – 95 – 10.40 = 1.60, or $160

Fig. 48 Short straddle (naked)

The outcomes based on this example are shown in Fig. 48.

To see a table showing outcomes at various price levels, link on **short straddle (naked)** at the website https://www.thomsettpublishing.com/option-strategies-n-z.

Short strangle – also called a strangle write, this strategy combines puts and calls with the same expiration but different strikes. A popular approach is to sell both options out of the money and about equal distance from the price of the underlying at the time the position is opened.

Example: The underlying is valued at $108.10. You open a short strangle by selling two options with April expirations. The 115 call is sold at the bid of 3.90 and the 105 put is sold at the bid of 4.55. Your total credit is 8.45. The advantage to this position is that both sides of the short strangle are out of the money. Either or both may be closed when time value declines, regardless of the movement in the underlying. The 8.45 credit provides a profit range equal to that value both above the call strike and below the put strike, for a total of 26.9 points (10 points between the strikes plus 8.45 above 115 plus 8.45 below 105).

Maximum profit occurs when the underlying is trading in between the two strikes, so that both options remain out of the money. In this range, profit is limited to the net credit received: 8.45, or $845.

Breakeven occurs at two price points. Lower breakeven is equal to the strike of the short put, minus premium received: (*105 – 8.45 = 96.55, or $96.55*). Upper breakeven is equal to the strike of the short call plus net premium received: (*115 + 8.45 = 123.45, or $123.45*).

Maximum risk is determined by the number of points the underline moves, either below the short put's strike or above the short call's strike. For example if the underline declines to $94 per share, the lower loss is determined by subtracting the current price from the strike, minus the net premium received: (*105 – 94 – 8.45 = 2.55, or $255*). If the underlying price rises to $128 per share, loss is the difference between the underlying price and the call's strike, minus the net credit: (*128 – 115 – 8.45 = 4.55, or $455*).

The outcomes based on this example are shown in Fig. 49.

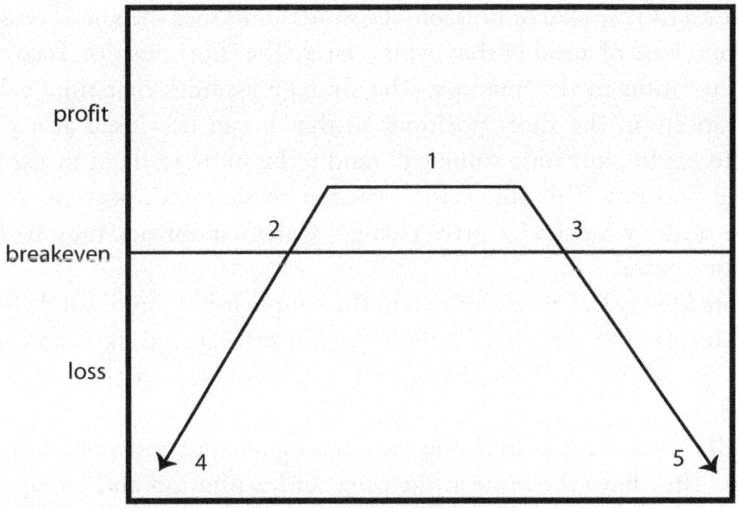

1 maximum profit 8,45, or $845
2 lower breakeven 105 – 8.45 = 96.55, or $96.55
3 upper breakeven 115 + 8.45 = 123.45, or $123.45
4 maximum loss (underlying declines to $94):
105 – 94 – 8.45 = 2.55, or $255
3 maximum loss (underling advances to $128):
128 – 115 – 8.45 = 4.55, or $455

Fig. 49 Short strangle

To see a table showing outcomes at various price levels, link on **short strangle** at the website https://thomsettsguide.com/options-strategies/

Simulated straddle *see* **Reverse hedge**

Spread – any combination of two option positions, one long and one short, with different terms. The spread enables a trader to reduce the risk on a short position with an offsetting long position. As long as the long position has the same expiration or a later expiration, the short position is covered.

Spreads may be vertical, horizontal, or diagonal. A vertical spread consists of the same expiration but different strikes. Horizontal refers to a spread with the same strikes but different expirations. A diagonal spread has different strikes and different expirations in the option positions.

Spreads may consist of calls, puts, or both. They may also be bullish, bearish, or neutral. A bull spread is going to produce the greatest profits when the underlying rises in price. Bear spreads are the opposite. A neutral spread will produce profits when price does not change significantly, and are characterized by a middle profit zone with limited loss zones above and below.

Another distinction focuses on the time of expiration. The calendar spread (also called a time spread or horizontal spread) combines the sale of one option and the purchase of another that expires later. The short position is covered by the long position in this manner. The strategy assumes that time value will decline rapidly in the short position, so that it can be closed at a profit or allowed to expire, but time value will tend to be more resilient in the longer-term long position. This allows for a smaller erosion and, possibly, for profit from the underlying stock's price change. Calendar spreads may be bullish, bearish, or neutral.

The spread may be more exotic than the simple inclusion of single long and short positions. The variations include the butterfly spread, ratio spread, ratio calendar spread, reverse calendar spread, calendar combination, backspread, and condor.

Straddle – a strategy combining the opening of a put and a call with identical terms. They have the same strike price and expiration and are opened on the same underlying stock. In a long straddle, price movement of the underlying has to be great enough in either direction to offset the cost of buying the options. In a short straddle, the trader hopes that the underlying price will remain within the profit zone created by the credit for selling the options.

The straddle can be varied in several ways. For example, a strangle involves two options with the same expiration but with different strikes. A straddle may also be covered, at least partially. If you own 100 shares of the underlying and you write a short straddle, it consists of a covered call and a naked put. If you do not own 100 shares of the underlying, the short straddle is uncovered.

Strangle – a variation on the straddle, in which expiration is the same for each side, but the strike price is different. Strangles are often used in short positions in place of the straddle, as they reduce the chances of exercise. In a short straddle, one side or the other is always in the money unless the strike is exactly equal to the underlying stock's current market value. The strangle, in comparison, is usually designed with both short positions both out of the money, one on each side of the current underlying price. For example, if the stock is selling at $95 per share, a strangle may include a short call at the strike of 97.50 and a short put at the strike of 92.50. The total credit received for opening a short strangle creates a profit zone equal to the points in that credit. The profit zone extends above the call strike and below the put strike. So a credit of 7.00 creates a 19-point profit zone when the strikes are five points apart: 7 + 7 + 5 = 19 points.

A long strangle is based on the assumption that the underlying stock's price will be volatile, but the direction of the underlying price movement is unknown. It requires considerable price movement to create a profit, since the entire debit paid for put and call is time value. Just as the short straddle creates a wide profit range, the long straddle fixed just as broad a loss range, requiring the stock's price to exceed that range above or below.

A short strangle is more likely to be profitable due to the breadth of its profit range. In addition, either side can be closed at a profit when time value declines, especially for the side that remains out of the money. In a short strangle, one side of the transaction is always out of the money. This is a primary advantage of the short strangle over the short straddle.

Strap – a variation on the straddle, in which more long calls than long puts are opened, at the same strike and expiration. This adds an upward directional bias to the long straddle.

Example: You create a strap on the underlying priced at $58.91 per share. You buy two 60 calls at the ask of 2.40 each, for a total of 4.80; and you buy one 60 put at the ask of 2.85. Your total debit is 7.65. In order for this position to become profitable, the underlying price must move enough points to overcome the debit of 7.65. Because the number of calls are doubled, the upward movement produces a profit more quickly.

Profit potential is unlimited. Profit in the event of a price decline must exceed the net debit of this position. In the example, the debit is 7.65 points. If the underlying declines to 50 per share, downside net profit is the difference between strike and price, plus the net debit: (*60 – 50 – 7.65 = 2.35, or $235*). Because a higher number of calls are included, upside profits are realized more rapidly. In the example, two calls were opened. Upside profit is equal to the underlying price minus the strike, and this net difference multiplied by the number of calls; and reduced by the net debit. If the underlying price rises to $67 per share, net profit is: (((*67 – 60*) × *2*) – *7.65 = 6.35, or $635*).

The position also produces two breakeven points. The downside breakeven is equal to the strike minus net debit: (*60 – 7.65 = 52.35, or $52.35*). Upper breakeven is equal to the strike plus one-half of the total debit: (*60 + (7.65 ÷ 2) = 63.825, or $63.82½*).

Maximum loss occurs at the strike and is equal to the net debit paid: 7.65, or $765.

The outcomes based on this example are shown in Fig. 50.

To see a table showing outcomes at various price levels, link on **strap** at the website https://thomsettsguide.com/options-strategies/

Strip – a bearish variation on the long straddle, in which more long puts are opened than long calls. As the opposite of the strap, profit will occur more rapidly if the underlying price moves downward; however, profits will result in two ways: when the underlying price moves far enough above or below the debit.

Example: You create a strip on an underlying priced at $93.69. You buy one 90 call for 5.90 and two 90 puts for 1.85 each, or a total of 3.70. Your total debit is 9.60.

Maximum profit is unlimited and is found both above and below the strike. However, based on the size of the total debit, considerable movement in the

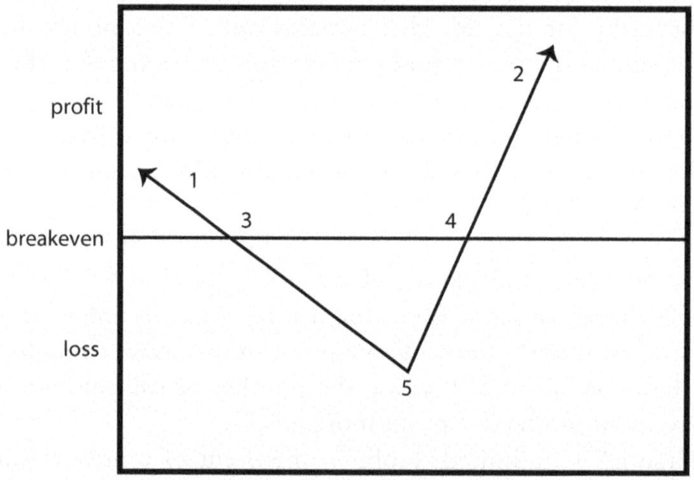

1 maximum profit (lower) (price declines to $50 per share):
60 – 50 – 7.65 = 2.35, or $235
2 maximum profit (upper) (price advances to $67 per share):
((67 – 60) * 2) – 7.65 = 6.35, or $635
3 breakeven (lower) 60 – 7.65 = 52.35, or $52.35
4 breakeven (upper) 60 + (7.65 ÷ 2) = 63.825, or $63.82½).
5 maximum loss 7.65, or $765

Fig. 50 Strap

underlying price is required. On the downside, maximum profit is equal to the strike, minus the price of the underlying, with the net divided by two; less the net premium paid. For example, if the underlying price declines to $82 per share, profit is: (((*90 – 82*) × *2*) – *9.60 = 6.40, or $640*). On the upside, profit is equal to the underlying price minus the strike, minus the net debit. For example, if the underlying rises to $100 per share, profit is: (*100 – 90 – 9.60 = 0.40, or $40*).

Breakeven takes place at two price points. On the downside, it equals the strike minus one-half of the debit paid: (*90 –* (*9.60 ÷ 2*) *= 85.20, or $85.20*). Upper breakeven is located at the strike plus net debit: (*90 + 9.60 = 99.60*).

Maximum loss is limited to the net debit paid: 9.60, or $960.

The outcomes based on this example are shown in Fig. 51.

To see a table showing outcomes at various price levels, link on **strip** at the website https://thomsettsguide.com/options-strategies/

Synthetic long call *see* **Married put**

Synthetic long stock *see* **Long stock (synthetic)**

Synthetic put – also called a protected short sale, the purchase of a call when short on 100 shares of the underlying stock. This limits the short stock

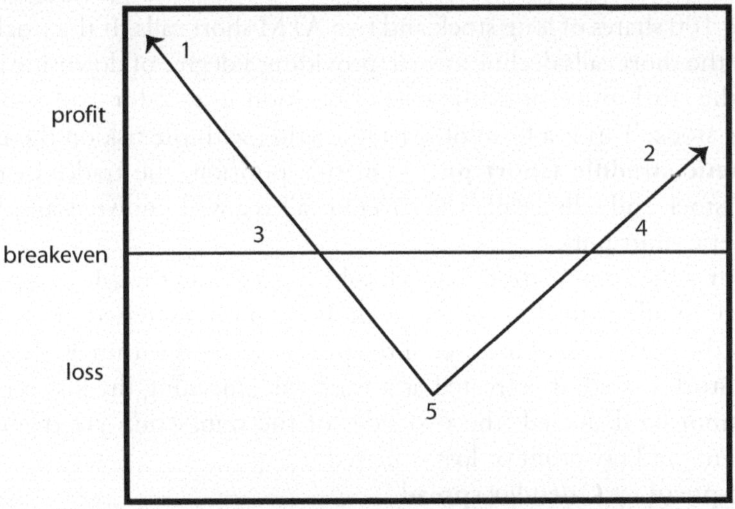

1 maximum profit (lower) (price declines to $82 per share):
((90 – 82) * 2) – 9.60 = 6.40, or $640
2 maximum profit (upper) (price advances to $100 per share):
100 – 90 – 9.60 = 0.40, or $40
3 breakeven (lower) 90 – (9.60 ÷ 2) = 85.20, or $85.20
4 breakeven (upper) 90 + 9.60 = 99.60
5 maximum loss 9.60, or $960

Fig. 51 Strip

risk. If the stock price rises, the call offsets that rise with point for point increase in intrinsic value. Maximum risk is equal to the strike price of the long call plus the call premium, minus the stock price.

Synthetic short call – the combination of 100 shares of short stock and a short put. This position has the same profit potential as a short call.

Synthetic short put – the combined long position in 100 shares of the underlying stock and a short call. The profit potential is the same as that of a short put. A well-known example of a synthetic short put is the covered call.

Synthetic short stock *see* **Short stock (synthetic)**

Synthetic straddle (long call) – a position combining 100 shares of short stock and two long calls at the money. For the cost of the long calls, the position is protected while creating profit potential. If the underlying price falls, the stock becomes profitable. If the underlying price rises, the short stock loses value, but the long calls grow 2-for-1 in intrinsic value over the short stock loss.

Synthetic straddle (long put) – a position combining 100 shares of long stock and two ATM puts. If the stock price rises, it becomes profitable but the puts lose value. If the stock price declines below the put strike, the puts gain two points of intrinsic value for every point lost in the stock.

Synthetic straddle (short call) – a variation on the previous strategy, involving 100 shares of long stock and two ATM short calls. If the stock value declines, the short calls decline as well, providing a degree of downside protection. If the stock price rises, the overall position loses 2-for-1 of short calls over long stock. This is a form of 2:1 ratio write, with the risk on the upside.

Synthetic straddle (short put) – in this position, the trader owns 100 shares of stock and sells a call. The covered call is a well-known example (also *see* synthetic short put).

Tax put – the combination of stock sold at a loss and the sale of a put. The put premium offsets the loss on the stock. If the put is exercised, stock is reacquired at the put's strike. However, if the put is exercised within 30 days of the date the stock is sold, it is treated as a wash sale, meaning the loss on sale of stock cannot be deducted; the two sides of the transaction are treated as a single event, and tax profit or loss is netted.

Time spread *see* **Calendar spread**

Uncovered option *see* **Naked option**

Vertical spread – a spread consisting of options with different strikes but the same expirations (see Fig. 10, diagonal spread). For example, opening option positions (either both calls or both puts) in the same expiration month but with different strikes is a vertical spread. If this is reversed and the strikes are the same but expirations different, it becomes a horizontal spread; and when both strike and expiration are dissimilar, it is a diagonal spread.

Option Glossary

abandoned option status of any option not closed or exercised, but allowed to expire worthless.

abnormal return any outcome from a trade or investment either above or below the expected rate of return.

absolute breadth index (ABI) a technical indicator used to track volatility without regard for price direction. The difference between advancing and declining issues is the key factor in ABI, on the theory that larger gaps between the advance/decline imply greater volatility in near-future prices.

accumulation (a) holdings in securities positions, including reinvested capital gains and dividends; (b) large purchases of stock by institutional investors; or (c) retention of net profits from operations to expand markets, versus paying out dividends.

accumulation/distribution technical indicator tracking momentum to determine whether buyers or sellers are dominant. Formula:

$$\left(\left(close - low\right) - \left(high - close\right)\right) \div volume$$

accumulation area technical indicator descriptive of the price range in which prices do not drop, anticipating near-term increased buyer activity.

acid test alternate term for the quick assets ratio; the current ratio excluding inventory. Formula:

$$\left(current\ assets - inventory\right) \div current\ liabilities$$

M. C. Thomsett, *The Complete Options Trader*,
https://doi.org/10.1007/978-3-319-76505-1_5

active market a market experiencing higher than average levels of volume.

actuals commodities underlying specific futures contracts or options on futures.

adjusted basis the basis in stock, reduced by profits or increased by losses in covered call trades.

adjusted option a non-standardized option allowing for changes in terms.

adjustments changes in value, such as stock splits or stock dividends, requiring adjustment in option valuation.

advance/decline index the accumulated advance/decline line's value.

advance/decline line (AD) a technical indicator summarizing the difference between advancing and declining issues and accumulating the trend. Formula:

$$\left(Advances - Declines\right) + previous \setminus AD \setminus value$$

after-tax breakeven point net profit after deducting tax liabilities, including federal and state income taxes applicable to investment profits.

against actual the exchange of futures for cash, arranged between two hedgers.

all-or-none (AON) a multi-contract option order specifying that the entire transaction has to be filled, and that no partial orders are acceptable.

alpha/beta trend channel the creation of a channel or band consisting of two trend lines, one above and one below a moving average; this provides an averaging of price ranges, used in technical analysis.

alternative order the adding together of two or more orders on the same underlying security or option position, in which one position offsets or cancels the other.

American-style option an option that may be closed or exercised at any time between the time a position is opened, and expiration date. *See also* European-style option.

amortization (a) payment of a debt over a period of months or years; (b) reduction of asset value to reflect deferred expense over two or more tax years; or (c) payments on a loan over a specified period of years.

annual report a publication issued by corporations to shareholders, summarizing financial results and explaining markets, conditions, and planned expansion. The report is part disclosure by way of financial statements and footnotes and part public relations.

annualized basis the net profit from a trade, adjusted to reflect the return if the asset had been held for exactly one year. Formula:

$$(N \div H) \times 12$$

where

n = is the net return
h = the holding period in months

annualized yield the percentage of yield or profit, when reflected on an annualized basis.

anti-straddle rules federal tax rules designed to prevent options traders from mismatching gains and losses in related positions (i.e., claiming a loss in the current year while deferring an offsetting straddle gain on the remaining straddle segment until the following year). In such cases, traders may be required to defer claiming the capital loss on the sold portion of a straddle. Capital gains treatment under this scenario.

appreciation (a) the growth of value in a capital asset. Although assets are depreciated and report declining value, they may appreciate over time so that market value is greater than net book value; or (b) increased value in an investment asset or trade, resulting from greater demand; for example, stock market value or option premium may appreciate during a holding period, creating profits for long positions or losses for short positions.

approved delivery facility in the futures market, any location in which contract deliveries are approved.

arbitrage a strategy in which the same or equivalent stocks or options are bought and sold on different exchanges, creating a net profit due to price differences.

Asian option a specific type of option for which profits rely on the average price of the underlying stock, versus value at expiration date; also known as an average option.

ask price the price a seller offers for options or shares of stock.

asset allocation a form of advanced diversification, involving spreading a portfolio among major asset classes, including equities, debt, real estate, and cash or cash equivalents.

asset ratios fundamental tests comparing values between assets, or from assets to other financial results (e.g., liabilities or sales).

assignable contract in the futures market, a condition allowing the holder to transfer rights or obligations to another person.

assignment (a) reference to notification of exercise by the OCC; (b) the act of obliging an option seller of the requirement to sell stock (when a call was sold) or to buy stock (when a put was sold), either at a contractual strike price; or (c) notice from the OCC to a clearing member that exercise of an option has taken place.

at the close a market or limit order that is to be executed at or right before a session's close; or canceled if execution does not occur.

at the money (ATM) condition of an option when the strike price is equal to current market value of the underlying stock.

at the opening order (OPG) an order requiring execution at the market open or, if that is not possible, to be canceled.

auction market any market allowing buyers and sellers to make competitive bids, with matching prices paired together for order execution. In comparison, over-the-counter markets involve negotiated prices rather than auction bidding.

automatic exercise the act of exercising options on the part of the OCC, occurring automatically at expiration and based on ITM price levels.

automatic reinvestment selection by investors, notably in mutual funds, to have all profits reinvested in the purchase of additional partial shares, creating compound rates of return on shares.

average down a systematic approach to buying securities when prices are falling, reducing average costs.

average option *see* Asian option

average price option an exotic option with a payoff at zero or formulated based on the amount an average price is greater than the strike (average price call) or lower than the strike (average price put).

average up the act of buying stock or options as prices rise.

average true range in technical analysis, the greater of (a) the current day's high to the previous day's low; (b) the current day's high to the previous day's close; or (c) the current day's low to the previous day's close. The third variation applies only if and when the previous close is outside the range of the current's day's trades.

averages general reference to indices used to track markets, including the DJIA and S&P 500.

back fee in a compound option, the premium changed in the second phase of trading, which is either at the close of the position or upon exercise.

back months the farthest-out expiration months or delivery dates for futures contracts on a specific commodity, the equivalent of expiration dates in option cycles.

back pricing a system for pricing futures contracts after positions have been taken in those contracts.

backspread an options spread when the trader has opened more long positions than short positions. This provides the potential for greater profits from rising prices in the underlying when using calls, or from falling prices in the underlying when using calls.

backwardation a theory that as expiration approaches, futures contracts trade at higher prices than those with more time until expiration.

balance sheet ratios any ratios comparing values found on the balance sheet, including current ratio and debt ratio as two of the primary balance sheet ratios.

barrier option a variation on the option contract specifying payoff only if the underlying stock reaches or passes a specified price level.

basis (a) the purchase price of stock, adjusted for transaction fees and option income, also known as cost basis; or (b) in the futures market, the difference between the spot price and relative commodity price for a related contract with the shortest current delivery.

basis grade the minimum standard for a deliverable futures contract, also called par grade or contract grade. Because actuals may vary in quality, basis grade sets the standard to maintain uniformity in the market.

basket option an option not in one underlying security, but in a basket of securities or futures contracts.

bear market condition when prices are broadly declining in the market, compared with a bull market.

bearish a pessimistic outlook; the belief that prices are falling or about to fall.

Bermuda option a hybrid of American- and European-style options, allowing exercise only on a specific series of dates, often only once per month.

Bermuda swaption an option on a swap with specified limits on timing of exercise.

beta a measurement of how a stock's price moves relative to movement in the broader market, quantifying volatility in the stock's price.

bid the current price a buyer is willing to pay to acquire stock or options.

bid wanted (BW) notice that a stock or option is available for sale; the initial step to finding a buyer without specifying the price.

bid-ask spread the difference between ask price and current bid; the difference between the highest price buyers are willing to pay, and the lowest price sellers are willing to accept.

big board slang name for the New York Stock Exchange (NYSE).

Black-Scholes a modeling equation used to measure option pricing volatility, based on outcome if an option were held to expiration, thus appropriate more for *European-style* options than for *American style*. The model is applied to American-style options, however, particularly on those stocks that do not pay dividends, based on the assumption that it is not advantageous to exercise an option prior to expiration in such cases. However, this conclusion is theoretical and not always practical.

block stock traded in large quantity, 10,000 shares or more.

blow off top a rapid run-up in a stock's price, followed immediately by a rapid decline; a price spike.

blue chip term for stock of large, established corporations with long-established earnings and dividend growth; or, in general, descriptive of any investment of high value and quality.

board broker a commodities exchange member authorized to execute and match orders, issue price quotations, and ensure order in trading.

boiler room a high-pressure sales operation in which potential investors are called from a list (the "sucker list"). Boiler rooms are known for promoting questionable products and, in many cases, fraudulent products.

Bollinger Bands a technical system for plotting moving averages and showing trading range trends. Three bands are used. The middle band is a 20-day simple moving average, and upper and lower bands are calculated as standard deviations of closing prices above and below that average; developed by John Bollinger in the 1980s.

bond a debt instrument issued by government entities or corporations, providing fixed contractual interest and used to finance growth and expansion. Bonds are either secured by corporate assets (or guaranteed by the issuing government) or unsecured (corporate debentures).

bond ratio a ratio comparing bonds as a percentage of total capitalization, similar to the better-known debt ratio. The bond ratio analyzes bonds only, whereas the debt ratio includes all long-term liabilities.

book value (a) the net value of a corporation, calculated as the difference between total assets and total liabilities. Most commonly used is *tangible* book value, which also excludes intangible assets like goodwill; or (b) the net value of a capital asset listed on a company's books, consisting of gross purchase price minus accumulated depreciation.

breadth indicator an indicator based on analysis of advancing and declining issues to track price trends in the market.

breadth of the market theory in technical analysis, the belief that trend strength can be tracked and anticipated by watching the number of advancing and declining issues.

break an unexpected or sudden movement in price, in either direction.

breakaway gap the difference between closing price one day and opening price on the next day, accompanied by high volume and price movement above or below established trading range or consolidation area.

breakeven point (a) the price required for an option position to have neither a profit nor a loss; or (b) the percentage yield required to break even after allowing for both inflation and taxes. Formula:

$$\left(rate\ of\ inflation \div \left(100 - effective \setminus tax \setminus rate\right)\right)$$

breakout price movement above resistance or below support.

Broad-based a trend or price movement involving a large number of stocks or industry sectors.

broadening formation in technical analysis, a trading range with widening breadth (a diverging trend line), often used to confirm trend reversal patterns.

broker an individual representing others in market trades.

bulge a rapid increase in commodities prices.

bull an individual who believes that market prices are going to rise in the immediate future.

bull market a market characterized by rising prices, usually as part of a long-term, or primary trend.

bullish an optimistic attitude, the belief that prices are going to rise in the immediate future.

business cycle a predictable pattern of growth and decline, applied to individual companies or sectors, or to the economy as a whole.

buy limit order an order to be executed only at or below a predetermined price.

buy minus an order to be executed at a predetermined price below the current market price.

buy on close an order to be executed at or near the close of the trading day at a specified price or, if not, to be canceled.

buy on open an order to be executed immediately upon the opening of the market at a specified price or, if not, to be canceled.

buy stop an order to execute a purchase above the current price, which goes into effect only when price moves through a predetermined price level.

buy the book an order to buy all available shares at the current price, used by institutional traders.

buy to close a trade that closes a short position in an option.

buy to open a trade that opens a long position in an option.

buyer an individual who opens a trade in stock or options on the long side; or a short seller entering a "buy to close" order to close out a short position.

buying climax a peak at the end of a long bullish period, when prices level out and then begin to retreat.

buying hedge alternative name for any long hedge, entered to protect against unexpected price increases that would adversely affect the value of another position.

buying power funds available to invest or, when applied to a margin account, the total of cash plus maximum available margin.

buy-to-close an order placed against a short position to close it out.

buy-to-open an order establishing a long position in stock or options.

calendar effect a belief, expressed through various theories, that the market acts in a predictable manner on certain days on in certain months. These include the Monday effect and the October effect.

call one of two types of options (along with the put); the call grants its buyer the right, but not the obligation, to purchase 100 shares of a specific underlying stock, at a fixed strike price, and at any time prior to a stated expiration date. A call buyer has three possible courses of action. First is *exercise*, in which 100 shares are purchased under the call's contractual terms at the strike price. Second is *sale*, or the closing of the call position at the prevailing market price. Third is *expiration*, or allowing the call to expire worthless.

call premium (a) the current market value of a call, paid by a call buyer or received by a call seller; or (b) the amount above par value of a callable bond, paid to bond holders when the bond is called by the issuer.

call price also called redemption price, the price at which a bond or shares of preferred stocks may be redeemed by the issuer.

call ratio backspread a strategy combining options into a spread with little or no risk but some profit potential. This involving combining short low-strike calls with a larger number of long higher-strike calls, or combining short high-strike puts with a larger number of lower-strike puts.

call warrant a warrant including the right to buy shares of the underlying stock on or before a specified date and at a fixed amount, beyond the other rights granted under the warrant.

called away the exercise of stock under an option contract. A call seller has an obligation to deliver 100 shares of stock at the strike price, for each short option if and when the call is exercised.

cancellation a notice issued by a brokerage firm, advising a customer that a trade was entered in error and has been reversed or corrected.

candlestick chart a type of stock chart revealing price movement via a rectangular box and vertical lines extending above and below. The distance between the extent of the vertical lines represent the trading range for the day. The top and bottom of the rectangle represent open/close or close/open prices for the day. The rectangle is white on an upward-moving day and black on a downward-moving day.

capital gain or loss the net outcome of an investment. A *realized* capital gain or loss is taxed at capital gains rates if the holding period exceeds one year. Capital gains or losses with holding periods of less than one year are taxed at ordinary rates.

capitalization (a) the total sources of funds used by corporations, consisting of both equity and debt. Equity capital includes all classes of stock and retained earnings. Debt capital includes bonds and notes listed as liabilities on the balance sheet; or (b) the entire market value of a corporation, also known as market capitalization or 'market cap.' The formula for market cap is:

$$shares\,outstanding \times price \setminus per \setminus share$$

capitalization ratios in fundamental analysis, ratios reflecting degrees of capitalization derived from various sources. These include total long-term debt (debt ratio), long-term bonds only (bond ratio), preferred stock (preferred stock ratio), and common stock (common stock ratio). Capitalization ratios are usually expressed as percentages of total capitalization.

capitalization-weighted index any index based on a selection of stocks, in which actual weighting within the total index is based on market cap.

capped-style option any option with a cap on either profit or price. A cap price is equal to the strike price plus a cap interval (for a call) or the strike price less a cap interval (for a put). Capped-style options are exercised automatically when ITM.

capping (a) placing of selling pressure on a stock to prevent the market price from rising; or (b) selling large blocks of stock near an option's expiration date to prevent the price from rising and moving into an ITM price range.

carrying charge the cost of holding securities or physically storing stock certificates or commodities.

carrying cost interest charged on funds borrowed on margin.

carry-over capital losses the excess loss above annual loss limitations for federal tax purposes, which must be applied to future periods. Annual limitation is $3000 maximum loss. Carry-over is applied to offset future capital gains or is absorbed at the annual maximum levels until used up.

cash-based settlement in cash upon exercise or assignment, without any physical delivery of the underlying security.
cash commodity the physical commodity to be delivered at delivery date, as opposed to a futures contract on the same commodity; also called actuals.
cash flow (a) in fundamental analysis, the study of how cash moves in and out of the company and the level of working capital available, expressed through ratios such as the current ratio; (b) the summary of cash movement in the financial statement called "Statement of Cash Flows," which adjusts operations results on a cash basis and accounts for how cash is derived and applied during a year.
cash market any market in which commodities are traded for cash in exchange for immediate delivery; also called spot market.
cash ratio a measure of a corporation's ability to liquidate assets and cover current liabilities, also called the liquidity ratio. Formula:

$$(cash + marketable\ securities) \div current\ liabilities$$

cash settlement contract a system for meeting obligations under an option contract, involving the transfer of cash equal to the ITM value, rather than by delivery of the underlying stock.
cash-on-cash return a return on investment based on annual cash income, divided by the initial cash investment
cash-or-nothing option an option with payoff set at a fixed price if and when the underlying is below the strike; if this does not occur, payoff is zero. This option is usually European style.
cemetery spread a spread involving so many segments that the trader is "buried" by transaction costs.
chain a grouping of options quoted across several strikes.
chartist a technician who relies primarily on price and volume charts as the means for anticipating near-term price movement of stock.
chooser option an exotic option in which the trader selects either a call or a put at a specified point in the contractual period.
Christmas tree also known as a ladder, a strategy involving the purchase and sale of calls at varying strike prices. The strike of the long positions resides below the strikes of short positions. As a variation of the ratio spread, it is entered assuming the underlying stock's price will rise. The profit from the long position will be profitable to a point; however, a substantial price rise would create losses due to a higher number of uncovered short positions.

Variations include covering the short positions with stock ownership, or creating a bear inverse Christmas tree with long and short puts.

churning the practice of high-volume trading in customer accounts to increase a broker's commission income; also called "churn and burn."

circuit breaker a measure or series of measures put into place by stock exchanges when large sell-offs are underway, to prevent larger drops in value. These include halts in trading or limitations on program trading.

class of option a grouping of call or put options associated with the same underlying stock.

clearing house an agency of a futures exchange or corporation allowed by the exchange to execute futures trades, collect and pay funds, maintain margin accounts, and execute delivery; facilitators of futures trading, serving as buyers to every seller and as sellers to every buyer.

climax the farthest extent of a price trend, after which a reversal or consolidation period follows. While usually associated with a market top, a bottom climax also may occur.

close the final step in a trade. A long position is closed with a sell order, and a short position is closed with a buy order.

closed position status after a closing order has been executed.

closing order an order to close out a position. A long position is closed with a 'sell to close' order, and a short position is closed with a 'buy to close' order.

closing price the actual price at which a trade was executed.

closing purchase the closing trade of a short position, also called a "buy to close" order.

closing sale the closing trade of a long position, also called a "sell to close" order.

closing transaction a trade that closes a position, consisting of a sell order for a long position, or a buy order for a short position.

collateral any asset placed as security for loans or for trading in margin accounts; in trading, the loan value of total marginable securities and cash.

commission payment to a salesperson or broker for executing a trade in behalf of an investor or trader, or for offering investment advice.

commitment a fee assessed by lenders for lines of credit or for credit to be used in the future; or an agreement for performance under a contract.

commodity a physical good serving as the basis for futures trading, including agricultural products, precious metals, cattle, market indices, and financial instruments (currencies and interest rates). The origin of the commodity-based futures contract was to fix a future price for agricultural products over the span of an entire season, to ensure that farmers would have a ready market upon harvest.

common gap a common minor price gap between one day's closing price and the next day's opening price.

common stock shares with voting rights and, when applicable, qualification for receipt of dividends. Common stock has lower priority when compared to preferred stock and bonds in the event of liquidation; also known as junior equity.

common stock equivalent an instrument convertible to common stock but traded like an equity, usually preferred stock or a bond.

common stock ratio a capitalization test, distinguishing the portion of total capitalization represented by common stock. Formula:

$$\textit{dollar value of common stock} \div \textit{total capitalization}$$

compliance process of ensuring a financial service company, investing banking operation, or securities broker/dealer is operating properly under federal and state law, especially law and regulation enforced by the Securities and Exchange Commission (SEC).

composite index a collection of stocks, commodities, currencies, or geographical interests, used as a benchmark for market performance or for performance of a segment of a larger market.

compound option any option related to another option rather than to an underlying stock or future. Because compound options involve two derivatives, there are also two strike prices and two exercise dates. The four types of compound options are calls on calls, calls on puts, puts on calls, and puts on puts.

confirmation (a) similar movement in an index or sector that verifies implied significance of the same movement elsewhere; or (b) a document or communication produced by a brokerage firm providing the details of an executed trade.

congestion (a) a trading pattern in which no specific price trend is established, or (b) differences between supply and demand for shares of stock or derivative contracts.

constant dollar plan also called dollar cost averaging, a system for investing a fixed amount of capital into the market each month or at other intervals, regardless of changes in price levels, most often employed by those buying shares in mutual funds.

constant ratio plan a method for maintaining a predetermined level of asset allocation, in which periodic investments are made based on increases or decreases in portfolio value in each allocated class.

constructive sales in tax law, a situation treated as a taxable event even though a specific sale was not executed. Examples include offsetting positions involving stock and options, or advanced offsetting option positions. IRC Code Section 1259 explains the rules and transactions to which these rules apply.

contango a situation occurring when a futures price is higher than the expected future spot price; the opposite of backwardation.

contingent order an order that is to be executed only if and when a related event takes place. For example, this order may specify an option trade if the underlying stock's price moves above or below a specified price level.

continuation pattern in technical analysis, price movement that will eventually lead to a continuation of a previously established trend; a false reversal or accumulation pattern.

contract month the month when a futures contract will expire; also called delivery month, the month delivery will occur unless open contracts are closed.

contract neutral heading a hedging strategy combining a long put or a short call for every 100 shares of the underlying held.

contract size the value of the underlying stock in an option; for listed options, 100 shares of the underlying stock for each open option contract (adjustable in the event of a stock split or stock dividend).

contract unit the dollar value of the physical commodity underlying each futures contract.

contrarian investing a strategy of investing that intentionally moves in a direction opposite of the majority opinion, based on the observation that the majority is more often wrong than right.

convergence movement in two or more prices, or between moving averages and the current price.

conversion arbitrage a three-part riskless transaction involving the purchase of 100 shares of stock, one long put, and one short call.

conversion ratio the ratio comparing shares of a preferred stock or value of a bond, to the equivalent value of common stock.

converted put a strategy representing a position equivalent to the purchase of a long put; consisting of the combination of short stock and a long call.

convertible security any product that is convertible into another product; a bond or preferred stock that are structured to include a call feature, exchangeable for a specified number of common shares of stock.

correction a change in the direction of a price trend, usually downward after a strong bullish trend; usually a temporary price decline that is resolved in a return to the established trend's direction.

cost of carry the costs of assuming positions, including interest on margin accounts, transaction fees or load fees, and the costs associated with committing capital and possibly losing other investment opportunities.

cost of tender charges for the delivery of commodities arising from fulfillment of a futures contract.

cover closing of a short position; buying stock or options to offset previously sold shorts.

covered status of a short call when offset by a long position in 100 share of the underlying stock. When traders have shorted 100 shares of stock, it can also be covered by a long call or a short put on the same underlying. Options cover one another as well, when combinations consist of offsetting long and short positions on the same underlying.

credit a sum of money on account or received or, in bookkeeping, a right-side transaction offset by a debit of equal value.

cross hedging a form of hedge in a different product with similar or identical price tendencies.

cum dividend literally "with dividend," the situation when a dividend has been declared but not yet paid. The time between declaration and ex-dividend date is described as trading cum dividend.

cum rights entitlement to dividend income based on ownership on the date of declaration, whether or not shares are still owned on the dividend payment date.

cumulative volume index a technical indicator tracking volume trends and adding together the net differences between advancing and declining issues.

cup-and-handle pattern a price pattern with a two-part shape. A 'U' shape (the cup) is followed by a down-trending or down-drifting price (the handle).

currency swap a swap between different currencies; a foreign exchange swap.

current delivery a requirement for delivery in a futures contract, either in the current month or the month following.

current market value (CMV) valuation of any asset based on the market price or equivalent, rather than on original cost; the value adjustment made to securities held as collateral in a margin account, to ensure continued compliance with margin requirements.

current ratio a balance sheet ratio quantifying working capital. The formula:

$$current\ assets \div current\ liabilities$$

curvature change in an option's delta, a comparison of differences in the movement of option value compared with changes in the price of the underlying stock.

cushion the protection sometimes built into a callable bond, when they are not callable for a predetermined number of months.

cycle the expiration months for series' of listed options. All options begin with expirations in the next two months, plus expirations in the next two months of one of the three cycles. Expirations on these cycles occur in (a) January/April/July/October (JAJO); (b) February/May/August/November (FMAN); and (c) March/June/September/December (MJSD). Longer-term options (LEAPS) expire in January in each year and may extend as far as 30 months out.

day order an order to be filled on the day placed or, if any part is not filled, to be cancelled.

day trade any trade opened and closed within a single trading session.

dealer the person who buys for his own account.

dealer option an option written with a commodity as the underlying, rather than stock.

debit (a) payment paid from an account, or (b) an option that reduces the trader's cash balance.

debt instrument a bond, note or money market instrument issued with a contractual obligation to pay interest and to repay principal with specific terms.

debt ratio a balance sheet ratio distinguishing the level of debt as a percentage of total assets; a test of corporate leverage employing debt. Formula:

$$total\ debt \div total\ assets$$

debt/equity ratio the primary capitalization ratio, which may be computed in two ways. As a comparison between debt and equity, the formula is:

$$total\ debt \div common\ shareholders' \backslash equity$$

The debt/equity ratio as a measurement of how corporations capitalize operations between debt and equity involves a comparison between long-term debt and total capitalization. The formula:

$$long-term\,debt \div \left(long-term\,debt + total\,shareholders' \backslash equity\right)$$

decay the reduction in value in option premium over time; the course of change in time value as expiration approaches.
decimalization system the pricing of securities in dollars and cents, the replacement of the historical system based on eighths or sixteenths.
deep discount broker a brokerage firm charging low trading fees and offering no investment advice, usually involving a flat fee per trade regardless of the dollar value or share value of the trade.
deep in the money (DITM) any option five points or more ITM based on current market price. A call is DITM when current market value of the underlying stock is at least five points above strike price; and a put is DITM when the current market value of the underlying stock is at least five points below strike price.
deep out of the money (DOTM) the opposite of DITM; this condition exists for a call when the underlying stock is at least five points below the strike price; and for a put when the underlying stock is at least five points above the strike price.
deliverables assets delivered to an option holder upon exercise.
delivery the transfer of stock or options upon completion of a transaction or when an option has been assigned.
delta a comparison between changes in an option's market value and changes in the value of the underlying stock; a measurement of variations in non-intrinsic value of the option and both option and stock volatility. Calls have positive delta, and puts have negative delta.
delta neutral positions equal in levels of delta so that an options position will not gain or lose based on small underlying movement.
derivative any security with value based on the value of an underlying security, including options and futures.
digital option an option with a provision that the payout amount is fixed if and when the underlying stock exceeds a threshold price level; also known as a binary option.
diluted earnings per share a calculated of earnings per share if all convertible securities were to be exercised, including convertible preferred shares, debentures, employee stock options, and warrants.
discount condition when an option trading below intrinsic value.
discount arbitrage the simultaneous transaction of a discount option and an opposite position (long versus short or vice versa) in the underlying stock.

discount broker a broker executing trades at very low commissions while offering no investment advice.

discount yield the yield on any security that was transacted at a discount.

discounted cash flow the present value of future cash flow, an analytical method used to compare investment opportunities when current terms are not identical.

discretion permission granted by an investor to a floor broker or account executive, to execute orders without first consulting with then account holder. Discretion may be limited to a range of points or order type.

distribution (a) condition when volume exceeds volume of the previous day, but with little or no price change; (b) payments from an account to the account holder, especially in a tax-deferred retirement account; (c) payments from mutual fund accounts for capital gains, dividends or interest.

divergence condition when stock or option prices move away from an index or moving average, used in technical analysis as a signal of impending price action.

diversification the spreading of risk to avoid a large loss. This is achieved by investing in different stocks, different sectors, or dissimilar markets (allocation); and by avoiding issues subject to the same market and economic forces.

dividend capture a strategy involving purchase of shares prior to ex-dividend date to earn the quarterly dividend; with the intention of selling shares on or after ex-dividend date.

dividend payment to stockholders for a portion of earnings upon approval by the board of directors. Payment occurs in cash or additional stock.

dividend payout ratio earnings paid in dividends, expressed as a percentage. Formula:

$$annual\ dividend \backslash per \backslash share \div earnings \backslash per \backslash share$$

dividend reinvestment plans (DRIPS) a system allowing stockholders to have dividends reinvested in shares or fractional shares of stock. This creates a compound rate of return in dividend income.

dividend yield the return from dividend income, based on a comparison of the dollar amount of dividends paid per year, and the market value of stock. Formula:

$$annual\ dividends \backslash per \backslash share \div current\ price \backslash per \backslash share$$

divisor the number used to calculate relative value of stock as part of an index, adjusted for stock splits in a price-weighted index, or for additional issues of shares in a capitalization-weighted index.

do not increase (DNI) condition attached to an order, to not increase the number of shares to be traded in case of a stock dividend or split.

do not reduce (DNR) condition attached to an order, to not decrease the limit price on the cash dividend record date.

dollar cost averaging the buying of a fixed dollar amount every month no matter how the share price changes; this technique can be applied to stock, but is more popular as a method of investing in mutual funds; also called constant dollar plan.

don't know (DK) description of a trade when unexplained discrepancies are outstanding.

double barrier option an option containing two separate price triggers. In order for the trader to receive a payout, the price must first reach or pass a range limit, or the price has to avoid reaching a specified limit (or limits).

double bottom in technical analysis, a pattern where price levels fall, rebound, and fall again to approximately the same level; believed to anticipate an upward price movement.

double top in technical analysis, a pattern with two price peaks and a decline in between, anticipating a downward trending price movement.

double witching the expiration of two classes of options or futures on the same day (any two of the three: listed options, index options, or index futures).

doubling option the right held by a bond issuer to redeem twice the debt level when repurchasing and closing out callable bonds.

Dow Theory a technical market theory based on the Dow Averages; identification of primary uptrends or downtrends based on advances in one average and confirmation in another.

down-and-in option an option with payout to occur only if the price of the underlying stock drops to a specified price level (the barrier price). If the barrier price is not reached, the option can be exercised at the strike value.

down-and-out option an option with payout to occur only if the price of the underlying stock rises to a specified price level (the barrier price). If the barrier price is not reached, the option can be exercised at the strike value.

downside protection a feature describing covered calls, in which the premium received is viewed as a cushion to protect against potential price declines in the underlying stock. For example, a covered call sold at 4 ($400) provides a four-point downside protection by reducing the net basis in the underlying stock.

downside risk the risk of losses resulting from price declines.
downtick the price immediately below a security's previous price level.
dual listing a listing on two or more exchanges.
due diligence reasonable care on the part of a company or investor, to ensure full understanding or an investment's features and risks.
dynamic analysis a form of analysis while positions are open and changing over time, versus post-closing analysis of a transaction.
dynamic hedging a form of hedging requiring continuous rebalancing to maintain a hedge ratio.

early exercise assignment of an option before expiration.
earnings growth a fundamental trend reflecting changes in annual net income from year-to year, reported as dollar value, percentage of increase or decrease, or in earnings per share (EPS).
earnings per share (EPS) total earnings reflected on a per-share basis, a popular fundamental indicator. To accurately report this value, the *average* number of outstanding common shares has to be calculated from beginning to end of the fiscal year. EPS Formula:

$$\textit{total earnings} \div \textit{average outstanding shares}$$

earnings report a quarterly or annual summary of operations, provided to investors and to regulators.
efficient market theory a technical theory premised on the belief that the market cannot be beaten because all available and known information has been factored in to stock prices at all times.
efficient portfolio a portfolio structured to provide maximum expected returns for a specified risk level; also called optimal portfolio.
embedded option an option whose price movement is tied permanently to another instrument, that cannot be removed. In comparison, a normal option trades separately from its underlying security.
end of day an order requiring execution at a specified price or better, that remains in effect only until the end of the current trading day. If the price is not reached or passed, the order expires.
equilibrium price a price when there is a match between supply and demand, seen in periods of sideways movement in a stock or index.
equity (a) a margin account's net difference between securities owned and loans outstanding, or net account equity; or (b) in fundamental analysis, the value of a corporation calculated as the difference between assets and liabilities.

equity investment ownership, a form of investment in the stock of a corporation, as opposed to a debt investment such as a bond.

equity option any options with equity (stock) as the underlying security, or options on exchange-traded funds (ETFs).

equity swap a swap involving approximately equal cash flow, usually between stock and fixed-income securities, usually entered to hedge other positions.

equivalent positions two or more strategies with identical or similar risks and profit potential. An example: a long vertical call spread is approximately equivalent to a short put vertical spread, although one creates a debit and the other creates a debit.

escrow receipt a document assuring that an option writer has placed the underlying stock on deposit and that it is available for delivery if and when the option is exercised.

European-style option a type of option that can be exercised only at expiration or during a brief period immediately prior to expiration.

even lot a benchmark value of commodities to be used in quoting futures prices.

exchange the marketplace for trading of stocks, bonds, commodities or derivatives, where an orderly market is maintained and current price information is published and announced; and where member or listed company activities are monitored and regulated in accordance with exchange rules.

exchange rate a currency price relative to the currency of another country.

exchange-traded funds (ETFs) mutual funds first created in 1993 and traded on public exchanges rather than directly with a fund's management. These are as liquid as stocks because transactions are executed at any time rather than based on prices at the end of the trading day. Each ETF consists of a pre-identified basket of stocks associated together in some manner (e.g., sector, country, or commodity). Many ETFs allow option trading, expanding the range of underlying securities.

exchange-traded options any option traded over an exchange based on that exchange's standardized terms (advance knowledge of underlying stock, quantity per option, expiration and strike price); also known as listed options.

ex-dividend reduction of a stock's price at the time dividends are applied.

ex-dividend date (ex-date) the day at which purchasers of shares will not qualify for the current dividend payments.

execution successful completion of a buy or sell order.

exercise the process of buying stock under the terms of a long call, or selling stock under the terms of a long put. At exercise, the transaction is completed at the fixed strike price regardless of current market value of the underlying stock.

exercise by exception processing a rule applied by the OCC for clearing members. A member is assumed to have placed exercise notices that are ITM, protecting option owners from the loss of intrinsic value. Unless instructed not to do so, all expiring options that are ITM will be exercised if they have reached predetermined threshold values.

exercise limit a limit on the number of options any individual owner is allowed to exercise within a specified period of time. This restriction prevents attempts to corner a market in the underlying security.

exercise notice a notice to an option seller, also known as an assignment, advising that 100 shares are required to be sold for each short call, or that 100 shares must be bought for each short put, when those options have been exercised.

exercise price the strike price; the price at which an underlying security is to be bought under terms of a call or sold under terms of a put if and when exercised.

exercise settlement the net price difference between exercise price and settlement value of the related index, on the day of exercise.

exhaustion gap a type of gap taking place following a strong uptrend or downtrend in a stock's price, signaling that the trend is coming to an end.

exotic option a complex option trading over the counter and not in conformity with the terms of listed options, including options on other options or containing terms and conditions not common to listed options.

expected return the return investors or traders expect to make based on statistical distribution analysis of historical returns.

expiration the end of an option's life, after which it becomes worthless.

expiration cycle the months during which options expire. All options have expiration dates in the next two months. In addition, there are four specific cycles. For listed options, three of these apply. In addition to the immediate two-month expiration months, expirations will also occur in the first two months of a four-month cycle: January, April, July, October (JAJO); February, May, August, November (FMAN); and March, June, September, December (MJSD). The fourth cycle applies only to LEAPS options. These have expirations in the immediate two months as well as in every January up to the third year out (maximum lifespan is 30 months).

expiration date for listed options, the Saturday immediately after the third Friday of the expiration month.

expiration Friday the last trading day before expiration; the third Friday of each expiration month. (If a holiday, the expiration day is moved to the last trading day preceding expiration Friday.)
expiration month the month when options are scheduled to expire.
expiration time the precise time of day when expiration notices are given out on actual expiration day. The expiration time is 5:00 p.m. EST.
extrinsic value the portion of an option's premium value excluding intrinsic value.

facilitation provision of a market in securities.
fail to deliver an order in which one side did not meet its requirements. In the options market, this means a seller did not have shares to meet a call, or cash/margin to accept a put; or a buyer did not have adequate funds or margin value to pay for the purchase.
fair market value (FMV) the current market price or value of securities or property, based on current trading levels *and* on the assumption that an adequate time period is allowed to complete a transaction.
fair value the value of an option contract, often used to describe only the intrinsic value portion of premium.
far option the segment in a spread with a later expiration date.
fast market description of a market experiencing heavy trading, especially when accompanied by high volatility in price levels.
February-May-August-November (FMAN) one of the three listed option cycles. In this cycle, options will have expirations in the next two months, plus the first two of the four indicated months.
fence a strategy involving a short call and a long put when the underlying stock is also held. The fence enables the trader to protect paper profits by building in downside protection. For short positions, a long call and short put provides protection in the event the underlying stock's price rises, which is a reverse fence position.
fiduciary call a trading strategy replacing the protective put with long calls at the same numbers.
fifty-two week high and low the range of highest and lowest price a stock reached during the previous 52 weeks.
fill completion of an order or satisfaction of transaction requirements.
fill or kill (FOK) an order requiring complete execution or cancellation. Similar to an all-or-none, the FOK is to be canceled immediately if all segments cannot be executed. The FOK cannot be employed in a GTC order due to this requirement.

financial futures a series of futures contracts based on underlying financial instruments rather than physical commodities. These include Treasury securities, currencies, and indices.

financial instrument an asset or investment having intrinsic value.

financial plan a systematic evaluation of financial assets and income, risk tolerance, and specific long-term goals, with the intention of identifying and selecting investment strategies to meet future goals while protecting current portfolio, investment, and personal assets.

financial statement a report subject to independent audit and published by listed corporations, summarizing the year-end values of all assets, liabilities and stockholders' equity (the balance sheet); the past year's operations including revenue, cost of sales, expenses, and net profit (the income statement); and an analysis of the sources and uses of cash during the year (the cash flows statement). Financial statements are filed quarterly and annually with the SEC and are also included, with extensive footnotes and explanations, in the company's annual report.

firm order an order within a brokerage firm's own account or a discretionary order executed by a broker in behalf of a client.

firm quote a guaranteed quote provided by a dealer or market maker.

first notice day the earliest day that a notice of intent to deliver a commodity may be forwarded to a buyer to satisfy the terms of a futures contract.

fiscal year a 12-month period used by a company for accounting purposes, calculation and payment of income taxes, and annual audit.

flag a pattern in a technical price chart, often called a pennant, in which the trading range is broadening or narrowing, used as a signal to anticipate short-term price direction.

flat market the condition when no specific trend is apparent.

flexible exchange option (FLEX option) an exchange-traded index option enabling a trader to specify exercise price and date, within limits.

float the number of currently outstanding common shares for a company.

floating security stock or other securities held in street name, in anticipation of a short holding period and quick sale.

floor broker a broker in an exchange responsible for execution of orders for customers.

floor traders members of the exchange who buy and sell for their own account.

follow-up action trading after establishing an open option positive, to reduce risk exposure or limit losses. An example includes buying shares to cover the position in an uncovered call write.

forced conversion exercise of an issuer's contractual right to convert a security, when investors to not favor the conversion.

forced liquidation brokerage action to sell securities in a customer's account when that customer is delinquent or to meet a margin call.

formula investing any system for placing money into securities based on a formula rather than on changing market conditions, including dollar cost averaging or asset allocation investing.

forward contract a variation of the futures contract involving a cash transaction, when delivery is deferred until the contract is made. In this arrangement, price is set on the original trade date rather than upon delivery.

forward market the market for over-the-counter futures trading.

forward price the set delivery price as part of a futures contract.

forward P/E the price/earnings ratio based on a forecast of future earnings per share (EPS) rather than on reported past earnings. Normally applied to a 12-month period, the formula is:

$$market\ price\ per\ share \div expected\ EPS$$

free market price the price of a security estimated by current supply and demand, based on a belief in the efficiency of the market.

front fee a premium assessed when a trader opens a compound option.

frozen account a brokerage account in which no transactions are allowed, due to the account holder's failure to make timely payments or to meet margin requirements.

full disclosure a requirement by the SEC that all regulated public companies provide investors and markets with all information concerning on-going business operations, especially to the extent that the information may affect investment value in the company's stock.

full-service broker also accurately called a full-commission broker, a firm charging full commissions for trades, while offering investment advice, research, and planning.

fully diluted earnings per share a company's EPS, calculated if all stock options and warrants were exercised, and all convertible bonds and preferred stock were converted.

fundamental analysis a form of analysis based on financial statements and other operational information. Although there may be no direct relationship between current stock price and financial results, most analysts agree that long-term price trends are affected by the company's revenue and earnings trends.

fundamental volatility a tendency for variation in year-to-year reported results of operations. A low-volatility report reflects steady and consistent revenue, costs, expenses, and profits; a high-volatility report is erratic and unpredictable.

fungibility the result of setting standardized terms on options; descriptive of listed options, whose terms are clearly distinguished and serve as part of the option contract.

futures contract an agreement for delivery of a stated amount of an underlying commodity, at a specific date in the future, the value of which is set as part of the contract regardless of changes in market value. Such changes make existing futures contracts more valuable or less valuable in the same way that option values change due to price changes in the underlying stock.

futures equivalent a comparative value between futures and options; the number of futures contracts equal to an option position.

futures market a market for the buying and selling of futures contracts, operating as an open outcry auction market.

futures option an option with a futures contract as the underlying security.

futures price the agreed-upon price between buyer and seller for a futures transaction at a later settlement date.

futures spread a position involving the buying on one exchange and selling on another, of the same futures contract; a futures arbitrage strategy.

gamma the rate of change in an option's delta; one of the "Greeks" applied to option analysis.

gamma neutral a trading strategy with zero or near-zero gamma, causing delta to remain unchanged regardless of underlying movement.

gap any space between a closing price on one trading day and opening price on the following day. Some gaps are viewed as strong technical signals based on current price movement, volume, and proximity of the gap to resistance or support; other gaps recur as a normal part of trading and are not technically important.

gilt-edged bond a bond issued by a blue chip corporation; a high-grade bond with little risk of default.

going concern value the value of a company with established assets enabling it to continue operations; a distinction used to identify companies unlikely to be able to continue as a going concern due to excessive debt or declining market share.

good delivery condition when a trade is in proper form and title.

good till cancelled order (GTC) a type of limit order that remains open as long as required to be executed (filled) or later canceled by the originator.

Greeks descriptive of various types of risk in option positions. The name comes from the use of Greek letters to distinguish them from one another (delta, gamma, theta, and rho). Vega is included with the Greeks, although not part of the Greek alphabet.

greenshoe option a provision in some underwriting agreements for new issues of stock, allowing the underwriter to sell more shares than the issuer intended; used when demand for shares is greater than anticipated and also called an over-allotment option.

growth stock any stock with earnings estimates greater than market averages.

gut spread a spread involving short positions in calls and puts that are both ITM.

haircut (a) the reduction in reported value of one or more assets for the purpose of calculating capital requirements or collateral levels; or (b) the spread between buy and sell prices for market makers.

hardening condition when futures price volatility is declining, or when market prices are rising gradually.

head-and-shoulders pattern a popular technical chart signal characterized by three price tops. The first and third (shoulders) are not as high as the middle top (the head). It is believed to signal a downward move resulting from a failed attempt to move through resistance. A reverse, or invested head-and-shoulders involves three price bottoms. The first and third (shoulders) are not as high as the middle bottom (the head). This reverse head-and-shoulders pattern is usually viewed as bullish, anticipating rising prices after a failed attempt for price to decline below support.

heavy a futures market tending toward declining prices.

high-low index (H/L) a technical moving average consisting of a comparison and accumulation of stocks reaching new high prices, versus those reaching new low price levels. Technicians use H/L to measure strength or weakness in the market.

historic volatility the measurement of stock price movement over a period of time.

historical yield actual yield earned and reported in a mutual fund over a stated number of months or years.

holder the owner of an open option contract.

holder of record the individual listed as registered owner of a security.

holding period the time an investment position remains open.

hot issue an IPO selling above its original offering price on its first trading day.

house rules internal rules mandating how customer accounts are handled in a brokerage firm.

hypothecation the rights held by a lender regarding collateral for the loan, including liquidation of securities without advance notice to satisfy a margin call.

immediate or cancel (IOC) a type of order allowing cancellation of part of the transaction or complete cancellation if not filled right away; the IOC cannot be attached to a GTC order. Unlike the AON or FOK order, the IOC can be partially filled.

implied volatility the volatility in the current option price, estimated based on underlying security volatility and assumptions of future price movement.

in and out a fast trade opening and then closing a position, often within the same day (a day trade), as opposed to employing a buy-and-hold strategy.

in the money (ITM) condition when the underlying security's current market value is higher than a call's strike price, or lower than a put's strike price. The number of points an option is ITM is equal to the option's intrinsic value.

incentive stock option an employee benefit, as a form of compensation, in which no income tax is payable by the employer at the time it is granted. Tax is deferred until the employee exercises the option *and* sells the stock. This type of stock option cannot be issued at a strike price lower than current market value of the company stock.

incremental return a covered call writing strategy intended to create higher returns on stock intended for eventual sale.

index a grouping of stocks reported together as a single value, based on an average that may or may not be weighted (by price or by capitalization). An index serves as a benchmark for investing, or as a tracking device for the overall market.

index arbitrage simultaneous buying and selling on an index future and stock, to profit from the net differences.

index fund a mutual fund with a portfolio consisting of or matching a market index, to provide broader market-wide returns with relatively low operating expenses.

index futures any futures contracts with a financial index, currency, or interest rate as the underlying security.

index option any option with an index as the underlying security.

indicated yield the yield on stock based on dividends paid during the past year, and assuming the same dividend will be paid in the coming year. It is expressed as a percentage. The indicated dividend is compared to current price per share. Formula:

$$indicated\ dividend \div price \setminus per \setminus share$$

individual volatility the volatility in option premium based on a pricing model and using the five pricing factors: time to expiration, strike price, underlying stock price, dividend, and assumed interest rate.
inflation risk type of risk associated with investments based on the rate of inflation. For example, if a rate of return after taxes is lower than inflation, an investment loses purchasing power.
initial margin the required cash or securities that have to be on deposit before an investor is allowed to trade on margin. Federal Reserve Board Regulation T requires 50% initial margin; some brokerage firms require higher minimum initial margin levels.
inside day a formation in candlestick charting in which a day's trading range is within the trading range of the previous day.
inside market the range of highest (bid) and lowest (ask) prices make by market makers for their own accounts.
insider information any material information about a company or its stock that is not available to the public.
insider trading illegal trading by insiders and based on knowledge not available to the general public.
institutional investor a mutual fund, pension plan, insurance company, or other financial institution actively trading in the market.
intangible asset an asset listed on a company's balance sheet but lacking physical value. The distinction is critical in applying certain ratios, such as tangible book value per share (in which intangible assets are excluded). Intangibles include goodwill, brand, patents, covenants, trademarks, and franchise values.
interest (a) a basic return, usually expressed as a percentage, on a debt investment. Basic formula:

$$dollar\ value\ of\ interest \div amount\ invested$$

To ensure accuracy, holding periods of varying times should be annualized so that expressions of interest income are truly comparable. Formula for annualizing return:

$$(yield \div months\ owned) \times 12$$

(b) fee for borrowed money, charged by a lender, expressed as an annual percentage as well as an annual rate based on compounding and additional fees charged; or (c) the holdings by an investor in an asset, as in a partial interest represented by stock or partnership equity.

interest coverage a company's financial capability to make scheduled interest payments on its outstanding debts. The lower the percentage of interest coverage, the greater the debt burden. Formula:

$$earnings\ before\ interest\ and\ taxes \div interest\ expense$$

interest rate the rate lenders charge for borrowed money or, for debt investors, the rate earned on a bond or money market instrument.

interest rate option an obligation with a debt obligation as the underlying security.

interim report any financial report issued during the fiscal year, normally on a quarterly basis for quarters one, two and three, reporting results of operations for the partial months from the beginning of the year until that time.

intermarket spread a simultaneous purchase and sale of options or futures contracts on different exchanges, to take advantage of price differences.

intermediate trend a trend of less time than a primary trend, but more time than a short-term trend, most often used to describe Dow Theory status, notably for reverse price direction within the primary trend.

internal rate of return (IRR) a discounted rate of return based on the present value of future cash flow and assuming a fixed interest rate.

Internet broker any brokerage firm offering services to clients via the Internet rather than in person.

intrasector spread a yield spread between two fixed-income securities in the same market sector and with an identical maturity date.

intrinsic value the portion of option premium equal to the number of points ITM. This occurs when the current market price of stock is higher than a call's strike price, or lower than a put's strike price.

inverse head-and-shoulders a head-and-shoulders pattern turned upside down, showing three price lows. The first and third (shoulders) are not as low as the second (head). Because this pattern is a failed attempt at price moving lower, it anticipates an upward price movement.

inverted market the futures market when the nearest-expiring contracts are set at higher prices than later-expiring contracts.

investment grade bond a safe bond, issued by a company with the higher levels of credit rating, generally BBB or above.

island reversal (island cluster) in technical analysis, a pattern involving a price gap, a period of trading in the newly established range, and then a gap returning price levels to the previously established trading range.

January-April-July-October (JAJO) one of the three listed option cycles. In this cycle, options will have expirations in the next two months, plus the first two of the four indicated months.

Japanese candlesticks alternate name for the candlestick charting system, which originated in seventeenth- and eighteenth-century Japan for use in trading of rice contracts.

kappa one of the Greeks, a measurement of option value based on assumptions of current and future volatility.

knock-in option an option that gains intrinsic value only if and when a specified price is reached or passed.

knock-out option an option that becomes worthless if and when a predetermined price level is reached or crossed.

know your customer a standard of the New York Stock Exchange (NYSE) Rule 405(1) and American Stock Exchange (AMEX) Rule 411. Also known as the suitability rule, a duty is placed on brokers to understand every customer's knowledge level, financial limitations, and risk tolerance as requirements for entering into investment positions.

ladder option an option with locked-in profits that go into effect if the underlying security reached predefined levels, effective even if the underlying prices retreat or the option expires.

lambda one of the Greeks estimating a change in option values compared to changes in the volatility levels of the underlying security.

lapsed option an option that expires without being exercised.

last trading day the third Friday in an option's expiration month; the day immediately prior to expiration day.

LEAPS long-term equity anticipation securities, long-term (or, long-dated) options. Expirations occur in the immediate two months from a current date, plus the next two years, in January.

leg a two-sided option transaction entered at different times. The first leg is opened with the idea that it will close profitably on its own, or seeking a more favorable price for the second leg at a later date. If this does not occur, the position is hedged by opening the second, offsetting leg.

letter of guarantee notification from a brokerage firm or bank stating that a customer with a short option position either owns the underlying stock, or guaranteeing delivery if and when the position is exercised.

leverage (a) the use of capital to control additional, borrowed funds to take trading or investment positions, as through a margin account; or (b) use of any product enabling control over an underlying security for a smaller amount of capital; for example, options limit capital risk by requiring relatively small investment, while providing control over 100 shares of the underlying stock.

limit move the greatest price movement allowed for a futures contract within a single trading day, set by the futures exchange.

limit order an order to either buy at or below a stated price, or to sell at or above a stated price. A limit order with discretion allows a broker to determine whether to buy or sell beyond the limit if necessary to fill the entire order.

limit price the specified price attached to a limit order.

limited risk an attribute of an investment, usually a long position and associated with the initial amount invested. A long option position's limited risk is the premium cost. An uncovered call has no limited risk because the price of the underlying stock could rise indefinitely.

limit-on-close order a limit order to be executed only if and when a closing price is more advantageous than the specified limit price, expanding on the market-on-close order.

limit-on-open order a limit order to be executed only if and when an opening price is more advantageous than the specified limit price, good only for the day's opening price.

linkage the opening of a position on one exchange and simultaneous sale of the same security on another exchange.

liquid market a market with a high volume of trading or volatility.

liquidation (a) closing of a business by selling its assets and paying its liabilities, with any remaining capital paid to shareholders; or (b) a trade that eliminates an offsetting position (long versus short or vice versa).

liquidation value the quick-sale value of a company, or the current tangible book value per share on the basis of selling all assets and paying off all liabilities.

liquidity (a) on the markets, a trading situation with high volume and narrow big/ask spreads; (b) for investments, the ability to match buyers and sellers easily or via the auction market; or (c) for companies, availability of cash adequate to pay current debts and fund on-going operations.

liquidity ratios financial tests used in fundamental analysis to compare and track a company's management of working capital and ability to pay its current debts. These include the current ratio, quick assets ratio, and other tests of operating cash flow. The trend in debt ratio also affects long-term liquidity.

liquidity risk any risk associated with how readily a position can be traded in the market. Highly liquid assets such as listed stock or options are more desirable than less liquid assets such as units of limited partnerships.

listed company a corporation whose stock is traded on a public exchange.

listed option an option traded on the public exchanges, with standardized terms, versus over-the-counter options, for which the terms are individually negotiated.

listed stock the stock of listed corporations, traded over public stock exchanges.

local traders futures traders who buy and sell on their own accounts.

locked in problem faced when closing a position would create a tax liability the trader or investor wants to avoid.

lognormal distribution a statistical analysis of price movement based on the shape of a bell curve, implying that outcomes of stock or option trades will occur within statistical distributions that are predictable.

long any position involving ownership in a stock, option or futures product. The sequence of events in a long position is buy-hold-sell (compared to the sequence of a short position, which is sell-hold-buy).

long jelly roll a time value spread including offsetting call *and* put positions. It usually consists of two separate spreads. First is a long put with a short call with identical strike and expiration. The second consists of a short put and a long call with the same strikes (but different than the previous spread) and later expirations than those of the first spread.

long market value (LMV) the total value of securities based on the previous day's closing prices.

long option position ownership in an open option entitling the owner to buy the underlying stock at a fixed price (in the case of a call) or to sell the underlying stock at a fixed price (in the case of a put). The amount of underlying is equal to 100 shares per option, and each must be exercised or closed before expiration date, or expires worthless.

long-dated options alternate name for LEAPS, long-term options.

long stock position ownership of stock.

long-term capital gains profits from investments or other capital assets that were held longer than one full year. These are taxed at lower rates than short-term gains, which are taxed at the same rate as ordinary income.

long-term equity anticipation securities (LEAPS) options with expiration longer than one year. Time erosion takes longer than for shorter-term expiring options, but these also tend to be less responsive to price changes in the underlying stock as long as expiration is far off. Expirations occur in the next two months and in the next two Januarys.

lookback option a variation on the option contract enabling traders to exercise based on the best possible prices of the underlying stock. A *fixed* lookback refers the option price, which is fixed upon purchase. Exercise can be made based on the underlying stock's highest price (for a lookback call) or lowest price (for a put). A *floating* lookback fixes the strike price at maturity. The call strike is the lowest price reached by the option and for a put it is fixed at the highest option price.

loss zone the price zone of an underlying stock at which an option position will produce a loss.

lost opportunity risk (a) the risk that by having capital invested in one position, other, better positions will be lost, or (b) in the case of covered calls, the lost profits in a rising underlying stock that are lost because of requirement to cover the short call position.

maintenance margin the lowest allowable value of cash and securities that has to be kept in a margin account when margin positions are open, also called minimum maintenance.

manipulation the practice of artificial adjustments in market value of a security, for the purpose of profiting from current positions at the expense of other investors.

March-June-September-December (MJSD) one of the three listed option cycles. In this cycle, options will have expirations in the next two months, plus the first two of the four indicated months.

margin (a) transacting in the market with a combination of cash and securities owned, and funds borrowed from a brokerage firm; (b) an account set up by a brokerage firm to enable investors to borrow money for the trading of securities; (c) an account in which investment activity may include borrowing funds from the brokerage firm; (d) a demand for payment to settle margin debt, or to increase holdings to meet minimum requirements within the margin account; (e) the level of debt in a trader's margin account, subject to interest, or at times a reference to the total of all margin debt on an exchange; (f) the requirement for dollar value of securities and cash that must be held in a margin account in order to borrow money; or (g) a minimum dollar amount required for uncovered option writers to leave on deposit, subject to daily adjustments as market values change.

market basket a collection or portfolio of stocks sharing attributes, which simulate an index's performance.

market capitalization the overall market value of a listed company, used to distinguish size in terms of capitalization (versus total revenue or earnings). Formula:

$$common\ shares\ outstanding \times price \setminus per \setminus share$$

market if touched (MIT) a conditional order that converts to a market order if and when a specified price is reached (a price below current price for a buy order, or above current price for a sell order).

market maker a member of an exchange who trades for his or her own account and maintains an orderly market by entering bids and offers for a stock or range of stocks and their related options.

market not held order a type of market order when the floor broker his discretion as to the timing of execution.

market on close (MOC) an order to be executed at or near the day's close of business.

market on open (MOO) an order to be executed at or near the day's opening.

market order an order asking for execution at the best available price.

market quote the current price or bid/ask for a stock or option, either in real-time, delayed, or after-hours.

market risk the actual risk from changes in the prices of stocks or options, also called systemic risk.

market value (a) the current value of shares of stock or options; or (b) in fundamental analysis, a company's total capitalization including equity and long-term debt.

marketability the degree to which a security can be traded. In an active, ready market, securities are easily traded and in this respect, marketability is the same as liquidity.

marketable securities current assets held by companies that can be converted to cash easily and quickly.

mark-to-market adjustment in the valuation of options in an account based on the prior trading day's closing market prices or latest quotes, settlement set by the OCC.

mark-to-model technique to assign value for assets that are otherwise difficult to price due to the lack of a ready market.

matching orders offsetting buy and sell orders, creating an illusion of trading at greater volume than is actually taking place.

matrix trading a bond swap involving varying yields from bonds with dissimilar ratings.
maturity date the date when a loan or debt security is repayable in full.
max pain the time of option expiration, based on the observation that many long option traders will hold their options until they expire.
member (a) a broker who belongs to the exchange and is authorized to enter trades for their clients; (b) a person or firm who owns a seat on the NYSE; or (c) a broker-dealer member of the exchange.
members' short sale ratio short sales opened in member accounts on the NYSE, as a percentage of total short sales. In technical analysis, a high percentage is viewed as bearish and a lower percentage of shorts as bullish.
mini options those options tied to ten shares of the underlying rather than to 100 shares.
minimum price contract a forward contract including guaranteed minimum delivery price.
minimum price fluctuation a tick; the smallest allowed price movement in a security.
minus tick a downtick, a trade taking place at the smallest allowable increment below the previous price.
misery index an economic indicator devised in the 1970s to describe current economic opinions among the general public. Formula:

$$\textit{unemployment rate} + \textit{inflation rate}$$

mixed account any account with a combination of both long and short positions in stocks, options, or both.
model a formula used to price options based on a series of known values and variables, including the price of the underlying stock, the strike price, time to expiration, dividends, and an assumed interest rate. The best-known of these is the Black-Scholes model.
momentum a technical method for analyzing price trends based on the rate of movement rather than simple price change. This is used to identify overbought or oversold situations to time trades.
momentum indicator a mathematical calculation of price or volume rates of change.
momentum trading a technical strategy employing momentum indicator trends to time entry or exit, including the study of price and volume.
money flow a technical system in which the high, low, and closing prices are added and then multiplied by daily volume, compared to the previous day's money flow, and quantified as either positive or negative.

Money flow index (MFI) a momentum indicator that compares daily price and volume levels, similar to the relative strength index (RSI).

money management a range of activities including portfolio diversification, savings, budgeting and long-term planning, to ensure availability of cash and liquidity levels, often part of a formal financial plan or investment strategy.

moneyness the proximity between current underlying price and an option's strike, broadly descriptive of ATM, OTM, and ITM status.

Monte Carlo Simulation a probability analysis system using random variables, so-called because games of chance (such as gambling in Monte Carlo) involve random outcomes in a way similar to investing and trading.

most active issue the stock with the highest trading volume during a trading day, driven by buyers or sellers.

moving average a technique used in charting, to smooth out volatility. In addition to tracking daily high, low, opening, and closing prices, moving averages are shown as a line moving along with price trend. Popular time periods include 14-day, 20-day, and 200-day MAs. These may also be weighted, giving more importance to the most recent price information. Calculation of weighted moving average is performed in many ways, the best-known being exponential moving average (EMA).

moving average chart a price chart focusing on the moving average rather than current price levels or trends.

moving average convergence divergence (MACD) a technical indicator used to identify overbought or oversold conditions. As two different moving averages move closer (converge) to current price or farther away (diverge), trend reversal signals appear.

multiple listed options those options listed and traded on more than one exchange.

mutual fund a pooled investment company, in which many investors contribute capital to create a managed portfolio of stocks, bonds, or both. Management identifies a specific investment and risk level for each fund. One variation, the ETF identifies a basket of securities in advance so that management decisions are removed from the equation. ETF shares are traded during a trading day like stocks rather than based on a fund's closing net asset value (NAV). Many ETFs also allow option trading on the basket of securities.

mutual funds cash/assets ratio a measure of a mutual fund's investment posture, comparing cash to the total value of the fund. Funds generally maintain approximately 5% of total assets in cash to settle redemptions. However, when the cash ratio rises, it indicates a bearish opinion among the fund's management. Formula:

$$cash \setminus on \setminus hand \div total\ fund\ assets$$

naked strategy any option strategy involving selling options without underlying stock as cover; a high-risk strategy.

naked writer the trader holding an uncovered option.

narrow-based an index made up of a relatively small number of stocks or other securities, as opposed to broad-based.

near option the portion of a multi-option position that expires the soonest.

near term short-term, meaning about to expire (options) or payable very soon (liability).

negotiated market unlike an auction market, one in which security prices are negotiated between buyer and seller.

net book value per share (NBV) the value of a corporation (assets minus liabilities) excluding intangible assets, divided by outstanding common shares. Formula:

$$((total\ assets\ intangible\ assets) - total\ liabilities) \div outstanding\ common\ shares$$

net change the price difference between the current day's closing price and the previous day's closing price, the most common financial indicator reported for individual stocks in the financial press.

net credit money posted as a transaction to increase an account's balance.

net debit money paid from an account, decreasing the balance.

net earnings revenue minus all costs and expenses, a key financial indicator.

net proceeds the amount received from the sale of securities or other property, after deducting all costs or liens.

net transaction any transaction not involving fees or commissions.

neutral an opinion about a security or the market as a whole, that does not favor either a rise or a decline in price.

neutral strategy any trading or investing strategy based on a neutral opinion about market direction.

new high/new low ratio a technical indicator, comparing new 52-week highs to new 52-week lows. As the rate changes, technicians see the ratio as bullish (number of new highs rising) or bearish (number of new lows rising).

ninety-ten (90/10) strategy a strategy combining 90% of a portfolio in Treasury securities and 10% in long calls or puts.

nominal yield the rate earned on a bond based on face value, which is paid by the issuer, regardless of the current premium or discount value of that bond; the coupon rate.

non-equity option an option with an underlying security other than stock, usually based on an index, commodity, debt security or financial future.

nonqualified stock option an employee stock option subject to income tax, to be based on the difference between grant price and exercise price and taxed at ordinary rates.

non-statutory stock option an employee stock option that creates a tax liability upon exercise; also called non-qualified stock option.

not held (NH) an order giving discretion to the floor broker in fulfillment.

note a debt obligation maturing between one and ten years. A *bill* usually matures in under one year, and a *bond* usually matures beyond ten years from issue date.

notice period the time during which a futures buyer may be asked to accept delivery, usually between three and six weeks before delivery date.

number of advancing or declining issues a basic technical indicator comparing issues rising in price to those declining in price during a single trading session.

NYSE Composite Index a widely used market indicator tracking movement in four other indices: industrials, transportations, utilities, and financials. Price per share is multiplied by the total number of shares listed to arrive at changes in the index each day.

NYSE rule 405 *see* know your customer

odd lot an amount traded other than the normal trading unit, usually referring to stock transactions of less than 100 shares.

odd lot theory a technical indicator based on the belief that odd lot traders are usually wrong. Thus, when odd lot sales rise, it is seen as a strong indicator to buy; and vice versa.

offer (a) the price a buyer is willing to pay for an asset; or (b) placing an asset for sale and stating the price.

offering circular a short-form prospectus for a new listing, disclosing the basic attributes and risk features.

offset eliminating an open position with its opposite (long versus short or short versus long) to reduce exercise obligation.

offsetting transaction a transaction that closes another open position or eliminates its risk. For example, a naked call seller may either buy the call in an offsetting transaction or buy 100 shares of stock to satisfy assignment if it occurs.

OHLC chart a chart showing open, high, low, and close price levels; *see also* bar chart.

on balance volume (OBV) a technical indicator entered onto a price chart as a means of identifying when the stock is being accumulated or distributed; a confirmation of price trends based on volume analysis.

one-cancels-other (OCO) an option order treating different transactions as a combination, when execution of one side will reduce the number of contracts to be executed in the other.

on close a market or limit order to be executed immediately before the trading session's close; also called at the close.

one sided market a condition in which either buyers or sellers dominate, distorting the orderly level of supply and demand.

open (a) the beginning of the trading day; (b) status when a placed order has not yet been executed or canceled; (c) the first price in a security in a trading day; or (d) the process of starting (opening) a customer account with a brokerage firm or bank.

open interest the current number of open option contracts within a specific series.

open order an order that has not yet been filled.

open outcry a method of trading in which market makers or floor brokers interact in person rather than electronically, employing voice or hand signals for placing orders.

opening purchase transaction creation of a long position.

opening sale transaction creation of a short position.

opening transaction a trade creating new positions, either long or short.

opportunity cost (a) the cost of deciding upon one investment over another; or (b) differences in yield from a selected investment or strategy versus another.

option a contract granting its owning the right, but not the obligation to buy (via call) or to sell (via a put) 100 shares of a specified underlying security, at a fixed price and by or before a specified expiration date. An option seller grants the same rights to a buyer, and may be required to sell 100 shares (via a short call) or to buy 100 shares (via a short put) under the specific contract's terms.

option account a brokerage account which includes approval for option trading.

option agreement (a) the agreement signed by an investor with the brokerage firm, laying out conditions and acknowledging risks in trading options; or (b) reference to the overall terms in every option contract to buy or sell shares of the underlying stock.

option chain the collective options available on an underlying security, listed in order by strike price and expiration date.

option contract *see* option agreement.

option cycle the distinctive expiration months for all options. Listed options have expirations in the next two months and in the following two months in one of three cycles: January, April, July, October; February, May, August, November; and March, June, September, December. LEAPS expire in the next two months as well as in the next two Januarys.

option exchange any physical or electronic exchange accepting option trades.

option margin the requirement stated under Federal Reserve Regulation T for the amount of cash and securities that must be maintained in an option account, which changes as the degree ITM changes.

option period the span of time between the opening of an option position and expiration.

option premium the current price of an option contract, reported in dollars and cents per share of the underlying security. For example an option currently valued at 2.60 has a premium of $2.60 per share, or a total of $260 (since each option is tied to 100 shares of the underlying stock).

option pricing curve a chart of the projected option price between the current date and expiration, based on predictable decline in time value and estimated price of the underlying stock.

option pricing model a mathematical estimation of an option's value, based on its attributes and assumed interest rates. The best-known model is Black-Scholes.

option series a grouping of calls or puts on the same underlying stock and with the same strike price and expiration date.

option writer a seller of options, either calls or puts.

optionable stock any stock allowing trading of listed options.

optionee the trader currently holding open options.

options on futures contracts traded based on underlying futures contracts.

options pricing curve a graph revealing projected option premium changes at various underlying prices, with changes due to time decay versus intrinsic value.

or better condition attached to an order to achieve a minimum price or lower as part of a buy order, or a minimum price or higher as part of a sell order.

order an instruction to buy or to sell securities.

order book official an employee of an exchange responsible for tracking orders placed by the public.

original issue discount (OID) a bond discount at the time of issue; the difference between par value and issue price.

oscillator in technical analysis, a trend indicator showing price variations and potential overbought or oversold conditions.

OTC option over-the-counter, an option traded without standardized terms, negotiated between buyer and seller.

out of the money (OTM) status of an option when strike price of a call is higher than current market value of the underlying stock, or when strike price of a put is lower than current market value of the underlying stock; an option with no intrinsic value.

outside day a candlestick charting pattern in which the current day's trading range extends above *and* below the range of the previous day.

over the counter (OTC) a market in which trading occurs electronically rather than on a physical exchange.

overbought a price resulting from excess demand for a security; price levels greater than those justified by technical indicators.

overreaction hypothesis an observation that investors and traders tend to create excessive priced movements by overreacting to current news, leading to price corrections in subsequent trading.

oversold a price resulting from reduced demand for a security; price levels lower than those justified by technical indicators.

overvalued status of securities trading above price levels justified through analysis.

owner the holder of an open long position in stock or options.

P/E ratio one the best-known analytical tools, combining technical (price) with fundamental (price) indicators. A measure of valuation, the formula is expressed on a per-share basis. The current market value is the latest market price per share. Total dollar value of earnings is divided by the average common shares outstanding. The formula:

$$current\ market\ value \setminus per \setminus share \div \left(earnings \div outstanding\ common\ shares\right)$$

pairs trading matching up a long and short position in two different stocks within the same market sector. This hedges the sector as well as the overall market. The strategy usually is applied to stocks, but the use of options also creates an equivalent position.

paper profit or loss any unrealized profit or loss, which is the current outcome if open positions were to be closed.

paper trading the practice of tracking trade decisions without actually investing or risking capital. The purpose is to check strategies in a real-time environment, but without the risks.

par the maturity value of a bond; face value. This is normally $1000 for corporate bonds. During their existences, bonds may trade at a premium above par or at a discount below par. These variations occur due to changing market interest rates, because the rates contractually attached to bonds are fixed.

parity for options, condition when current premium consists entirely of intrinsic value so that it is said to be trading at parity.

participate but do not initiate (PNI) an order including instructions to trade in a security only after trading has been started by others, but restricting initiation of a position.

pattern day trader an individual who trades a specific security in a margin account, within a single trading day, repeated four or more times in five or fewer consecutive trading days; based on FINRA Rule 4210.

payback the time required to recapture the initial cost of investments, calculated on cash income. The overall cost is divided by yearly cash received to calculate the time; this may be adjusted to include interest cost on the original investment.

payoff diagram an options-based chart used to calculate profits or losses before execution of a position or combination strategy. It includes profit and loss zones as a means for estimating overall risk and opportunity.

pennant a technical charting price pattern including converging trend lines that form a pennant or flag-like shape, often anticipating a price breakout.

perfect hedge the elimination of all risk in a position or portfolio.

phantom option plan employee compensation equaling a specific number of shares, with the added feature that those shares can be sold later including any subsequent price appreciation.

physical option an option written against an actual amount of a commodity rather than on futures contracts or shares of stock as the underlying security.

pin risk the risk that the expiration-date price of underlying stock will exactly equal the strike price of a short option. The risk arises in the contingency of exercise and subsequent price movement in the underlying stock.

pinning the strike a tendency for the price of the underlying stock to move close to the strike price of options being traded heavily immediately prior to expiration.

pit the location on an exchange's trading floor where trading occurs in a specific stock, options, or range of securities.

pivot price set in technical analysis, which becomes significant if and when the trend moves beyond that level.

plus tick an uptick; trading one increment above the previous trading level.

portfolio a collection of securities held by an investor in an account, including stocks, options, mutual funds, and debt securities; and both long and short positions.

portfolio insurance (a) a hedging system involving long positions in stocks with short selling index futures; (b) insurance for brokerage accounts provided by the SIPC; or (c) a system of using options to protect positions in stocks to avoid losing paper profits.

position status of holdings in a portfolio, such as long or short.

position limit the greatest maximum number of calls or puts an individual is allowed to have open at any given time.

position trading a strategy based on holding positions over a period of time, versus short-term or swing trading.

positive carry holding of two offsetting positions when one side's inflow of cash is greater than the other side's outflow.

positive yield curve the yield when long-term debt instruments offer yields greater than short-term debt instruments; also called nominal yield curve.

preliminary prospectus the initial draft of a prospectus, published prior to the initial public offering date. This has been called a "red herring" because the SEC requires the use of red ink on a portion of the cover.

premium (a) an option's price including intrinsic and time value; or (b) for bonds, status when the current bond value is greater than par value.

present value current worth of money or cash flow, based on an assumed rate of interest; also called discounted value.

price limit a range of prices that options or futures are allowed to extend in either direction during a single trading day; the daily trading limit.

price risk *see* market risk.

price/book ratio a financial ratio comparing current price per share to book value per share; specifically, the denominator is usually the tangible books value per share, which excludes goodwill, patents, trademarks, value assigned to brand names, covenants, and other intangible assets shown on a company's books. Formula:

$$price \setminus per \setminus share \div (tangible\,book\,value \div outstanding\,common\,shares)$$

price/core earnings ratio (P/CE) a variation of the P/E ratio, employing only core earnings, or earnings only from a company's core business and excluding non-recurring income or expense. Formula:

$$price \setminus per \setminus share \div (core\,earnings \div outstanding\,common\,shares)$$

price/earnings ratio (P/E) a comparison between current price per share and latest reported earnings per share. Formula:

$$current\ market\ value\ per\ share \div (earnings \div outstanding\ common\ shares)$$

price/sales ratio (PSR) a comparison between current price per share and sales reported for the most recent 12 months. Formula:

$$current\ market\ value\ per\ share \div (sales \div outstanding\ common\ shares)$$

price-weighted index any index based on a computation of each price of stocks in the index, divided by a set divisor.

primary market the exchange where securities are traded in the highest volume, when also traded in lower volume on other exchanges.

principal (a) a loan's repayment amount or the amount remaining due; (b) face value of a bond, to be repaid upon maturity; (c) the amount invested, without considering earnings; (d) a legal term describing an owner of a business or of property, or a party in a contract or other transaction.

pro forma a Latin term meaning "for the sake of form," used for calculating financial reports including projections or forecasts of future revenues, expenses and earnings.

pro forma earnings estimated future earnings based on assumptions, often used in business plans or budgets; reports beyond GAAP-based rules.

profit graph a graph reporting profit or loss from a specific investing strategy at a single moment or over a period of time, often used to summarize option strategies at various expiration dates.

profit margin a financial ratio comparing net profit and revenues, expressed as a percentage and used as a means for comparison between different companies in the same sector, or for a single company over a period of years. Formula:

$$net\ profit \div revenue$$

profit range the range, or zone, in which a strategies will realize a profit, often used in combinations or situations where two separate breakeven levels and profit ranges may occur.

profit table a compilation of prices and profits or varying levels, reported as a table or graph.

profit taking closing positions to take available profits, even when the original strategy involved a longer holding period or higher profits.

profit zone the profit range, or price level or levels where a strategy produces profitable results.

program trading method for large-volume and large-dollar trading, involving automatic execution generated from an automated source.

prospectus the offering document for an initial public offering, disclosing risks and other important information required by the SEC.

protected strategy a strategy with limited risk, such as a covered call or protected straddle write.

protective call a hedging strategy combining calls with short stock.

prudent man rule a requirement stating that anyone managing funds or providing investment advice should limit that advise to what a prudent or reasonable person would do.

public book a collection of buy and sell orders maintained by as market maker or specialist.

pullback a reversal of prices downward from a peak or upward from the lowest point of decline; a signal of a pause in momentum of the dominant trend.

purchasing power (a) credit in a margin account available for additional transactions; or (b) currency valuation in a trend influenced by inflation or lost value relative to other currencies.

put an option granting its owner the right, but not the obligation, to sell 100 shares of a specific underlying stock, at a fixed strike price and by or before a specific expiration date.

put swaption a position providing a put buyer to enter into a swap with a floating rate.

put warrant a warrant including the right to sell at an agreed-upon price before a specified expiration date.

put/call parity the price relationship when puts and calls in the same class are static, enabling traders to create positions equivalent to stock ownership.

put/call ratio a technical indicator used to judge bullish or bearish sentiment, measuring the number of outstanding put contracts to the number of outstanding calls.

pyramiding growing a position with the use of unrealized profits.

quadruple witching the third Friday of calendar quarter ending months (March, June, September, and December), when index options, index futures, stock options and stock futures expire, characterized by volatility and high trading volume.

qualified covered call in federal tax rules, a covered call entitling the seller to claim long-term tax rates on the underlying stock if the call is exercised. An unqualified covered call either tolls the 12-month period or requires that it begin anew after closing the call position. Qualification is based on the degree the short call is ITM. Deep ITM short calls will probably be unqualified.

quality of earnings a distinction of earnings resulting from higher revenues accompanied by lower costs and expenses, rather than as the result of accounting restatements or gimmicks.

quality spread a spread between Treasury debt securities and non-Treasury debt securities with identical rates but different credit ratings.

quanto option an option on a specific currency, which makes payment in a different currency.

quarterly options any options expiring on a quarterly cycle.

quick assets ratio a variation of the current assets ratio, also called the acid test. It includes current assets with the exception of inventory value. As a general rule, a quick assets ratio of 1 or better is considered acceptable (in comparison, the standard for current ratio is 2 or better). Formula:

$$(current\ assets - inventory) \div current\ liabilities$$

quote the current or latest price of a security.

rally strong and sustained increases in price, either in individual issues or in the market as a whole.

random walk hypothesis a belief that market prices cannot be predicted or anticipated, and are independent of one another. Under this theory, past trends are not reliable indicators of future price movements.

range also called trading range, the distance between support and resistance. On a day-to-day basis, the distance between highest and lowest price levels.

rate of change the rate of change, usually used in reference to price, which is usually expressed as a ratio between two variable factors.

rate of return basic calculation of investment yield expressed as a percentage, which should be compared among dissimilar holding periods on an annualized basis. Formula for rate of return:

$$net \setminus gain \div basis$$

Formula for annualized yield:

$$(basic \div months\,owned) \times 12(months)$$

ratio analysis any form of comparison between two or more factors, normally used as part of fundamental analysis. Comparisons are made between two current values, or between a current value and historical value.

ratio strategy any strategy involving a dissimilar number of long and short options, or covered calls greater than shares of stock (e.g., four short calls against 300 shares) or less than shares of stock (e.g., two short calls against 300 shares of stock); the most common strategy involves more short calls than stock, and is also called a ratio write.

reaction a movement in prices opposite the prevailing direction.

real time quotations system when prices are current, as opposed to lag time, commonly involving a 20-minute delay.

realized profits those gains that have been taken, as opposed to paper gains (unrealized gains); a closed transaction, with the net subject to capital gains tax.

record date the date used to determine which investors are entitled to dividends.

red herring name given to a preliminary prospectus, so called because of the required use of red ink on the cover as part of SEC-mandated disclosures.

redemption return of principal adjusted for gain or loss in a security, realized upon closing of an open position.

registered options principal (ROP) a brokerage firm employee who has successfully passed the FINRA Series 4 examination, qualified to provide investment advice concerning option trading.

Regulation T Federal reserve Board rule specifying the amount of cash and securities that must be maintained in a margin account and limiting credit a brokerage firm can extend; also known as initial margin, current limitation calls for a limit of 50% that can be invested on margin.

rehypothecation a pledge of securities held on margin, used as collateral for a loan.

reinvestment rate an assumed rate available from income, usually applied to fixed-income positions, that is available for reinvestment. This is used to compare investment strategies and to calculate total return.

reinvestment risk the risk that upon closing a position, the rate available on alternative future investments of similar risk will be lower than the rate currently being earned.

relative strength a measurement of price performance in relation to a sector or related index. Price performance for a stock is divided by price performance for the sector as a whole or by price performance of the index.

relative strength index (RSI) a momentum indicator used in technical analysis, to quantify price trends and flag overbought or oversold conditions. The RSI range, also called the RS (relative strength), moves from zero to 100. When the indicator exceeds 70, it indicates an overbought situation; and when it falls below 30, it indicates the stock is oversold. Formula:

$$100-\left(100\div\left(1+RS\right)\right)$$

relative value any comparison in value between two or more positions. In fundamental analysis, this may involve comparative analysis of key financial ratios to determine higher-quality or safer companies.

relative volatility comparison of risk levels in different instruments, or between portfolios or indices.

reload option a type of employee stock option providing for the grant of additional options when the employee exercises the initial positions.

resistance level an important technical concept, which is the highest price in the current trading range of a stock. Prices are expected to not exceed resistance; however, if and when it does, the breakout may signal a rally to the upside and eventual establishment of a new trading range (or anticipate a retreat to the previously established range).

retail investor an individual; anyone who trades for his or her own account, rather than acting as a broker or trading in behalf of an institution such as mutual fund, pension plan or insurance company.

return the net gain or loss from opening and closing security positions, expressed as a percentage. Formula:

$$net\backslash profit\div basis$$

return if exercised the net return from a short option position that will be realized if and when the option is exercised. The calculation may include dividends earned on stock when a covered call is open, or may be limited to the comparison between call premium and strike price of the underlying stock.

return if unchanged the return from a short option position if there is no ITM movement and the option expires worthless or is sold at a reduced premium.

return on equity (ROE) the calculation of net profit based not on revenue, but on the value of shareholders' equity, often involving calculation of average equity within the range of a complete fiscal year. Formula:

$$net\ profit \div shareholders'\ equity$$

return on investment (ROI) the calculation of profit based on the initial net amount invested, often referred to simply as return. Formula:

$$net\ profit \div basis$$

reversal arbitrage riskless arbitrage combining short stock with a short put or a long call, also called conversion arbitrage.

reversal day in swing trading, a trading day in which price direction first moves opposite the direction of the established short-term trend.

reverse conversion a synthetic long position (a short put with a long call) combined with a short position in the underlying stock, creating a position equivalent to owning the underlying stock.

reverse split a stock split which reduces, rather than increases, the number of shares. For example, in a one-for-two split, the owner of 200 shares at $25 before the split would end up with 100 shares worth $50.

reverse strategy any strategy with attributes those of the assumed positions (e.g., short versus long or backspreads)

rho one of the Greeks, expected change in option premium compared to changes in a risk-free interest rate.

rights the privileges associated with ownership in a security. For example, holders of shares of stock may also acquire rights to purchase additional shares at a fixed price; also called subscription rights. Option investors also acquire specific rights of exercise at a fixed strike price.

risk potential losses or inconveniences associated with security positions. The best-known is market risk, or the risk that a position will lose value. Liquidity risk means that it is difficult or impossible to resell securities at market value, or that it may take time to close out positions.

risk arbitrage a form of arbitrage with a degree of risk.

risk averse condition of an investor who wants minimum risk in a portfolio and seeks safer, more conservative investments; an individual with low risk tolerance.

risk free rate an assumed interest rate that could be earned in any position that was completely riskless. Investors used the rate on the three-month Treasury Bill rate as an approximately risk free rate.

risk tolerance an investor's willingness or ability to live with risk. Low risk tolerance means the individual is risk averse, and high-risk tolerance means more speculative positions may be appropriate.

risk/return trade-off the unavoidable relationship between the two sides to any investment: Greater returns require taking greater risks, and safer, less risky investments yield lower returns.

rollover (a) movement of funds in a qualified retirement fund to a different fund, in a manner that does not create a taxable exchange; or (b) reinvestment from a maturing debt security into a new one with a later maturity date.

rotation strategy in which one sector is weighted more than another, subject to readjustment later based on changing sector and market conditions, also called sector rotation.

round lot a normal trading unit, such as 100 shares of stock.

round trip transaction cost total cost for completion a transaction on both sides, also called a round trip.

run a panic, a time when large numbers of bank customers or investors in the market attempt to withdraw or sell at the same time.

runaway gap type of gap occurring during periods of strong upward or downward trends, when either buying or selling activity is so strong that prices move in a rapid series.

Russian option a type of lookback option that has no expiration date.

S&P 500 a widely used, market-weighted index of 500 widely-held stocks; one of the most popular market benchmarks.

same-day substitution a change in a margin account in which one asset is replaced by another within a single trading day.

scale order an order consisting of several incremental limit orders with either increasing (buy scale) or decreasing (sell scale) price limits.

scalping strategy aimed at creating large volume of profit on small price increments.

secondary market a market for resale of securities or assets traded in the primary market.

sector index an index that includes stocks within a single market sector.

secured put a short put opened when cash in an account covers the position in the event of assignment.

security (a) an investment, including equity (stock), debt (bond or money market instrument) or derivative (option or future contract); (b) property used as collateral for a loan or in a margin account; or (c) an investment objective aimed at protecting capital worth.

sell limit order an order to sell at or above a specified limit price.

sell the book an order placed by an institutional investor to sell the maximum amount possible of a currently held position, at the current market price.

seller (a) one who disposes of holdings with a sell to close order or, in short selling, who opens a position with a sell to open order.

selling hedge a short hedge.

selling short the act of opening a position with a sell to open order, either in stock or options.

sell-plus an order requiring the sale of a position above current market price.

sell to close a trade that closes a long position in an option.

sell to open a trade that opens a short position in an option.

senior security any security with seniority in the case of liquidation, usually a bond (following by preferred stock and then common stock).

sentiment indicators technical tests of investor opinion within the market, or to define long-term opinion as bullish or bearish.

serial option an option on a futures contract in which expiration of the option will occur prior to the future contract's own expiration.

series the collective options of the same class (call or put), expiration date, strike price and underlying security.

settlement date the date executed trades must be settled, including payment by the buyer and delivery by the seller. This is normally three trading days for stocks, and one trading day for options.

settlement price an option's final premium at the end of a trading day, set by the OCC, through a process called mark-to-market.

share ownership in a corporation or mutual fund, a portion of the total equity.

shock absorber a trading restriction or halt resulting from a high volume of trading and large-scale losses within the session.

short any position opened with an initial sale transaction. Shorted stock involved borrowing the stock from the brokerage firm, paying interest, and holding the short position in the belief its value will fall. Shorted options may include uncovered or covered calls, or uncovered puts. In the event of exercise a short call writer is required to deliver stock at the strike price; a short put writer is required to accept delivery of stock at the strike price.

short interest shares sold short and currently open.

short interest ratio the short interest in a company's stock, divided by the average trading volume in the same company; as a technical indicator, this ratio measures the current sentiment in the market for the specific company; also called short ratio. Formula:

$$short\,interest \div average\,daily\,volume$$

short interest theory a belief that growth in short interest anticipates an increase in price; a contrarian indicator.

short position any position in stock or options initiated with a sell order, and remaining open until a buy to close order is entered.

short sale in stock, a position opened to sell shares in the hope that share price will fall; in options, covered or uncovered sell transactions that expire worthless, are closed before expiration, or are exercised.

short selling the sale of securities not owned, anticipating a decline in value leading to profits at a later date.

short squeeze excess demand arising from declines in supply of a security.

short the basis a strategy in the futures market involving the purchase of a futures contract to offset a delivery commitment in the future.

short-term capital gains the profits from the sale of securities or other assets owned less than 12 months and subject to ordinary tax rates.

simple moving average an unadjusted average in which the values in a field are added together and then divided by the number of values (n) in the field. Each new calculation involves dropping the oldest value and adding the newest one, and recalculating the average. Formula:

$$(value1 + value2 + value\,n) \div n$$

single option a solitary call or put position, versus combinations involving multiple contracts.

single stock future (SSF) a future on a stock as the underlying security in place of a commodity or financial value. Stock futures include no dividends or voting rights.

slippage the net difference between estimated transaction cost and actual costs incurred.

small-cap stocks the stocks of companies with total market capitalization smaller than mid-cap or large-cap companies.

specialist exchange member allowed to both buy and sell for his or her own account, and to execute public orders.

speculator an investor willing to accept higher than average risks in exchange for the opportunity for short-term profits (or losses), likely to trade in options and futures.

spike a large price movement either above or below the established trading range, which immediately retreats back to that range. For the purpose of tracking price volatility, spikes should be removed from the averaging equation.

spin-off issue of shares of stock or dividends in a subsidiary corporation, or the sale of an operating segment to another company.

split an adjustment in the total outstanding common shares. For example, with a two-for-one split, shareholders are given twice the number of shares worth half the per-share value; thus, overall value remains unchanged. This often occurs when the market price per share becomes too expensive for small investors.

spot commodity a commodity trade occurring on the spot market, meaning delivery is expected; in comparison, trading in futures contracts usually does not include likely delivery of the underlying commodity.

spot price the price of an underlying commodity based on delivery date and time.

spot trade transaction in currency or commodity on the condition that delivery takes place immediately.

spread order an order with two or more options in a spread position. This usually includes both long and short sides of a related option strategy with the same underlying stock.

spread strategy an option strategy with two sides, one long and one short, on the same underlying stock.

standard deviation a statistical concept to measure the degree of change in a value; in technical analysis, this is applied to analysis of price movement compared to the average over time.

standardization a system ensuring conformity among different exchanges for all listed options. So classes of options trading on multiple exchanges are defined by the same terms under standardization.

static return the return earned by options traders when the price of the underlying stock remains unchanged.

statutory stock option an employee stock option providing the employer with tax benefits, but which also has greater restrictions than a non-qualified stock option. These restrictions include the number of options that can be granted to an individual employee, and options must be equal to or greater than current market value at the time they are granted.

stochastic indicator a type of technical indicator based on observations about price behavior. As prices of stocks rise, closing price levels tend to move closer to high prices in each trading session; and as prices fall, closing prices tend to be closer to the low trading levels of the range. This observation is used to anticipate likely price levels as trends become established.

stock a security with the feature of equity, or ownership, in a corporation. Common stock provides the holder with voting rights, participation in shareholder meetings, and dividends, if declared. Preferred stock excludes most of these rights, but gives owners priority in the event of liquidation.

stock dividend a dividend to be paid in the form of additional shares rather than in cash.

stock market overall, the market for buying and selling shares of stock and related derivatives such as options or stock futures.

stock option a contractual right to buy 100 shares of stock (call option) or to sell 100 shares of stock (put) in a specific underlying company, at a set strike price, and at any time before a specific expiration date.

stock option plan a company benefit allowing employees to buy options in stock issued by the corporation. The number is normally limited within specific time frames, and rules for exercise and strike price are included in the option agreement.

stock split *see* split.

stockholder of record the registered owner of stock on a specific date, for the purpose of identifying who is entitled to dividends. Because the record date is not the same as payment date, the stockholder of record on the declaration date receives dividends even if stock is sold prior to payment date.

stop and reverse order a stop order that, once reached, leads to a close of the current position and an open in the opposite direction.

stop-limit order an order that is converted to a limit order when the security is traded at the stop-specified price. (In comparison, a stop order is converted to a market order in the same circumstances.)

stop-loss order an order to sell a security if and when it reaches a specified price.

stop order a contingent order that is converted to a market order if and when the security trades at or through the specified price. Buy stops are placed above current market value, and sell stops are placed below current market value.

strategy a plan of investing or trading, usually including related long or short positions and actions leading to closing and taking of profits; or a means for limiting or eliminating risk through the use of options in offsetting positions with one another or with the underlying stock.

strike price the unchanging price per share at which calls or puts can be exercised. No matter how market price per share changes, the option owner is allowed to call stop away from a call writer or put stock to a put writer at the fixed strike price. Also called striking price, strike, or exercise price.

strike price intervals the incremental prices for a series of options. When the underlying stock is valued at $25 or less, intervals are usually $2.50. When underlying values are between $25 and $100, strike price intervals are usually $5; and above $100 in the underlying, intervals change to $10.

structured product a pre-set investment plan that consists of stocks, bonds, options, futures contracts, or an allocated combination of investment types and risk levels.

suitability a concept stating that anyone investing or trading in a particular way should be able to tolerate the risk associated with the trading strategy.

supply and demand a basic economic concept recognizing that prices of any goods vary based on buyer and seller levels. Excess supply causes price reduction, and excess demand drives prices upward. This principle applies to the overall economy as well as to stock and options markets.

support level the opposite of resistance; the lowest price level a security is expected to fall, given current conditions. As the lowest price that sellers are willing to accept for a security, support defines the lower end of the existing trading range.

swap exchange of one security for another, to extend maturity or to avoid exercise.

swaption an option for entry into an interest rate swap, also called a swap option. The premium is paid to acquire the right to fix an interest rate until a specified date.

switching the liquidation of a position for other securities.

synthetic stock a combination of options to create an artificial position approximating stock ownership. This usually involves a long call and a short put (synthetic long position) or a long put and a short call (synthetic short).

systematic risk *see* market risk.

tangible book value per share the book value (assets less liabilities) excluding intangible assets, with the net divided by the number of outstanding shares. The number of shares is usually computed as the average of shares outstanding at the beginning and end of a fiscal year. Formula:

$$\left(\left(Assets - Intangible\,Assets\right) - Liabilities\right) \div outstanding\ shares$$

tangible asset an asset with physical value and form, as opposed to an intangible, or non-physical asset.

tax basis the purchase price or acquisition value of an asset or investment, reduced by trading costs and other buyer's fees. Tax basis is applied to calculation of capital gains or losses; also called cost basis or basis.

tax loss carryover the excess loss in a year, which cannot be deducted and must be applied to future tax years. For capital losses, the annual loss limit is $3000, so any net losses above that amount are carried forward.

technical analysis market analysis focused on price and volume as well as trading patterns, all designed to anticipate upcoming price action.

technical rally an upward price movement immediately following a downtrend, caused by technical factors rather than by fundamental developments.

terms option features, including strike price, expiration date, underlying stock, and type of option (call or put).

theoretical pricing model a formula designed to estimate an option's future value based on underlying volatility, risk-free interest rate, volatility, and other variables.

theoretical value the price estimated to be proper for an option, based on a price model rather than the actual current market value; this modeling includes analysis and comparison of strike price, time until expiration, stock volatility, and an assumed rate of interest.

theta a measurement of the change rate in an option's value, compared to changes in time until expiration.

tick the minimum incremental price change in a security.

ticker symbol the combination of letters used to distinguish trading in a stock or its options.

time decay the erosion of value in an option's premium due to the time remaining until expiration.

time order an order to be executed at a specific time or, if not so executed, to be canceled or converted to either market or limit order.

time spread a type of option spread in which each side has the same strike price but different expiration dates, also called a horizontal spread.

time value the portion of an option premium outside of intrinsic value, which is associated with the time remaining until expiration.

time value of money a concept observing that the value of money varies based on (a) the time it remains on deposit or loaned out, (b) the interest rate in effect, and (c) the method of compounding applied.

time-weighted rate of return the return from investment based on compound growth rate of interest, exclusive of new transactions that follow the initial deposit.

total return a method of calculating return from an option and stock strategy, that includes all forms of income. Usually applied to covered call writing, this provides a means for accurate comparisons between different strategies and various outcomes. Total return includes profit from the short option write, dividends, and capital gains if and when the short call is exercised. This concept is also applicable to combined strategies involving multiple option positions, both long and short, as well as positions in the underlying stock.

tracking error the net difference between a portfolio's performance and the index it tracks.

trade date the date when a trade is executed, as opposed to settlement date.

trader (a) an individual who trades in the market, often in short time increments, with trading as a short-term activity opposed to longer-term investing; or (b) an exchange member conducting business on the floor of an exchange.

trading floor the floor of an active exchange, where traders bid with one another.

trading limit the limit imposed by various exchanges on the number of option or futures contracts that can be bought or sold in a single trading day.

trading pit a trading floor location designated for trading in a particular class of stock or option.

trading range the price span between highest and lowest prices within the current trend, defined by resistance level on the top and support level on the bottom.

trailing stop a type of stop-loss order set below a long position's market price, or above a short position's market price.

transaction costs fees and charges involved with trade execution, which include brokerage fees, assignment and exchange fees, and interest on outstanding margin balances, as well as penalties involved with any trade completion.

Treasury Bill/option strategy also called 90/10, a strategy in which 90% of capital is invested in interest-bearing debt securities such as Treasury Bills, with the remaining 10% used to buy options.

Treasury stock shares of common stock that have been repurchased on the market by the issuing corporation. Treasury stock is retired permanently, has no voting rights, and pays no dividend. It is also excluded from the calculation of outstanding shares.

trend direction of price movement, usually associated with technical analysis and divided into time periods (short, intermediate, or long-term) or, under the Dow Theory, divided into primary and secondary market-wide trends.

trendline in technical analysis, a line drawn onto a chart indicating the general price direction of a stock or index.

triangle a pattern seen on a price chart, in which the trading range narrows due to declining tops, bottoms, or both.

triple bottom a technical chart pattern in which prices decline to support three times. The third unsuccessful attempt to break through support anticipates a price reversal to the upside.

triple top the opposite of a triple bottom, a pattern in which prices rise to resistance three times and, failing an upside breakout, precedes a price decline.

triple witching day the third Friday of a month with three expirations: stock index futures, stock index futures, and stock options. This occurs in March, June, September, and December each year.

true strength index a momentum indicator used to identify overbought or oversold conditions. Short-term purchasing momentum is compared to the 25-day and 13-day exponential moving average of price. When current price is compared with the two EMA trends, the price status and anticipated next move are more easily interpreted.

turnaround descriptive of the price of stock in a company whose performance has been poor in the past, but currently is experiencing a price rally.

type one of the four option terms, the distinction between call or put (the other three terms being strike price, expiration, and underlying stock).

uncovered call writing a strategy in which calls are sold when the trader does not own 100 shares of the underlying stock. This presents theoretical unlimited risk because the stock price could rise indefinitely. In comparison, a covered call contains less risk because the writer owns 100 shares per short call; so in the event of exercise, the shares are used to satisfy the assignment.

uncovered option a call or put that is sold without offsetting stock position.

uncovered put writing a short put not offset by a position in the stock. To cover a short put, the trader would need to be short 100 shares of the underlying stock.

underlying security the security on which an option or future are based. In the case of options, the underlying security is stock; for futures, it is a commodity.

undervalued a security trading at a bargain price, or at a price below fair market value.

underwater status of a call when strike price is greater than the underlying stock's market value, or of a put when strike is lower than current market price of the underlying; more commonly known as being out of the money.

unit of trade the minimum quantity of a security in a normal trading increment. Stock unit of trade is 100 shares, and for options it is one contract (which relates to 100 shares of the underlying stock).

unlisted security a stock or other security not listed on an exchange, often because the company has not met listing requirements.

unsystematic risk any form of risk other than market risk, or a form of risk unique to a particular sector or in various kinds of markets.

up-and-in option an option that cannot be exercised unless or until the underlying stock reaches or passes a predetermined price level; also known as a knock-in barrier option.

up-and-out option an option that expires not on a specific date, but if and when the underlying stock reaches or passes a predetermined price level; also known as a knock-out barrier option.

upside the profits that may be realized in the best outcome of a strategy. As applied to stock prices, this is the likely price estimated for the stock. For combined option strategies, it refers to the profit zone or maximum profit when that profit is limited by the components in the strategy.

upside/downside ratio a ratio of advancing issues to declining issues on the NYSE.

uptick the incremental minimum advance in the price of a security, based on how it is listed and valued; a plus-tick.

value investing a concept for selecting stocks currently available at bargain prices, in some cases below their tangible book value. Such stocks are also perceived as dominant in their sector, well capitalized, and characterized by moderate or low P/E ratio or higher than average dividend yield.

vanilla option a listed option with no exotic features or limitations.

variable ratio write a strategy involving ownership of 100 shares of an underlying stock and writing of two calls with dissimilar strike prices.

vega a measurement of option premium movement in relation to assumed volatility.

vertical line chart a technical price chart including the opening and closing prices (represented by small horizontal lines) and the day's trading range (represented by a vertical line from top to bottom); an OHLC (open, high, low, close) chart.

VIX an index developed in 1993 by the CBOE to measure implied volatility in the stock market, based on the S&P 500 index.

volatility price risk; the degree of change in price over a specified period of time. As a measurement of the breadth of a stock's trading range, volatility affects option pricing as a reflection of market risk in the underlying stock.

volatility quote trading quotation system for option contracts with quotes based on implied volatility instead of prices in the underlying stock.

volatility smile a technical chart pattern in which a grouping of options' strike prices and volatility are plotted using the same expiration.

volume shares traded on a single trading session in a particular stock or on the market as a whole, often divided into volume on advancing versus declining issues.

warrant a derivative similar to an option but usually associated with a debt issue, used as an inducement to attract investors. The warrant allows the debt investor to purchase additional positions at a pre-set price; also called subscription warrant.

wash sale rule a rule disallowing any losses on trades when closed positions are reopened within 30 days of the closing date. In such a case, the loss cannot be claimed, but is rolled into the original position.

wasting asset any derivative asset whose value deteriorates over time, such as options experiencing time decay.

watered stock shares of stock with issue price greater than the value of corporate assets.

wedge a technical price pattern with converging trading range lines.

weighted moving average a moving average including mathematical adjustment of the latest fields to provide greater impact. The exponential moving average (EMA) is popularly used as a weighted calculation.

whipsaw price pattern in which a movement in one direction is immediately followed with a reversal.

wild card option an option with Treasury securities as the underlying, providing for a delayed delivery for the short side of the transaction.

wild card play the right to deliver commodities at the last available price, even when the specific contract is no longer in effect.

working capital a fundamental test of a corporation's ability to pay current debts from available current assets. "Current" assets are cash and any assets convertible to cash within one year (accounts receivable, inventory, marketable securities); and "current" liabilities are all debts payable within one year, including 12 months' payments due on long-term liabilities. Expressed as a dollar amount, the formula is:

$$current\ assets - current\ liabilities$$

working capital turnover a ratio used in fundamental analysis, comparing revenue levels to working capital, designed to estimate the use of working capital to generate income. Formula:

$$revenues \div (current\ assets - current\ liabilities)$$

write action of selling an option; a short option position, operating on the sequence of sell-hold-buy *or* sell-hold-exercise. When a written option is exercised, the writer is required to deliver 100 shares of the underlying stock (for a short call) or to accept 100 shares (for a short put), both at the specific strike price of the option contract.

writer the trader who sells short one or more options.

yield income from an investment consisting of interest or dividends, expressed as a percentage. Yield is distinguished from capital gains or losses that are realized upon closing positions in a security.

yield equivalence the rate earned on a taxable security that is equivalent to the rate earned on a tax-free security when tax liability is taken into account. Formula for the taxable yield equivalent:

$$tax - exempt\ yield \div (1 - effective \backslash tax \backslash rate)$$

Yield for the tax-exempt equivalence:

$$taxable\ yield \times (1 - effective \backslash tax \backslash rate)$$

zero-minus tick a security price identical to the previous transaction price, but lower than the most recent trade price.

zero-plus tick a price level identical to the previous transaction price, but higher than the most recent trade price.

Elements of Value

The cause and effect of option premium value is elusive to many traders. Many factors come into play, and no simple formula can predict how premium values will change. The influencing factors include:

– time to expiration
– proximity between option strike price and underlying stock current market value
– direction of change in price (in or out of the money)
– volatility of the underlying stock (historical volatility)
– implied volatility of the option

The current premium of any option involves three distinct parts: extrinsic, time, and intrinsic value. Each of these values contains specific attributes and behaviors that can be predicted to a degree. But the formulation of change and the weight of that change in option premium is a great variable. Not only do some options react more than others to underlying volatility (the feature known as implied volatility of the option), but the attributes of this volatility are constantly changing.

In academic circles, reliance is placed on pricing models, notably Black-Scholes and binomial versions. However, this is an imperfect method, since:

> standard models predict that only six factors enter into the option pricing formulas: the price of the underlying asset, exercise price, time to maturity, risk-free interest rate, volatility, and dividends on the underlying asset. Other factors that may affect the price of the underlying asset, such as expected future stock returns and investors' preferences about the higher moments of the underlying asset return distributions, are not priced.[1]

M. C. Thomsett, *The Complete Options Trader*,
https://doi.org/10.1007/978-3-319-76505-1_6

This multitude of influencing factors clearly is a disadvantage for those relying on pricing models. Over-emphasis on pricing models at the theoretical level ignores a practical reality: Options are *derivatives* of the underlying security, meaning an attempt to anticipate changes in the option's value is correctly a factor of underlying price behavior. The historical volatility of the underlying may be adequate for analyzing options pricing, versus the use of estimates for implied volatility of the option. The role of volatility is the primary determinant of risk in not only options, but larger portfolio positions, affecting construction of hedges and awareness of risk overall:

> The problem of pricing options is one confronting not only option traders but also, increasingly, a broad spectrum of investors. In particular, institutional investors' portfolios frequently contain options or securities with embedded options. More and more, risk management practices of financial institutions as well as of other corporate users of derivatives require frequent valuation of securities portfolios to determine current value and to gauge portfolios' sensitivities to market risk factors, including changes in volatility.[2]

A stock investor knows that the current status of stock in terms of trading range, technical strength or weakness, and fundamental attributes (e.g., earnings) is always evolving from past to future, and this evolution creates a continuum of changing market attitudes and perceptions concerning that company. The same is true for options, but on an accelerated plane (especially when close to expiration). The looming reality of expiration—during the last month, for example—tends to bring option price variables into focus, but in the period prior to this (estimated one to five months), many changes in the factors affecting value are in play.

Proximity and Price

Traders will observe that the closer the price of the underlying stock to the strike price of the option, the greater the responsiveness of that option. When the option is deep in the money or deep out of the money (underlying price is farther away from the strike), option value tends to be far less responsive to underlying price movement, when compared to ATM options behavior. DITM options display the expected point-for-point changes in intrinsic value, which may be offset by movement opposing intrinsic price. For example, an option 12 points in the money may not always be expected to change in value for every point of movement in the stock (especially with a lengthy time until expiration).

When option strikes are in close proximity to the underlying price—at the money or close to the money—the phenomenon of *pinning* augments responsiveness and may even distort the underlying price:

> Pinning describes the tendency of the underlying future to be attracted to strike prices on expiration Friday of the option. Such behavior is surprising in light of our typical understanding of finance, which suggests that any closing price of the underlying is reached with equal probability.[3]

This potential distortion caused by pinning is an example of how the theory of pricing for an underlying security is imperfect. A rational observer assumes that options pricing is always derived from underlying price behavior; however, there are instances in which the underlying price acts irrationally—notably at or close to expiration, when the price may be attracted to the closest strike of options.

The behavior of the underlying in such cases is likely to take by surprise the purely technical trader, whose understanding of price movement is how price, volume, and momentum signals anticipate the next move.

> The impact of option listing on the underlying security market has been a source of intense debate. Proponents argue that options provide investors an expanded opportunity set, thus improving market efficiency … Opponents argue that institutional investors will destabilize market prices by taking large positions and attempting to arbitrage price differentials between the derivative and underlying markets.[4]

This popular error in perception affects how ITM and OTM option risks are understood by traders. This error is the tendency to see "risk" as a binary attribute of trading. It is either low or high, translating to greater chances for profits or for losses as absolute factors. In fact, *loss aversion* plays a role, so that the risk element becomes distorted among options traders:

> Although escalating concerns about potential loss may be related to increasing risk, it is not clear if mounting optimism about potential profit has the opposite relation to decreasing risk. The behavioral finance literature posits a phenomenon known as "loss aversion," in which losses loom larger than gains. Loss aversion could translate into a greater responsiveness of downside price pressure on raising risk relative to the responsiveness of upside price pressure on lowering risk.[5]

The phenomenon of intrinsic value behavior contradicts the simplified observation concerning its nature. It is supposed to reflect changing stock prices on a point-for-point basis. In reality, there often is a trade-off between intrinsic and extrinsic value. Although intrinsic value increases or decreases exactly with changes in the underlying price, extrinsic value may contradict changes in stock prices, translating to little or no option pricing responses. This is especially true when the stock price is far removed from the strike of the option. It occurs because implied volatility is a predictive force. Every trader who has bought a long option only to see it lose value in spite of favorable underlying price movement knows this occurs. So as a predictive feature of value, intrinsic movement is checked by extrinsic adjustment when the price movement of the stock is not acknowledged as part of a permanent trend. So a multi-point price movement is not mirrored in overall premium change because the prediction includes the possibility of a price correction in coming sessions. Long traders know that growth in intrinsic value is offset by decline in time value; but the adjustment made in extrinsic value exceeds even the predictable effects of time decay.

For this reason, analysis of option strategies always compares possible outcomes on the assumption that positions are going to remain open until the day of expiration. That is the only time that intrinsic value is likely to move at or close to the movement of the underlying stock.

The three proximity levels of the option—in, at, and out of the money—further influence how this interaction between intrinsic and extrinsic value works. ITM options contain intrinsic value equal to the number of points of difference between strike price and current value of the underlying. For example, when stock is at 47 and the strike of a call is 45, there are two points worth of intrinsic value (47–45). So the call will always be worth at least 2 ($200) at this moment. Value above 2 is a mixture of time and extrinsic value. For puts, ITM is the opposite; the current value must be below the strike in order for any intrinsic value to occur, and when this occurs the put is ITM. For example, if the strike is at 47 and the strike of the put is 50, that put is three points ITM (50–47). The put will be worth at least 3 ($300) at this moment, with any additional premium value consisting of time and/or extrinsic value.

The price movement of intrinsic value tracks the underlying point for point. This only means that the option will always be worth its intrinsic value at the very least. However, it may also occur that intrinsic and extrinsic exchange offsets this, but rarely to the point that premium is going to fall below intrinsic value (this does occur when options are deep in the money, but only marginally). As expiration nears, the delta of the ITM option increases. When options are deep ITM, the intrinsic value is going to be equal to the ITM points, but extrinsic value may include little or no additional premium. In some cases, extrinsic and time value may even be negative so that the deep ITM option's value is *lower* than its intrinsic value.

Calls and puts are both ATM when the underlying stock value is exactly at the option strike. In practice, whenever the proximity is close (e.g., within one point in either direction) it is considered to be ATM. A casual observation of the option's delta might lead to the assumption that delta will always be at 0.50 when ATM, but this is not the case. It is usually somewhat above 0.50 for calls and somewhat below for puts, because upward price movement, in theory at least, has greater potential than the more finite downward movement. This recognition as a risk factor defines the difference between a naked call and a naked put. The put has a finite risk while the call's risk is simply unknown, but certainly greater. Since delta is one way to predict an option's likely price movement relative to the underlying, ATM option movement is worth observing. The responsiveness of the ATM call or put in comparison with OTM price action demonstrates why proximity is so critical.

OTM options include underlying trading below the strike of a call, or above the strike of a put. OTM options have zero intrinsic value, so it is easier to observe how time and extrinsic value behave. Time value is going to decline in a predictable curve, so extrinsic value accounts for all of the variables in OTM premium. The closer to the strike the underlying stock's price moves, the more responsive the premium will be, as though anticipating how the whole premium picture will change if and when the option moves ITM. A deep OTM option will see little or no change in premium other than decline in time value, often accelerated by the same direction of change in extrinsic value. The deeper OTM the option and the closer its expiration, the less action in the premium. So even a sharp favorable change in the price of the underlying stock will have little or no effect on the deep OTM option. Its delta is at or close to 0.00 and as long as the likelihood of gaining any intrinsic value is remote, the status will remain the same.

Expiration and Option Valuation

Time and price are intricately related in all option premium. Time value is predictable in a very specific manner. The decay in time value is known to accelerate as expiration approaches, but is often cloaked by the volatility of the underlying stock and the resulting adjustments in extrinsic value. A common but inaccurate explanation of option premium value includes only intrinsic and time value, mixing extrinsic and time together as a single factor. So predictability of time value decay is not easily recognized when it is combined in this way.

Although time to expiration is a major factor in premium levels, it is best observed in conjunction with the evolving proximity between underlying price and strike. The relationship between time and proximity is related, understandably. This is seen in the emerging trends of extrinsic value. So just as intrinsic value may be offset by contrary adjustments in extrinsic value, the time value premium may be similarly distorted or altered. Time value premium in isolation will decline predictably, but when the combination of proximity (underlying to strike) and time to expiration are considered as a single feature of premium value, it will be seen that (even in OTM options) time value and extrinsic value often counter-balance one another. With a deep OTM option quite unresponsive to movement in the underlying stock (especially as expiration approaches) the expected rapid acceleration in time value decay may appear even greater than normal. This occurs when extrinsic value has been inflated in the past, and after movement of the underlying far from the strike, that extrinsic value declines rapidly. This may look like an increase beyond a normal curve in time value decay. As extrinsic value falls away, it appears that time value is moving more quickly than normal.

With the proximity a factor in this alteration of otherwise predictable forces, the entire matter of premium tracking becomes quite complex. It is helpful to remember a few key features of how premium values work:

1. Intrinsic value is specific and predictable, and is always equal to the number of points the option is in the money (underlying above a call's strike or below a put's strike).
2. Time value premium is also predictable, regardless of proximity factors. The closer the time to expiration, the greater the time decay. Time value reaches zero on the day of expiration, without exception.
3. Extrinsic value, a measure of volatility, is where all of the variation is going to occur. This includes a measurement of implied volatility expressed in the changing option delta and historical volatility of the underlying stock. It is further influenced by the proximity between strike price and underlying stock's current market value; by the time to expiration; and by whether the option is in, at, or out of the money.

Most traders are aware of expiration and the decay of time value, even when the other mitigating factors (specifically related to implied volatility) are not as evident. However, traders (both long and short) may also benefit by observing how implied volatility changes based on proximity. It would be reasonable to attempt to assign a "proximity value" to option premium, and to a degree this is what delta achieves. A deep OTM option, for example, displays a delta of 0.00, and when at the money, calls tend to be slightly above 0.50 and puts slightly below. If a trader considers delta a predictor of whether the option is likely to end of in or out of the money, it becomes easier to predict likely success of particular strategies.

This proximity value is used to greatest advantage by long traders. A long position trader has to overcome time and extrinsic value changes *and* experience an option ending up far enough in the money to create a profit on the day of expiration. However, long position traders may also profit by closing positions early when implied volatility inflates premium value. This may be predictable to a degree when the timing of entry into long positions allows for swings in the prices of the underlying stock. There are no guaranteed methods, but attempting to time entry into long option positions with such swings improves the outcomes. When prices fall considerably in a very rapid move, long call entry is signaled and may easily produce immediate profits when implied volatility is high. This is made more so when the option is close to ATM or even ITM. For example, on a weaker than expected earnings report, a stock's value may fall as much as 10 or 15% in a single trading session. This over-reaction invariably corrects over the following two to three sessions.

The same swing trading approach can take advantage of implied volatility using puts. For example, when a stock's price spikes upward in a single session on momentary news or even a rumor, it is likely to correct within two to three sessions following, especially once other traders recognize the over-extension of the price. Buying puts at this price spike creates a situation where correction is likely. ATM or ITM puts will benefit the most from this tendency.

Short sellers may use the same swings even more advantageously. Time value decay creates profits for short sellers in both ITM and ATM situations. Even OTM options may be sold short with some confidence. Remembering that 75% of all options expire worthless unless closed or exercised early, short selling presents a considerable advantage and the trader will be able to wait out the last phases of time decay and extrinsic narrowing. An ATM option is somewhat higher risk for the short seller because exercise is always a possibility. However, if movement is away from ITM, the higher delta will produce short profits rapidly.

Even ITM short sellers can be profitable when close to strike, because any decline in intrinsic value is likely to be close to a one-to-one point change as expiration nears, especially within one strike increment of ATM. In fact, short traders have considerable advantage over long traders because (a) they receive payment rather than making it, broadening their breakeven point spread; (b) time decay always favors the short positions, (c) short options can be rolled forward to further exploit time value; and (d) the strategy can be quite conservative when covered (coverage includes short calls with long stock as well as short options with longer-expiring long options).

Interest and Dividends

Among the factors affecting and influencing option value are proximity of underlying stock and the options strike price; time to expiration; historical volatility of the stock and implied volatility of the option; and two additional features that, while not directly involved with the setting of premium value, are certainly a part of the equation. These are interest rate and dividend yield.

Interest rate applies regarding a trader's account. Interest is paid on credit balances and charged on debit balances (also known as the cost of carry of open positions on margin). So if a trader is highly leveraged and using maximum margin, interest will be relatively high. Another trader, limiting positions only to cash available, will have no debit on which interest is charged and may earn interest income on credit balances, albeit only at a minimum rate. The open options and stock positions in a portfolio are influenced by interest rate, most notably when the margin balance is high and interest is being paid. This cost increases when time to expiration is extended (i.e., through rolling forward or legging open to new positions). If this extension requires additional margin, interest will also be part of the net outcome.

Dividend yield has a direct affect as well, and in several respects. For example, when a company increases its dividend, it usually causes lower call premium levels and higher put premium levels. Knowing this may represent valuable information, especially for short sellers. A higher dividend often makes a particular company more valuable as a long-term investment, but at the same time richer put premium levels may make short put writing more profitable and even less risky. But the same argument also applies in reverse. When a company decreases or suspends its dividend, call premium levels tend to rise and puts to fall.

Dividends play an additional role as elements of value. Clearly, the value of an outcome in any position relies on the net profit or loss. This is especially true in analyzing comparable returns for positions such as covered calls. The net income from a covered call on two different underlying stocks is going to vary based on different dividend yields. Even if the annualized return from dividends is identical and even if potential capital gains are also identical, dividends represent a significant portion of overall return. If one company pays a 4% dividend and another pays nothing, it makes no sense to ignore the dividend.

This observation is more important than its relevance to an accurate net profit calculation. It also affects which companies are to be selected for writing options. Because accurate comparisons rely on annualized returns, the difference between dividend yields cannot be ignored in this comparative analysis. For conservative investors interested in long-term price appreciation, covered calls are excellent vehicles for enhancing current profits; but so are dividends. The basic selection of stocks for option writing should include dividend yield and, for some investors, may even exclude companies whose annual yield is low or which do not pay any dividend.

Stock Selection as Part of the Option Value Equation

It is often true that option traders ignore or minimize stock risks. For speculators who may never take a long position in stock, the distinction between growth and value (or between volatile or safe stocks) may be less important than the implied volatility of options and relative differences in the volatility skew (relative value of options on one stock which vary based on differences in strikes and their distance from current market value). For those who combine long-term investing with option trading, the question of stock selection is clearly an important consideration in selecting both stocks and option strategies.

The selection of companies in which to invest has two aspects for options traders. First is consideration of the basic investment value of that stock, and second is the analysis of option premium value and implied volatility. Ideally, option traders seek a degree of historical volatility adequate to enrich option premium (on the short side) and implied volatility to provide momentary bargain pricing (on the option side). However, if the option side of the matter is allowed to over-rule basic stock selection, it is likely that traders will choose the wrong stocks, especially if they will be taking up positions in those companies.

For example, covered call writing should be led by the stock and not by the option. It is a common practice to review option opportunities and compute various outcomes and the yields they represent, and then buy shares of that stock specifically to write covered calls. This is a popular method for picking covered calls, but it ignores the requirements of sound stock selection as a first step.

Basic Investment Value of Stock

Every investor and trader has to determine what levels of risk are appropriate and what positions belong in the portfolio. This is not a simple matter, nor are the standards identical for everyone. Some investors are interested in short-term profits (and, consequently, also need to accept short-term risk). Others want to fill their portfolio with value investments, high-yielding dividend stocks, or stocks of companies which dominate their industry or offer exceptional and rapid competitive growth. All of these criteria may be in the mix for stock selection.

The criteria for stock selection (see chapter "Options and Stock Selection") used by option traders is likely to cover a range of fundamental and technical tests, preferably a combination of both. However, in picking companies in which to trade options, several questions should be addressed:

1. *Will you take long positions in the stock or simply trade options?* If you are only going to trade options, analysis of a stock can be limited to short-term technical features such as price volatility, strength or weakness of movement, recent breakout patterns or trading gaps, and the beta tendency of the stock (a measurement of price volatility relative to the overall market).

   However, if a trader plans to take positions in the short such as covered calls, the technical analysis should be augmented with a careful fundamental review as well. The fundamental tests should be designed to test capital strength, profitability, price/earnings trend, and dividend yield. More detailed tests beyond these basics are often unnecessary. Applying tests is a reasonable method for eliminating unsuitable companies for stock purchase and option trading.
2. *Are you willing to accept the market risk of owning this stock?* Even with a sound or conservative option policy, accepting the risk of long positions in stock may be considerable. In recent years, investors in financial companies, for example, discovered that the once solid and safe industry went through a serious credit crises and many of the larger financial institutions lost 50% or more of their value. For example, Citicorp (C) was once considered an exceptionally safe blue chip investment with an attractive dividend yield and strong capitalization. In 2007 and 2008, the company lost more than half of its market value. Even a rich program of option trading would be unlikely to offset such losses entirely. Positions can be protected with short calls to a degree or with long puts for a period of time. But why

would an investor take long positions unless they can live with the risks as well? Buying shares in "safe" companies like Citicorp is far from a sure thing, and options can protect long stock positions only to a degree.

3. *What is your long-term goal involving stock and option trading?* Too often, investors buy shares of stock with the initial intention of holding those shares for long-term appreciation, only to change the goal later. This may be unintentional. Writing covered calls may expose traders to exercise and, even though profitable, the unintended consequence is that desirable investments are moved out of the portfolio. These must be replaced with other, equally desirable shares of companies; but if traders misuse their portfolios by trading options in ways that are contrary to their long-term goals, the purpose of investing capital is contradicted.
   Traders will improve their overall portfolio performance by defining their goals in advance. For example, it could make sense to distinguish long positions in two categories. First are those stocks intended as long-term hold investments, on which no option trading should occur that could threaten this long position. (However, as prices rise or fall traders may swing trade in long options to take advantage of short-term volatility or to protect paper profits.) A second group may include those stocks whose primary purpose in the portfolio is to provide coverage for unusually rich premiums in a covered call strategy.

Selection of Appropriate Option Positions

When investors begin mixing their stock and option trades, it is easy to lose track of the initial goal and risk tolerance levels. For this reason, definition of appropriate strategies not only helps to keep goals on line; it also helps traders to identify value within both stock and option positions.

Value itself is a variable. For example, for some investors, using short puts makes sense as a form of contingent purchase that also generates short-term income. As long as a trader is willing to acquire shares at the strike price, and would be happy to have that company's stock in the portfolio, naked puts present a reasonable strategy. For other investors, this approach would be inappropriate and a violation of risk tolerance standards. The value of long or short strategies further depends on the portfolio goals as well as the individual's experience and knowledge, income, available capital, and size of the portfolio.

As an individual's portfolio grows, option strategies are likely to evolve as well. A base of covered calls on exceptionally high-quality shares is sensible in most portfolios because it represents a conservative and high-yield strategy. But as the dollar value of the portfolio grows, additional strategies may acquire value as well. These may include strategies of greater risk, or strategies of more conservative requirements.

Higher-risk strategies include straddles, strangles, and spreads as well as ratio writes and even the use of multiple-option combinations. As traders acquire experience in trading options, risk tolerance levels evolve too, and this may lead to more exotic levels of trading, and acceptance of greater risks. For others, more conservative hedging strategies will become desirable. For example, the use of long puts to protect paper profits may become highly desirable for many investors, notably those tending to be more conservative than average or beginning to think about retirement and preservation of capital as a primary goal.

In many stock-focused portfolios, option strategies may also be considered as a means of recovering paper losses when market values fall within stock positions. The rescue strategies available with options can make up losses far more rapidly than simply waiting out the market. If a company has been selected for its high quality, a temporary decline in market value is simply one possible outcome in a stock position; however, the recovery of a loss position can be accelerated in three specific ways:

1. *Covered call writing*. This provides downside protection from the premium received. In addition, a moderate loss in stock may be recovered with subsequent covered call writes; however, traders have to take care to avoid programming capital losses by picking the wrong strike prices for covered calls. The covered call is one of the more conservative strategies, but strike selection is essential in controlling and managing profits and losses. If the strike is lower than the net basis in stock, it makes no sense to write the covered call.

   Covered call writing is a conservative strategy, with one qualification: The strike must be greater than the net basis in stock (original cost minus premium of the covered call). Judgment should prevail as well. If the margin is minimal between net basis and strike, is it sensible to write the covered call? It could make more sense to wait out the price trend and (a) write a higher-strike call later, (b) simply wait for the price level to return, or (c) employ one of the other recovery strategies below.
2. *Short straddles against long stock positions*. Although many consider this a high-risk strategy, the short straddle is actually not that risky; it is a com-

bination of a covered call and a naked put. Remember that either or both sides of a short straddle can be closed when time value declines. In addition, both positions are initially out of the money in the properly structured short straddle, and exercise of either side is often more of an advantage than a disadvantage. The receipt of a two-part credit may be substantial and may even make up all or most of a paper loss. If the short call is exercised, the stock is called away at the strike, and as long as the net basis of stock (original cost minus straddle premium income) is lower than the strike, exercise will be profitable. If the short put is exercised, the trader acquires an additional 100 shares. This presents the opportunity for subsequent covered calls on more shares, or multiple-contract short straddles.

3. *Naked put writing.* When a trader would be happy to acquire additional shares of stock at the put's strike, the naked put is an advantageous strategy. It produces income so even the strike is discounted if and when the put is exercised. If it is not exercised, the premium income is entirely profit. Upon expiration or close, the strategy can be repeated indefinitely. If exercised, the opportunity to repeat any of the three rescue strategies is not only present, but expanded. Exercise also represents acquisition of more shares, which averages the cost of stock and also helps to reduce the paper loss.

The reasons for acquiring stock often mandate how option trading occurs. The kinds of option trading undertaken may also dictate which companies end up in your portfolio. As long as the risks are understood and accepted by an options trader, those consequences may be quite acceptable. The goal, however, should be to avoid unwanted surprises. Some option strategies are assumed to offer one level of outcome, where the actual outcome is quite different. Many covered call writers are surprised when their stock is called away, and naked put writers may be equally surprised when they are required to accept stock at inflated value based on current market value. Neither outcome should come as a surprise.

The next chapter involves calculation of returns from option trading. This may seem a rather straightforward process but in practice, it is quite complex. The goal should be to achieve consistency and accuracy for comparative analysis, and to ensure that risks of specific positions are acceptable given the potential returns.

Notes

1. Amin, K., Coval, J. & Seyhun, H. (2004). Index Option Prices and Stock Market Momentum. *The Journal of Business, 77*(4), pp. 835–874.
2. Abken, P. A. & Nandi, S. (December 1996). Options and Volatility. *Economic Review*, pp. 21–35.
3. Golez, B. & Jackwerth, J. C. (2012). *Journal of Financial Economics, 106*(3), pp. 566–585.
4. Kumar, R., Sarin, A. & Shastri, K. (April 1998). The Impact of Options Trading on the Market Quality of the Underlying Security: An Empirical Analysis. *Journal of Finance, 53*(2), pp. 717–732.
5. Low, C. (2004). The Fear and Exuberance from Implied Volatility of S&P 100 Index Options. *The Journal of Business, 77*(3), pp. 527–546.

Return Calculations

Figuring out profitability for a particular strategy is not as simple as it sounds at first glance. The variations of both outcome and calculation are complex, and this makes valid comparisons difficult.

Return calculations are valuable primarily as a means for monitoring the results of strategic decisions, for tracking portfolio performance over a period of time, and for making accurate comparisons between separate outcomes. This continual monitoring helps traders to fine-tune their strategies, abandoning strategies that did not work out or that were too risky, and focusing on higher-yield or lower-risk approaches to options.

These calculations are also used to anticipate likely outcomes given a set of facts. So calculations like *expected return* are designed to apply probability to option trading outcomes. For most traders, this is not a useful calculation because it includes estimates and is complex. Most people want to restrict their calculations to an analysis of risk and reward for a series of possible strategies.

Expected Return and Pricing Models

Expected return is simply the return you *should* earn if trades were made many times in identical situations. In other words, it is a statistical average. However, as most option traders quickly discover, the averages only apply historically. In the real world of trading, numerous new variables make the past useful only in comparison between different options, but not as actual estimates of return.

The likely return from a trade is also likely to be influenced by the current price. If an option's premium is exceptionally high based on a model of what

M. C. Thomsett, *The Complete Options Trader*,
https://doi.org/10.1007/978-3-319-76505-1_7

it should be, the advantage goes to the short seller; and if the price is exceptionally low, option long positions have a momentary advantage based on these models. However, models are just that; they predict and estimate, but they do not provide any guarantee of outcome. The best-known option pricing model is the Black-Scholes Model. First introduced in 1973, this has become the industry standard for estimating what an option's price should be. However, there are several problems with this model. It is accurate for European-style options (which may be exercised only at or near the time of expiration). Thus, the formula applies to most index and sector options but not to listed options and LEAPS premium values, which can be exercised at any time (American style). In addition, the formula is accurate for options on stocks that do not pay dividends but less so for dividend-yielding stocks and their options: "It is well known that the Black-Scholes model misprices options in the marketplace and there have been many competitive explanations for these pricing biases."[1]

Among these pricing biases are risk aversion and selection preferences (e.g., a trader may be exclusively bullish even when technical signals appear bearish). Beyond these obvious biases, many academic observers promote Black-Scholes even with its many well-known drawbacks, including the lack of allowance for dividends. A like-kind comparison made between one stock paying a dividend and another not paying a dividend is inaccurate on its face, and attempts following the original pricing model to correct this exclusion have not satisfied all of the requirements that would lead to an accurate pricing model.

Because dividend yield is excluded from the calculation of Black-Scholes, it is a difficult formula to use comparatively. Dividends reduce call premium as they are increased, so the importance of dividends in price modeling cannot be ignored in the attempt to discover an accurate price. The originators of the model recommended that by discounting the current stock price to adjust for dividend payments until option maturity, this flaw could be offset. The formula can also be adjusted by weighting call premium when dividends are applicable. The formula also is based in part on fixed volatility; however, stock volatility changes with the passage of time without fail, so the formula is lacking in more ways than one.

The importance of Black-Scholes was that it demonstrated how option pricing could be calculated to identify an *ideal* risk-free hedge. This works as a theory, but the model also serves as a means for making pricing calculations universal within the industry. The inaccuracies of Black-Scholes can be adjusted for by discounting the present value of dividends, which is the current stock price minus that discounted dollar value of dividends to be paid until option expiration. Models allowing for this include adjustments for option yield, discount of the dividend, and historical volatility. Additional methods for calculating premium include Robert C. Merton's jump-diffusion model, put-call parity modeling, and many other complex calculations.

Pricing is valuable to the extent that it sets a standard, which also leads to observations and calculations of return from specific strategies. Option traders select specific options for their trades based on preferences of risk level, particular stocks and the implied volatility of their options, and favored strategic approaches to trading. However, the selection of a specific option within a stock's choices (based on proximity between strike and stock value, time to expiration, and the richness of each option's price). If you study a range of option premium levels at any particular time, you will easily stock inconsistencies. In other words, even given the same expiration time, strike patterns alone do not predict a uniform change in option values.

The volume of trading in each option creates disparities in premium value, and these are best quantified by applying models such as Black-Scholes. However, because of that model's inconsistency, it is only fully accurate when applied to the options that (a) are available on a single stock and (b) that pay no dividend, and (c) if a dividend is paid, on options that expire at the same time. By limiting the application of any pricing model, these restrictions are acceptable because they are equally applied to all of the options being studied. Once the analysis moves between stocks, it loses accuracy. Once it is applied to varying expirations, the existence of a dividend further distorts the pricing model.

The anticipated or expected return based on pricing models is an interesting exercise and at times useful for comparing options to one another. However, the majority of traders are going to be more interested in selecting strategies with profitable outcomes or with limited and well-understood risks. The following sections provide guidelines for this level of option return analysis.

Annualized Return

The starting point for return calculations is ensuring that comparisons between dissimilar holding periods are expressed on a valid basis. If you have one position open for three months and another for 18 months, their identical stated yield is not really identical. Because the holding periods are not the same, the returns have to be annualized.

A word of caution: Annualizing return should not be performed to estimate consistent outcome from a particular strategy. In short-term trades, it is quite easy to produce double-digit annualized returns and, in some instances, triple-digit returns. But any claims that this is a likely consistent type of yield is going to be inaccurate. Annualizing is useful in comparing and selecting options based on their holding period.

The first application of annualized return applies in the selection of particular options. For example, in a covered call strategy, which option is going to produce the best yield? If you seek only the highest dollar amount from a covered call strategy, it will make sense to always sell the one that has the longest possible expiration, especially with a strike close to current value. However, this is not always going to produce the most desirable yield. The selection of a particular strike is going to affect the likelihood of exercise, a factor that cannot be ignored in picking an option. The higher the strike, the lower the option yield but the higher the capital gain on the underlying stock if and when the call is exercised. In the basic comparison between calls, begin by the relatively simple comparison of possible covered call candidates of the same strike but with different expirations.

Assume you bought 100 shares at $100 per share on February 1. Current value as of December 31 was $108.10. You consider writing covered calls at 110, based on the observation that exercise will produce not only income from the short call, but 10 points of capital gain in the stock position as well. The following calls were available at the 110 strike as of December 31, 2007:

Expiration	Time (months)	Last trade
January 08	0.70	2.15
February 08	1.70	3.63
April 08	4.70	6.00
July 08	7.70	8.30
January 09	12.70	11.70
January 10	24.70	16.64

Based on the current price of $108.10 at the time of these premium levels, it is clear that—as is normally the case—the longer the time to expiration, the higher the dollar value of the call. Many inexperienced covered call writers are immediately attracted to the higher dollar values, failing to realize the two flaws in this approach. First, the longer the time to expiration, the more time for the stock's price to develop and move; this means the longer the term, the higher the odds of exercise. Second, picking the highest dollar amounts ignores the probability that shorter-term options yield a higher annualized return; writing several shorter-term options is going to be more profitable than writing one very long-term option.

To annualize return, first calculate the unadjusted yield based on current option price and current stock value. The January 2008 call is worth 2.15 and the stock value is 108.10:

$$2.15 \div 108.10 = 1.99\%$$

Next, divide the unadjusted yield by the number of months in the holding period (in this case 0.70); and then multiply by 12 (months) to calculate the annualized return, which is the return that would be earned on this option if it were open exactly one full year:

$$(1.99 \div 0.70) \times 12 = 34.1\%$$

Annualizing is intended to serve as a comparative tool to determine which options are most feasible for a particular strategy. It would be reckless to perform this calculation and conclude that a covered call strategy will consistently yield 34.1% per year. The strategy might yield that well, but annualizing should not be applied to draw that conclusion.

The complete formula for annualized return is:

$$((d \div s) \div h) \times 12 = a$$

when

d = dollar amount of return
s = current price of underlying stock
h = holding period (in months)
a = annualized yield

Annualized return for all of the positions in the example is:

January 08	((2.15 ÷ 108.10) ÷ 0.70) × 12 = 34.1%
February 08	((3.63 ÷ 108.10) ÷ 1.70) × 12 = 23.7
April 08	((6.00 ÷ 108.10) ÷ 4.70) × 12 = 14.2
July 08	((8.30 ÷ 108.10) ÷ 7.70) × 12 = 12.0
January 09	((11.70 ÷ 108.10) ÷ 12.70) × 12 = 10.2
January 10	((16.64 ÷ 108.10) ÷ 24.70) × 12 = 7.5

Annualized return declines with time. The higher time value premium looks rewarding, but actual yield is invariably better with short-term covered calls, as this example demonstrates.

Annualized return is useful in the initial analysis of positions for short writing. The opposite is true for long call positions. You may also consider annualized return as annualized cost when trying to decide which long call to buy. The longer-out expirations cost more money, but the cost as a percentage of stock value is less. This provides greater time exposure for the long position. Accordingly, there is greater potential for a profitable outcome in distant expirations, if the trader believes that stock value will rise high enough to surpass the time value premium.

For example, a trader would like to buy 100 shares and pay no more than $110 per share. Buying a January 110 call provides a very low premium but only a remote chance of profit. However, a January 2010 call with a strike of 110 can be bought for 16.64, providing more than two years for the stock value to grow. The price of stock would have to reach a level of 126.64 per share by expiration in January 2010 in order for this trade to be profitable. However, for $1664 in option premium, the trader controls 100 shares at 110. Buying those shares today would cost $10,810. For an annualized cost of 7.5%, the trader controls shares and fixes the future exercise price.

Annualized return is valuable in comparing calls for any strategy. On the short side, annualized return enables traders to study comparable yields for a range of expiration times. On the long side, the cost of a position can be compared on the same annualized basis among a series of possible option positions.

Strike Selection for Covered Calls

Picking an expiration date is one-half of the covered call equation. Determining how long you are willing to remain at risk, versus the dollar amount and yield of the premium for each option, is the exercise that covered call writers go through. The other half of this equation is selection of the most appropriate strike.

The first guideline in this regard is based on the assumption that exercise is always a possibility, for any short call at any strike. Exercise is most likely to occur on the last trading day, but it can occur at any time. Covered call writers must be willing to accept this risk and to structure call selection with the possibility in mind that exercise can occur. So the strike must conform to an important limitation: If the call is exercised, the strike price must be greater than the net basis in the underlying stock. "Net" basis is the original net cost, minus premium received for writing the call:

$$\text{Basis in stock} - \text{Call premium} = \text{net basis}$$

If strike price is lower than this net basis, exercise will create a net loss. For example, if original basis was $54 per share and premium from writing a covered call is 6, net basis is $48 per share ($54–56). Acceptable strikes include 50 or above, but anything below the net of $48 per share will not be appropriate.

The selection of the right strike should be undertaken in the same way as selection of the expiration date. Premium levels are going to produce varying returns, and the balance between one strike and another has to consider a number of factors, including time to expiration, net basis in the underlying stock, and annualized return. The higher the strike, the lower the premium income will be, and the more remote the chances of exercise. At the same time, the higher that strike, the greater the capital gain on the underlying stock if exercised. Most covered call writers will select a call that is out of the money by one increment or less (e.g., a 45 call when the underlying is currently worth between 40 and 44, or a 60 call when the underlying is between 55 and 59). This tends to produce maximum return premium. Once this limitation is set, selection can be coordinated between strike and expiration, all on an annualized basis to make comparisons accurate.

It is not accurate to include capital gain in the underlying stock in the comparison between premiums. However, this is a very real consideration. So strictly for the purposes of comparison, this does have to be included in the decision-making process. A two-part analysis is recommended. First, check various annualized returns on options with acceptable strikes and expirations. Second, evaluate and select a covered call with one eye to the contingency of exercise. When two different options are close in terms of annualized return, the differences in strike and consequential capital gain may become a determining factor.

Returning to a previous example, that of share value as of December 31, 2007 at $108.10. Various expirations for the 100 call were compared on an annualized basis. However, this analysis may be expanded to also consider other strikes within the possible ranges for covered calls. The analysis is limited to strikes of 110 or above (even though, in the example, the original basis in stock was $100 per share). This limitation is appropriate since the current value is at $108.10; most covered call writers will prefer writing OTM calls based on current value. The distinction of net basis becomes most critical when original net basis is higher than current value of the stock. In that situation, writing a covered call that will exercise below net basis is self-defeating. Writers may need to wait until prices evolve, or accept lower margins of profit in that situation. However, original cost will be brought into the equation to make the final determination of which option to write.

Return If Exercised or Unchanged

Expanding the example to additional calls, the following are included in the range of possibilities, all calculated on the basis of annualized returns:

Month, year	Strike	Option premium	Stock value	Holding period	Full year	Annualized return
January 08	110	((2.15 ÷	108.10) ÷	0.70) ×	12 =	34.1%
February 08	110	((3.63 ÷	108.10) ÷	1.70) ×	12 =	23.7
February 08	115	((1.71 ÷	108.10) ÷	1.70) ×	12 =	11.2
April 08	110	((6.00 ÷	108.10) ÷	4.70) ×	12 =	14.2
April 08	115	((3.90 ÷	108.10) ÷	4.70) ×	12 =	9.2
July 08	110	((8.30 ÷	108.10) ÷	7.70) ×	12 =	12.0
July 08	115	((6.10 ÷	108.10) ÷	7.70) ×	12 =	8.8
July 08	120	((4.30 ÷	108.10) ÷	7.70) ×	12 =	6.2
January 09	110	((11.70 ÷	108.10) ÷	12.70) ×	12 =	10.2
January 09	115	((9.40 ÷	108.10) ÷	12.70) ×	12 =	8.2
January 09	120	((7.30 ÷	108.10) ÷	12.70) ×	12 =	6.4
January 10	110	((16.64 ÷	108.10) ÷	24.70) ×	12 =	7.5
January 10	120	((12.30 ÷	108.10) ÷	24.70) ×	12 =	5.5
January 10	125	((11.30 ÷	108.10) ÷	24.70) ×	12 =	5.1
January 10	130	((9.30 ÷	108.10) ÷	24.70) ×	12 =	4.2

If the writer wants double-digit returns, that is one way to narrow down this list. Of the 15 options listed, only six calculate out at double digits. These are:

January 08	110	34.1%
February 08	110	23.7
February 08	115	11.2
April 08	110	14.2
July 08	110	12.0
January 09	110	10.2

The original January and February 110 calls remain the most promising. However, both of these are only 1.90 points from strike price. It may be possible to reduce chances of exercise by selecting the February 115. Although this yields only 11.2% on the option, it may be favored for two reasons. First, it remains a fairly short-term option with much more remote chances of exercise than the February 110. Second, if exercise does occur, the capital gain on the underlying stock will be much greater. In the example, you had bought 100 shares the previous February 1, making these options even more desirable; exercise will produce long-term capital gains, which are taxed at a lower rate. A comparison between the two February calls including option premium and capital gain is as follows:

			Stock capital gain		
Month	Strike	Option yield	Gain	Adjust to annualized	Total yield
February 08	110	23.7%	((1000 ÷ 10,000)	÷ 12.7) × 12 = 9.4%	33.1%
February 08	115	11.2	((1500 ÷ 10,000)	÷ 12.7) × 12 = 14.2	25.4

In this example, the 110 call is more profitable in either case. Considering the option alone, income is 23.7% versus 11.2%. The only important benefit of the 115 call is that exercise is much more remote due to the distance to the strike. A trader may prefer this smaller net return in exchange for the greater likelihood that the option will expire worthless. The gap in net profit is narrowed somewhat by inclusion of the capital gain. The after-tax benefit relies on the overall tax rate for the trader and, of course, the larger question of whether exercise would occur.

In developing a truly comparable calculation of return if exercised, it is important to also include dividend income in the equation. Covered call writers continue to earn dividends on the underlying stock until exercise occurs. In comparing possible selection of calls on the same stock, as in the preceding example, this is not critical. However, in comparing overall return if exercised among different stock possibilities, dividend yield can make a significant difference.

For example, the underlying yielded between 1.5 and 2.0% dividend during the year. This may be in line for numerous other stocks on which options will be written as part of a covered call strategy. However, many other stocks yield no dividend or a far higher dividend. For example, Macy's (M) 2017 was paying nearly 6% by the end of 2017; and Tesla (TSLA) paid no dividend in 2017. Comparable covered call returns if exercised may be quite close, but when dividend income is added, higher-yielding stocks may be far more attractive.

A higher than average dividend is by no means the end of the story, however. Markets assume a positive correlation between increased dividends and stock price increases. However, outcomes are contrary to expectations:

> dividend changes should be followed by changes in profitability (earnings growth rates or return on assets) in the same direction … earnings growth rates of firms that increase dividends do not subsequently increase. Firms that decrease dividends, on the other hand, experience significant increases in earnings growth rates in the 2 years following the dividend decrease.[2]

With this surprising outcome in mind, the equity investor may change opinions about dividends as a factor in long-term growth. For options, traders, however, who tend to think in shorter time spans, dividend yield represents a significant portion of any option strategy involving holding long positions in the stock, most notably for covered call writing. If different companies are involved in the comparison between calls, dividend yield could influence a decision to pick one call over the other. Given the lower likelihood of exercise with an incrementally higher strike on a short-term expiration, if the call was associated with an issue paying three times more dividend yield, the selection might have been quite different.

As a consequence, any comparisons between two or more different companies have to include the dividend yield as part of the picture. This raises yet another question: Should you base dividend yield on (a) original price paid, (b) current value of the stock, or (c) the yield at the strike? Arguments may be made for any of these three selections. However, the strongest and most compelling decision is to base the yield on the yield at the time the stock was purchased. Since the amount of investment at that time and at that price determines the actual yield that will be received, it is justified to keep dividend yield at this original level. However, if one of the two alternatives is picked, it should be used consistently among those different stocks being compared.

A second calculation involves a covered call that expires. The premium from this call is entirely profit. However, the yield should be based on the original price of the stock, since that is what provides cover for the short position.

Annualized return is calculated in this instance based on the day of expiration. The reference to "unchanged" means that OTM stock remains OTM (or ATM at worst) and so the option expires worthless. This is a less complex calculation because no stock sale is involved, and dividend income is unaffected by the net outcome. In other words, the trader owned the stock before and continues to own the stock after the option expires. The previously demonstrated method of calculating return and then adjusting it for annualized return applies in this case as well. An alternate method of calculation involves basing the return on the strike rather than current value or original basis of stock. However, since the covered call was entered at the time the current value prevailed, it is that value that most affects the value of the option premium. To remain consistent in a comparative analysis, return if unchanged should be calculated based on the market value of the underlying stock at the time the position was opened; and annualized based on the period between opening date and expiration.

Also note an inconsistency in the consideration of underlying stock capital gains when brought into the overall calculation. Option return is calculated as a percentage of the current value of the underlying at the time the position is opened; but the capital gain is based on original cost of the stock. Remember, though, that the inclusion of the stock profit is used only to make valid value judgments concerning the selection of one strike price and expiration over another. The disparity in methods is justified because the exercise is not a "total return" calculation, but rather a comparative analysis. Since option premium varies based on proximity between underlying stock current value and the strike price, it is only accurate to base return from the option on the value of the stock. However, since the capital gain is only accurate when original cost is compared to sales cost, the exercise price (and variation of the strike between calls) affects the overall yield and has to be calculated on that basis, even though dissimilar from the method used in calculating the option return.

Return If Closed

For any option position, long or short, a final method of return calculation occurs when that position is closed before expiration. For covered positions, calculation of return is normally related to the underlying stock position as explained in the previous section. When you are dealing only in option positions return calculations are going to be based on net cash invested (in the case of long positions) or the return based on changes in premium value (for short positions).

For example, if you enter a long position for $300 net, and close that position at $600, the return is 100% (before annualizing). If you close it at $150, it represents a 50% loss (before annualizing). Remember, the process of annualizing returns, whether for profits or for losses, is only meaningful for purposes of comparison between positions and not to calculate what you should expect to experience throughout an entire year of option trades.

With short positions, the calculation is performed in reverse, just like the trade. If you enter a short position and receive \$400 and close that position at \$200, your profit is 50% (before annualizing). If you close at a loss, the process is also reversed. For example, a \$400 short closed for a net of \$500 represents a 25% loss. Because short positions are transacted in reverse order from long positions, it is not entirely accurate to treat these calculations as "return on investment" because of this reversal in sequence. In fact, return if closed is an oddity for either long or short trades, because the basis is not the same as that for covered calls.

In the covered call, option profit or loss is a percentage of the long stock position and, very much like dividend yield, that profit is a percentage of the long investment. For short positions, the return if closed calculation is an approximation only. With this in mind, the calculation itself is useful only when applied to compare a series of option-only trades. It is not the same as a covered position, but it does provide a means for tracking performance. It allows you to judge your timing and option selection, based on the artificial but comparative "yield" percentages.

A more accurate method for calculating a return on investment would be to identify a fixed dollar amount you have put aside strictly for option trades; and to track profits and losses as trades are entered and then closed. The net profit (or loss) as a percentage of that fixed amount would be a more accurate measure of return on investment. For a majority of traders, this is not a practical approach, even though it makes sense mathematically. Most traders do not isolate a fixed dollar amount for option trades, but move in and out of positions as part of the overall portfolio. The decision to increase or to decrease trades relies on market prices, perceptions, and volatility levels. Traders tend to leave idle cash in a money market account as part of a portfolio, and use a more generalized portfolio fund to execute trades, or even combined with the use of margin. So identifying a fixed fund is a great concept, but one that is going to be difficult to apply for most traders.

The purpose of attempting to identify return on any type of option strategy, or on a range of different strategies, is not so much to specifically define return itself, but to (a) measure timing and success, (b) compare different outcomes by strategy and risk level, and (c) to simply measure performance in option trading over time. Ultimately, the real measure of return is going to be based on annual net profit or loss in the entire portfolio, including capital gains or losses on stocks, dividend and interest income, and profits on option trades.

To calculate annual return at the end of each year, begin with the basic dollar value of profits and losses. Next, calculate the percentage this represents of the portfolio's value. If your portfolio has not been increased during the year with additional investment dollars, or decreased by withdrawals, this is simple. The dollar value of profit or loss is divided by the initial portfolio dollar value to arrive at the annual return.

Most investors experience a change in their portfolio throughout the year, consisting of additional investment deposits and withdrawals at various times. In this case, the annual return has to be calculated using a weighted average. This requires adding together portfolio value at various times during the year and finding the average value (excluding the addition of profits).

For example, your portfolio began the year with a value of $26,000. Your overall profits during the year were $3714. You added $3000 each on March 1, June 1, and September 1. On December 1, you withdrew $2000. Your pre-profit/loss portfolio value during the year was:

January–February	$26,000 (2 months)
March–May	29,000 (3 months)
June–August	32,000 (3 months)
September–November	35,000 (3 months)
December	33,000 (1 month)

Weighted average is so called because longer periods are given more weight than shorter periods. The calculation isolates each period; in this example, there were five separate periods, each with different dollar values. To calculate:

$$\left((26{,}000\times 2)+(29{,}000\times 3)+(32{,}000\times 3)+(35{,}000\times 3)+(33{,}000\times 1)\right)\div 12$$

Reducing the formula:

$$52{,}000+87{,}000+96{,}000+105{,}000+33{,}000\div 12=\$31{,}083$$

In this example, the weighted average value of the portfolio for the year was $31,083. This can also be calculated with partial months when changes occur midway, or even with the exact number of days. As long as the total of the months adds up to 12, or the total of the exact days adds up to 365, the formula works. Your profits for the year were $3714, so the overall yield on this portfolio for the full year was:

$$\$3714\div\$31{,}083=11.95\%$$

Any discussion of return on investment has to include the success of stock selection as well as of option trading. A basic premise of any portfolio program, even one heavily focused on options, is that isolating trades to high-quality and well-selected stocks is a sensible and wise concept. This increases net return not only short term but long term as well. The selection of the best and safest stocks depends on both fundamental and technical tests and comparisons. The next chapter examines stock selection for option trading.

Notes

1. Câmara, A. (2005). Option Prices Sustained by Risk Preferences. *The Journal of Business, 78*(5), pp. 1683–1708.
2. Grullon, G., Michaely, R. & Swaminathan, B. (2002). Are Dividend Changes a Sign of Firm Maturity? *The Journal of Business, 75*(3), pp. 387–424.

Options and Stock Selection

The selection of options based on appropriate risk levels and stocks makes more sense than the selection of stocks to maximize option returns. In other words, any position combining option and stock positions should be based on well-selected stocks held in a trader's portfolio as long-term investments. The alternative, for those interested solely in speculating in options, is to (a) accept higher-risk positions from speculation trading, (b) hedge high-risk positions with option-based coverage, or (c) be aware that long positions in stock are taken up not as investments but as hedges for option positions.

The speculator often is perceived as a negative player in the market, especially in the options market. To the conservative investor (who is likely to shun options trading altogether as too risky), speculation is considered as a negative influence on the market. However, the speculator plays a critically important role in the market. He

> helps to establish an equilibrium between supply and demand. He promotes an expedient rate of consumption by stimulating it when the supply promises to be abundant and checking it when the supply is likely to be small. He makes the daily market price conform to the seasonal market price and thus minimizes the very price-fluctuations out of which he draws his profit. Thus he stabilizes the economic life of the community as well as secures for it the largest possible satisfaction from the goods consumed.[1]

If you buy stock strictly to provide cover for short call positions, it may be a poor strategy. This is especially true for those traders seeking the richest possible option premium. That invariably leads to focus on high-volatility stocks. This means the portfolio ends up with many risky stocks, which is often

M. C. Thomsett, *The Complete Options Trader*,
https://doi.org/10.1007/978-3-319-76505-1_8

contrary to long-term goals. An assumption that most option traders want safety in their stock positions is granted for the following discussion; the assumption is that the majority of traders begin with the premise that the core portfolio should consist of long-term hold stocks (value investments) and that option activity is undertaken to increase current income, hedge long positions, or accept exercise if and when it occurs.

The following sections provide very basic criteria for stock selections, whether for trading options or simply for narrowing down a list of potential investment candidates. In picking options, remember these key points:

1. Higher historical volatility usually is accompanied by higher implied volatility in option premium *and* by higher market risks in both stock and option positions.
2. Stock selection should rule the decision about which stocks to buy and which ones to avoid, based on the risk profile for most traders. If this guideline is not followed, traders should acknowledge that they are accepting higher risks, or select alternative methods for covering short option positions (e.g., through buying longer-term expiring options as offset to shorter-term ones).
3. In narrowing down a list of potential stocks, remember that dividend yield represents a significant portion of overall return on investment. So dividends should always be part of a comparative analysis between stocks being considered. The relationship between dividend yield and call value may not be completely offsetting, so comparisons may have to include valuation of implied volatility as well as dividend yield.
4. Both technical and fundamental tests may be used to narrow the list of candidates for investment. However, the long-term value and safety of stocks should be a primary selection standard, with potential option trading a secondary consideration.

Diversification by Risk Profile

The methods used to diversify an individual portfolio may be varied. A preliminary opinion about diversification is that investors should not place all of their capital into a single stock. However, additional, perhaps more subtle, expansions of this concept are important. These include:

- diversification among stocks of different sectors
- selecting sectors not subject to the same economic cycles or forces

- utilizing mutual funds as an alternative to direct ownership of stocks
- allocation among non-stock investments (real estate, long-term debt, money market, futures)
- using options to hedge market risks or increase income
- diversification by risk profile within the stock market

The last method in this list is similar to the preceding one, the use of options to hedge risk or to eliminate risk altogether. Risk profile varies by individual of course; but for many, it is not a question of managing risk to ensure that *all* investments reside at the same risk level. Rather, portfolio management may also involve dividing up segments of total capital into different risk profiles. For example, a core of 75% may be invested in value companies with long-term appreciation in mind; and the remaining 25% used to speculate, swing trade, or pursue positions with exceptionally high current income. This diversification by risk profile is the most appealing for many investors who recognize that they do not want to be restricted to a single risk level.

Options play a role in this level of diversification. Not only are options valuable for hedging risk (e.g., buying puts to insure existing paper profits in long positions) and for increasing current income (via covered call writing and limited risk positions like butterflies or strangles), but also for seeking varying levels of historical volatility.

The moderate to conservative trader is likely to stay away from highly volatile stocks, simply because the market risks are not acceptable—at least not over the entire portfolio. However, such risks, because they may also produce exceptionally high returns, may be appealing for a segment of capital. In this situation, diversification by risk profile can improve the overall return potential for a portfolio without also increasing the overall risk beyond acceptable levels.

Most investors will be drawn to covered calls with risk diversification in mind. This is an appropriate method for portfolio management and return enhancement, as long as the primary objectives are allowed to remain intact. A great risk in using options is a volatility trap. This comes up when stocks are selected because they have high premium value in their options, rather than on other, sound technical and fundamental criteria. Any trader who gives in to the temptation to pick stocks based on option income potential is likely to increase market risks beyond levels they would otherwise consider acceptable.

With this trap in mind, a few guidelines for selecting stocks will help avoid this trap:

1. Always select stocks based on stock-specific analysis, and never due to the current implied volatility in option premium.
2. Be aware of volatility levels on a technical basis when including companies on a short list, making certain that the selection criteria are valid and not based on opportunities for option profits as an overruling factor.
3. Track stocks in the portfolio to identify changes in volatility levels, remembering that even when you use an appropriate set of criteria for picking stocks, it may change over time.

Fundamental Selection Indicators

Numerous possible fundamental criteria may be used for picking stocks. The individual risk profile will lead each investor to a range of attractive analytical tools. However, the relationship between fundamental and technical attributes often is ignored or discounted by options traders:

> Perhaps no researcher would deny the role of fundamental variables in determining stock prices. The question often centers on whether the variation in stock prices is fully explained by changes in the fundamental variables. A growing literature on behavioral finance emphasizes investors' irrational behavior as an additional explanation for the variation in stock prices that is not explained by the fundamentals.[2]

In practice, it is not realistic to ignore fundamental strength or weakness in the underlying security. The degree of volatility in the fundamentals directly impacts the volatility in the stock price and, in turn, defines volatility in the options market. A starting point in entering into an options trading program may begin with a basic but limited analysis of financial status. The following five general categories provide a general overview of the analytical tools that are most useful for most investors.

1. *Revenue and earnings*. The most obvious of all fundamental indicators is tracking revenue and earnings. Both the current year's status and longer-term trend are crucial indicators of a company's ability to continue growth and to expand in a competitive environment. Tracking both top-line and bottom-line results over a ten-year period is quite revealing, because this reveals the overall direction in which the company is moving. If revenue and earnings are declining over many years, it is unusual for the company to recover or to reverse the trend. A flat movement is an indicator that the markets for a company are not expanding. A growing level of both revenue and earnings is a

strong sign of improving markets and profitability. Earnings are most often tracked through EPS, or earnings per share, which is a valuable indicator to track but not to compare. EPS varies between companies based not only on dollar amount of earnings but also on the number of outstanding shares. So this is useful only for tracking within one company over a period of years.

A sensible fundamental rule: *Limit your list of investment candidates to companies whose revenue and earnings are improving over the long term.*

2. *Fundamental volatility.* The degree of variation in financial results from year to year, or "fundamental volatility," enables a trader to test a company's long-term trading risk. When a company's revenue and earnings are erratic and inconsistent from year to year, it is very difficult to predict long-term growth. Such companies, with frequent higher than average changes, are fundamentally higher risk than the opposite, companies with low fundamental volatility.

A sensible fundamental rule: *Limit investment candidates to those with long-term steady trends in revenue and earnings (low fundamental volatility) as well as consistent trends in dividends, price-earnings ratio, and working capital.*

3. *Working capital tests.* Two very critical tests of working capital are the current ratio and the debt to total capitalization ratio. The current ratio compares current assets to current liabilities. A current ratio consists of cash and assets that are convertible to cash within 12 months (accounts receivable, inventory, marketable securities). Current liabilities are payable within 12 months (accounts payable, taxes payable, and the current portion of long-term notes or other obligations). When the current assets are divided by the current liabilities, the result (expressed as a single digit) is the current ratio. As a general guideline, a current asset of 2 or higher is considered the norm of acceptable working capital control.

The debt to total capitalization ratio is a test of equity versus debt. This refers to the sources of capital for a company, either equity (stock) or debt (long-term bonds and notes). The higher the debt relative to the total, the worse the news. To calculate the debt to total capitalization ratio, add together all capitalization (shareholders' equity and long-term debt) and then divide long-term debt by the total. The resulting percentage is the debt to total capitalization ratio. If a long-term trend shows this level steady or declining, it is a positive sign. However, if the debt to total capitalization ratio is rising, that is a red flag; if it is exceptionally high (e.g., above 65%), it is going to be very difficult for the company to expand in the future. The larger the debt, the more profits have to go to paying interest and repaying the debt itself; and the less remains for paying dividends or for financing market expansion.

A sensible fundamental rule: *Seek consistency or improvement in both current ratio and debt to total capitalization ratio; avoid investing in companies with high or rising debt to total capitalization ratio.*

4. *Dividend yield and history.* The dividend yield represents a significant portion of overall portfolio income. Yet, it is most often overlooked, by both stock investors and option traders. The yield you earn is the yield based on the price you pay for shares of stock. This remains true no matter how much the value of stock changes. The yield after purchase date changes only if the company changes its declared dividend per share. Higher than average yield is accelerated when dividends are reinvested to buy additional shares. The long-term history of dividend yield is a valuable tracking tool. Reduce your list of candidates by looking for those companies that have increased their dividend every year for at least the last ten years. This test is valuable because a company must have funds available (profits) to be able to afford dividends. So a consistent record of growth in dividend payments indicates high quality in the investment itself.

A sensible fundamental rule: *Invest in stock of companies that pay better than average dividend yield, and that have increased their dividend per share every year for at least the last ten years.*

5. *P/E ratio.* P/E (price per share divided by earnings per share) is a hybrid indicator. The price is a technical indicator, and the earnings a fundamental. This ratio is calculated on a per-share basis, with the ratio expressed as a single number, also called the multiple. The P/E is the number of years' earnings equal to the current share price. When P/E is exceptionally high, shares are expensive and, if also volatile, it is also likely that option premium will have higher than average implied volatility. However, high-P/E stocks are overpriced. A reasonable P/E level is generally between 10 and 25, although this depends on the trend for the company and for its industry. In narrowing down your list of potential stocks, seek companies with moderate P/E ranges and trends.

A sensible fundamental rule: *Limit investment candidates to those companies whose P/E has been consistent through the past decade, and whose P/E is not excessively high (e.g., above 25).*

Technical Selection Indicators

Fundamental indicators are focused on profit and loss and valuation of the company. In other words, it is backward-looking and tests market success and financial strength. On comparison, technical analysis is a study of current price trends and related issues, such as volatility in price itself and the volume of trading activity. Many technicians are also chartists, those who study price charts to seek trading patterns and to anticipate the most likely price direction to evolve in the near future.

Technical indicators, like the fundamentals, come in many different varieties, from very simple to quite complex. However, the essential technical analysis science can be broken down into four major divisions:

1. *Price volatility*. The study of price volatility is most often expressed over a 52-week period and is quantified and compared in terms of how far price has varied off its 52-week low. This is inaccurate in many ways. It would be more accurate to compare the oldest 52-week price and study the range of deviation either above or below that price to get a realistic view of price volatility. Otherwise, the outcomes are vastly different for a stock near its 52-week high and another near its 52-week low.

This method does not allow for spikes. Statistically, an accurate range allows for exclusion of unusually high or low spikes in relation to a "normal" distribution. A price spike should be excluded when (a) it happens as an isolated price movement; (b) trading range returns fairly quickly to the previously established trading range; and (c) the aberration does not recur during the 52-week period.

For selection of stocks and their options, analyze historical volatility to determine levels of risk, for both the underlying stock and the options derived from the underlying price.

A sensible technical rule: *In placing a value on volatility, exclude price spikes and also be aware of the trend itself, remembering that price direction affects the importance of 52-week volatility.*

2. *Breadth of the current trading range and its general trend.* A trading range may move only within two to three points in a typical five- to ten-day trading

period; or it may cover many more points. The breadth of the trading range is important not only as it relates to the price per share, but also in how quickly it moves within the range. In addition, a trading range may be defined as a specific number of high-to-low points, but it may also demonstrate an overall trend. Interpreting the technical aspects of price should also take into account whether the price trend is moving upward, downward, or sideways; and whether the breadth of the trading range is widening or narrowing.

A sensible technical rule: *Analyze trading range of a stock over recent periods, remembering that farther-away ranges are less important to the current price direction. Be aware of price breadth itself as well as whether the overall price direction is upward, downward or sideways; and whether it is narrowing or widening.*

3. *The trading range today compared to the past.* It is a mistake to view a narrow or brief series of trading days and try to draw conclusions from it. The trading range a stock experiences today is built on past price direction and the interaction among buyers and sellers. The supply and demand affects the trading range just as the range affects buying and selling behavior. Although technicians focus on price patterns and trends, the impact of economic and earnings news on a company and its sector (not to mention the overall market) is likely to further impact trading range. From the technical point of view, one difficulty is in determining whether a recent change is a temporary one or the beginning of an important change in the trading range.

A sensible technical rule: *Remember that short-term analysis is difficult because reading the latest trend is not reliable. Evaluate today's trading range in the light of its past volatility, price direction, breadth trends, and trading volume.*

4. *Occurrence and frequency of support and resistance tests or breakouts.* Technicians look for strong price indicators that change the existing breadth of a stock's trading range. Resistance (the highest price in the trading range) and support (the lowest price level) establish order and predictability, but only for as long as the current trading range remains in effect. Eventually, trading ranges evolve and change, sometimes gradually and at other times quite dramatically. Certain price patterns predict breakouts above resistance or below support. These include head and shoulders patterns, double and triple tops (or bottoms), and changes in volume relative to price. When a breakout occurs—meaning price moves beyond the established trading range—it may continue to move in the breakout direction, or it may retreat back to the

trading range. This trend may be interpreted by price gaps (space between one period's close and the next period's open) and by the speed of price movement, changes in volume, and entry of buyers or sellers into the action.

A sensible technical rule: *Look for strong signals of important changes in price movement and trading range. Especially important are tests of resistance or support and breakouts, followed by price retreat or continued movement.*

Option traders focused on analyzing stocks, notably for any strategies involving the combined positions of options with stock holdings, will have an improved chance of making smart equity selections.

A related topic every option trader needs to remember is option taxation. The federal law includes many quirks and special rules affecting option trades, timing and recognition of tax losses, and even the possibility that long-term capital gains on stocks could be lost by entering an ill-advised option trade. These topics are covered in the next chapter.

Notes

1. Hutcheon, R. J. (1922). Speculation, Legitimate and Illegitimate. *International Journal of Ethics, 32*(3), pp. 289–305.
2. Wei, S. X. & Zhang, C. (2006). Why Did Individual Stocks Become More Volatile? *The Journal of Business, 79*(1), pp. 259–292.

Option Taxation

Taxes are complex no matter what kinds of investments are involved. However, if you trade options, the complexity of taxation is exponentially greater. Many rules apply only to option trading, and poor planning or unawareness of the rules may lead to expensive mistakes. These mistakes may even include the loss of favorable long-term capital gains rates on stock profits even when positions were open for more than the required 12 months.

This chapter provides an overview of the rules related to option taxation, limitations, and special rules that apply to wash sales, constructive sales, and short call positions.

Capital Gains and Losses

The general rule for capital gains is that long-term gains are taxed at lower rates than ordinary income. Short-term gains, those on investments held for less than one year, are taxed at the higher ordinary income rates. Qualified dividends are also taxed at the same rate as that for net capital gains.

Short-term capital gains apply on investment held for less than one full year, and are taxed at the federal level. Long-term gains are taxed based on calculated "net" capital gains (long-term net gains minus any short-term losses). Gains and losses on investments are required to be recognized and reported in the year that positions are closed (thus, a short position is not taxed until it is closed, exercised, or expired). Gains and losses may not be deferred. However, the maximum annual net capital loss is limited to $3000. Any excess must be carried forward and applied to capital gains or losses in

M. C. Thomsett, *The Complete Options Trader*,
https://doi.org/10.1007/978-3-319-76505-1_9

future periods, perpetually limited to the $3000 ceiling. These net losses do not expire but are carried forward indefinitely.

Long calls are taxed under the holding period rules if they expire or are closed with a closing sale order. They may be short-term (held less than one year) or long-term (held over one year, as in the case of long LEAPS positions). If a long call is exercised, a different calculation is involved. The premium paid for the call, net of brokerage commission, is added to the price of the stock acquired at the strike. The holding period for stock acquired under exercise of the call begins on the day following exercise, and may not include the holding period of the call.

Long puts, like calls, may be long-term or short-term depending on the holding period of the option. If a long put is exercised, resulting in the sale of the underlying stock, the cost of the put, net of brokerage commissions paid, is deducted from the amount realized upon sale of the stock.

Short calls result in receipt of premium upon opening the short position. However, this receipt is not taxed until the position has been closed by way of expiration a closing purchase order. If a short call is held until expiration, it is always treated as a short-term capital gain regardless of the holding period. If the call is closed with a closing purchase order, the net gain is also treated as a short-term capital gain in all cases. If the short call is assigned, the stock price consists of the strike price plus net premium received. A covered call that is assigned creates a profit in the underlying stock equal to the difference between original net basis (purchase) and strike plus short premium received net of brokerage costs (sale). This overall transaction is treated as either long-term or short-term depending on the holding period of the stock. An exception: If the covered call is unqualified, the stock profit may be treated as short-term gain regardless of its holding period (see the next section).

Short puts result in the receipt of premium, but this is not taxed until the position has been closed. If the short put is closed prior to expiration with a closing purchase order, it is always treated as a short-term capital gain regardless of the holding period. The same rule applies if the short put is held until expiration. If a short put is assigned, the basis of the acquired stock is reduced by the net premium received in writing the put. The stock's holding period begins the day after the stock is acquired in this manner, regardless of the holding period of the short put.

Qualified and Unqualified Covered Calls

An exception to the general rule of capital gains applies to some covered calls. In order for the rules in the previous section to apply, the covered call must be "qualified." This generally means that the call has to have at least 30 days to go before expiration, and the strike may not be less than the first strike price level below the closing price of the stock on the day prior to writing the call. This definition varies based on the time to expiration and the strike price range.

For example, if you write a covered call that expires in two months, it is qualified as long as the strike rule applies. If the previous day's closing price was $32 and the call's strike is 30, it is a qualified covered call. However, if the strike is 27.50, or 25.00, it is unqualified. This affects the calculation of capital gains on the stock, even if the call is never exercised. Another restriction: If the stock's market value at the opening of the day is higher than 110% of the prior day's close, that opening price is used to determine qualification rather than the previous day's close.

The distinction between qualified and unqualified covered calls varies with the stock price and with time to expiration (see Table 1).

Investors and traders are not barred from writing unqualified covered calls. However, there will be consequences in the way their capital gains will be calculated and taxed. In addition, if a covered call is ATM or OTM, based on the definitions above, the call cannot expire within the next 30 days to be considered as qualified.

Unqualified covered calls result in capital gains adjustments under the anti-straddle rule. This is a tax rule designed to limit or prevent mismatching of gains and losses in related transactions (e.g., long stock and short calls). There are five possible consequences to writing unqualified covered calls:

Table 1 Qualified covered calls

Prior day's stock closing price	Time until expiration	Strike price limits
$25 or below	Over 30 days	One strike under close of the prior trading day (however, no call can be qualified if the strike is lower than 85% of stock price)
$25.01–$60	Over 30 days	One strike under close of the prior trading day
$60.01–$150	31–90 days	One strike under close of the prior trading day
$60.01–$150	Over 90 days	Two strikes under close of the prior trading day (but no more than 10 points ITM)
Above $150	31–90 days	One strike under close of the prior trading day
Above $150	Over 90 days	Two strikes under close of the prior trading day

1. *ATM and OTM covered calls.* There is no change in the treatment of capital gains on stock as long as those short calls do not expire within 30 days. The status of these calls is based on a comparison between the short call strike and closing price in the stock on the prior day (or opening price on the current day if it exceeds the prior close by 110% or more).
2. *There is no effect on capital gains as long as ITM calls meet the qualification rules.* Traders are able to write ITM short calls, but qualification is restricted to those close strike prices. As long as these limitations are observed, long-term gain rates remain in effect for the underlying stock.
3. *The holding period to calculate capital gains on the underlying stock is suspended with an unqualified covered call is written.* For example, if you owned stock for five months and wrote an unqualified covered call, the count is suspended until the short position is closed, expired, or exercised. So if the short position were open for six months, it would require a total holding period in the stock of 18 months before long-term capital gains rates applied (12 months plus the holding period of the unqualified covered call).
4. *Covered call losses are treated as long-term losses.* Regardless of the holding period, any losses on covered calls, qualified or unqualified, are treated as long-term capital losses, even when underlying stock profits are treated as long-term capital gains.
5. *The stock holding period is affected when short call positions have been closed.* When qualified short calls are sold at a loss, the underlying stock must be held for at least 30 days in order for the call to be treated as qualified.

Rules for Offsetting Positions

Under the wash sale rule, traders are not allowed to sell and then repurchase the same positions within 30 days. For example, you may sell shares of stock on December 15 and claim a loss in the current year, with plans to repurchase the stock on January 5. This strategy would not work; the loss would not be deductible because the position is a wash sale (repurchase occurred within 30 days).

The definition of a wash sale is applied not only to identical positions, but also to "substantially identical" ones. This is where options enter the picture. For example, if you sell stock and, within 30 days, you sell an ITM put anticipating exercise, that is a substantially identical security. So the intent would be to claim a loss on the stock, but to also replace the stock at a selected strike through the short put. This transaction would result in disallowing the deduction of the stock sold.

These offsetting positions are carefully defined under federal rules to prevent a mismatching of profits and losses between tax years. Any time offsetting positions involve "substantial diminution of risk or loss," additional restrictions apply. Any time a strategy includes one position designed to reduce or eliminate the loss in another on the same security, four more rules also apply:

1. The holding period for purposes of capital gains is suspended during the period that offsetting positions are open.
2. Wash sale limitations are applied in many straddles, requiring that losses are deferred on one side until the second position has also been closed.
3. No tax deductions are allowed as long as "successor positions" are open. A successor position is on the same side as the original, position (long or short), but replaces that original position and entered within 30 days before or after the loss occurred. (Essentially this boils down to a rule stating that losses are not deductible in the year incurred if other portions of the offset remain open into the following year; those losses are deferred so that all profit or loss is reported in the same year.)
4. All costs of carry, including brokerage fees and margin interest, are added to the basis of the long position, and may not be deducted during the period the offsetting position remains open.

Exceptions to the "offsetting position" rules generally applied to straddles include two specific strategies. These are qualified covered calls and married puts. A married put is the same-day acquisition of shares of stock and a put on that stock. If the put expires in this situation, its cost is added to the price of the stock rather than being separately deductible; but the offsetting positions disallowance of losses does not apply.

Strategic Considerations

Some traders want to force exercise of covered calls, and have an incentive to write deep ITM calls. However, because this strategy may affect the taxation of gain on the underlying stock, it is important to ensure that the call in question meets the definition of qualified covered call. If the 12-month qualifying period has already been met, there is no tolling of the time period to count up to that requirement. However, it is important to know how the rules affect this when additional offsetting positions are involved.

If you trade options within a qualified retirement plan, the restrictions associated with qualified and unqualified covered calls are not an issue. Some self-directed plans allow covered call writing. However, because net gains are all deferred in these accounts, there is no long-term capital gain at risk.

Some conditions may be optimal for writing unqualified covered calls. Specifically, if you are carrying over an exceptionally large capital loss each year, you cannot deduct more than $3000 per tax period. However, writing unqualified covered calls produces high premiums with one of two outcomes. First, if stock value falls, the deep ITM calls can be closed at a profit. Second, if exercised, these covered calls result in capital gains. Even if long-term rates are not allowed due to the rules governing option taxation, current-year gains can be used in this situation to reduce the net carry-forward to capital losses. This provision shelters the unqualified gain and the fully taxed short-term capital gains on stock.

It is possible for traders to create unqualified covered calls unintentionally. For example, a trader originally acquired 100 shares of stock 11½ months ago at $35 per share. Today, market value is $62 per share. The trader sells a covered call with a strike of 60. However, the call expires in three weeks, which makes it unqualified. In this situation, since shares were owned for less than 12 months at the time the short call was opened, the count to the 12-month long-term holding period is suspended. If the call is exercised, it will result in a short-term capital gain.

Another situation arises when a covered call writer rolls forward to avoid exercise. For example, a 60-strike call on stock valued at $60 per share is qualified as long as the call does not expire within 30 days. Later, though, if the stock price rose to $67 per share, the covered call writer may want to roll forward to avoid exercise. Replacing a soon-to-expire 60 call with a 60 call expiring in 45 days makes sense to avoid exercise; but it closed out the original qualified call and replaces it with a new, unqualified call. If stock was owned for less than 12 months, this suspends the period counting up to the required long-term gain holding period. If that replacement call is exercised, it will result in short-term capital gain treatment for the underlying stock.

The tax rules for options are complex and often illogical. The purpose in many of the rules was to prevent option traders from using combination and hedging positions to defer tax liabilities, or to create tax losses in ways that got around the 30-day wash sale rule or the constructive sale rules. However, anyone trading options based on hedging positions or employing multiple-option positions like butterflies, straddles, or strangles, needs to consult with a tax professional to ensure that the tax consequences are as well understood as the potential tax benefits.

To see a summary of the options tax rules, download the free publication from the CBOE, https://www.cboe.com/LearnCenter/pdf/TaxesandInvesting.pdf.

Index[1]

A

Acquisition and merger risk, 47
Alligator spread, 56, 69
Allocation of risk, 26
Alpha risk, 45–47
Amazon.com, 47
American Stock Exchange (ASE), 166
Anchoring, 51
Andersen, Arthur, 48
Annualized return, 206, 207, 215–220, 222, 223
Anti-straddle rule, 56, 139
Aristotle, 5
Asset allocation risk, 44–45
Associative thinking, 52
At the money (ATM), 14, 18, 19, 32, 75, 102, 136, 140, 200, 201, 203, 205, 222, 239, 240

B

Bankruptcy risk, 48–49
Bear call spread, 56–58
Bear put ladder, 57, 58
Bear put spread, 58, 59
Bear spread, 56, 59, 60, 68, 73, 90, 95, 120, 124, 132
Beta risk, 45–47
Bid/ask spread, 55
Black-Scholes pricing model, 21
Blue chip stocks, 142, 208
Bollinger Bands, 17, 18, 75, 142
Boston Stock Exchange (OMX BX), 8
Box spread, 60–62
Breadth of trading, 16
Breakeven rate of return, 38
Breakouts, 143, 208, 234, 235
Bull call ladder, 62, 64
Bull call spread, 64, 65
Bull put ladder, 65, 66
Bull put spread, 66, 67
Bull spread, 60, 67, 68, 90, 95, 120, 124, 132
Bureau of Labor Statistics (BLS), 38
Butterfly spread, 33, 56, 68, 69, 132
Buy-write, 69

[1] Note: Page numbers followed by 'n' refer to notes.

M. C. Thomsett, *The Complete Options Trader*,
https://doi.org/10.1007/978-3-319-76505-1

C
Calendar combination spread, 69, 104, 107, 108
Calendar spread, 70, 71, 73, 104, 107, 109–111, 116, 132, 136
Calendar straddle, 70, 71
Capital gains and losses, 145, 224, 237–238
Chicago Board of Trade (CBOT), 8, 10
Chicago Board Options Exchange (CBOE), 8, 10, 41, 43
Chicago Mercantile Exchange (CME), 10
Collar, 71, 72
Collateral risk, 39–41, 56, 116
Combination, 1, 20, 22, 26, 28, 34, 40, 42, 43, 56, 62, 63, 72, 73, 78, 79, 86, 87, 89, 92, 94, 107, 120, 132, 136, 204, 208, 210–211
Condor, 73, 74, 91, 121, 132
Confirmation bias, 51–52
Consumer Price Index (CPI), 36, 37
Contingent buy, 73
Contingent sell, 75
Conversion, 75, 76, 149, 160, 185
Cost of carry, 150, 206
Covered calls, 2, 13, 21–22, 31–34, 36, 39, 41–43, 45, 56, 69, 71, 75–80, 113, 119, 120, 128, 132, 136, 206–211, 216–224, 229, 238, 241, 242
Covered combination, 78–80
Covered put, 102
Covered short straddle, 80
Covered strangle, 80, 81
Credit spread, 80, 84
Current ratio, 150, 231, 232

D
Debit spread, 58, 61, 81
Debt to total capitalization ratio, 231, 232
Delta hedge, 81
Delta spread, 82
Derivatives, 10, 16, 26–28, 152, 200, 201
Diagonal spread, 64, 82, 103, 132, 136
Diversification risk, 44–45, 228–230
Dividend yield, 31, 153, 206–208, 214, 221, 222, 224, 228, 232
Dow Jones Industrial Average (DJIA), 46, 47
Downside protection, 76, 77, 113, 126, 154, 210

E
Earnings surprises, 29, 49–51, 116
Earnings test, 208, 231
Eastman Kodak, 49
Effective tax rate, 37–39, 143, 197
Enron, 48
Equifax (EFX), 48
Exchange-traded fund (ETF), 1, 12, 156
Expected return, 157, 213–215
Experience risk, 42–43
Expiration, 7, 8, 10–12, 14–16, 22, 28–32, 34, 35, 40, 42, 43, 55–57, 60, 63–65, 68, 70–73, 75–78, 80, 82, 84, 86, 89–95, 97–99, 103, 104, 107, 109, 113, 116–126, 128, 130, 132, 133, 157, 158, 199–206, 211, 214–216, 218, 219, 222, 223, 238, 239
Extreme events, 13
Extrinsic value, 16, 35, 158, 202–205

F
Fortune 500, 48, 49, 53n13
Forward roll, 32, 34, 35, 43, 118
Fundamental risk, 27, 47, 48
Fundamental volatility, 161, 231

G

Gould, Jay, 7
Government National Mortgage Association (GNMA), 10
Gut strangle, 82, 84, 85

H

Hedge, 1, 2, 4, 5, 20, 25, 33, 44, 47, 75, 86, 94, 116–118, 122, 132, 200, 214, 227–229
Hedge ratio, 86
High-beta stocks, 27
High-risk trading, 25
Historical volatility, 16–18, 28–30, 199, 200, 204, 206, 207, 215, 228, 229, 233
History, options market, 5–11
Horizontal spread, 70, 82, 86, 132, 136

I

Implied volatility, 16–18, 28–30, 35, 163, 199, 200, 202, 204–207, 215, 228, 230, 232
Inflation risk, 35 36, 164
Interest, 1, 6, 8, 10, 17, 40, 94, 126, 164, 165, 199, 206–207, 224, 232, 241
International Stock Exchange (TISE), 8
In the money (ITM), 14, 16, 18, 19, 29, 31, 32, 34, 35, 42, 58, 60, 65, 67, 73, 77–82, 84, 94, 102–104, 116–119, 128, 133, 163, 200–205, 239–242
Intrinsic value, 15, 16, 18–19, 29, 31, 34, 35, 60, 63, 70, 72, 75, 79, 81, 86, 89, 94, 100, 102–104, 112, 136, 165, 199, 200, 202–205
Investor, 51
Investor psychology, 51
Iron butterfly, 86, 122

J

Jump-diffusion model, 215

K

Kansas City Board of Trade (KCBT), 8
Knowledge risk, 3, 42–44, 209
Kroger, 47

L

Leg in/leg out, 89
Leverage, 6, 10, 26, 28, 39, 40, 45–46, 89, 98, 167
Liquidity risk, 39, 41–42, 168
Long call, 19, 20, 23, 33, 35, 41, 42, 57, 60–65, 70, 73, 75, 82, 86–89, 91–94, 98–100, 104, 107, 109, 112, 115, 116, 119–123, 133, 134, 136, 205, 218, 238
Long call butterfly, 90, 91, 120
Long call condor, 91, 92
Long combination, 72, 92
Long iron butterfly, 86, 87, 92–94
Long put, 19–21, 23, 28, 41, 44, 57, 58, 60, 61, 66, 68–72, 75, 82, 89, 93–96, 99, 103, 104, 109, 116, 122–124, 126, 127, 133, 134, 208, 210, 238
Long put butterfly, 95–97
Long put condor, 96–98
Long stock (synthetic), 21, 23, 33, 44, 76, 92, 94, 98, 99, 113, 120, 128, 135, 136, 206, 209, 224, 239
Long straddle, 70, 99, 100, 132–134
Long-Term Equity Anticipation Securities (LEAPS), 10, 15, 23n7, 29, 30, 73, 75, 166, 169, 214, 238
Loss aversion, 51, 201
Lost opportunity risk, 21, 32–33, 41, 169

M

Magical thinking, 51, 52
Margin calculator, 41
Margin risk, 39–41
Market risk, 2, 3, 13, 15, 21, 22, 25–52, 72, 75, 94, 102, 128, 170, 200, 208, 228, 229
Married put, 100, 101, 135, 241
Merton, Robert C., 215
Moderate and neutral strategies, 33–35
Moneyness, 18, 19, 89, 172
Money spread, 101
Monsanto, 50
Monsanto (MON), 50

N

Naked option, 3, 34, 42, 101, 136
Naked put, 20, 22, 34, 102, 128, 132, 203, 209, 211
Neutral hedge ratio, 102
Neutral position, 102
New York Stock Exchange (NYSE), 7, 36, 174

O

Offsetting positions, 44, 56, 86, 89, 94, 120, 240–241
Option selection, 28, 224
Options Clearing Corporation (OCC), 8, 12
Out of the money (OTM), 14, 18, 19, 31, 32, 34, 35, 41, 58, 60, 62, 65, 67, 70, 71, 77, 80–82, 102, 103, 113, 116, 119, 128, 130, 131, 133, 177, 199–205, 211, 219, 222, 239, 240

P

Pacific Stock Exchange (PSE), 8
Paper loss, 33, 78, 210, 211
P/E ratio, 177, 232
Philadelphia Stock Exchange (PHLX), 8
Pinning, 178, 201
Portfolio risks, 4, 21, 39, 41, 46
Premium, –216, 2, 11–23, 28–31, 34–36, 40, 41, 43, 55, 67, 72, 76–82, 84–86, 88, 89, 91, 93–98, 100–103, 113, 119, 120, 127, 129, 131, 139, 199, 202–207, 209–211, 213, 218–219, 221–223, 227–229, 238, 242
Price discovery, 13
Price spikes, 16, 34, 50, 205, 233
Price volatility, 15, 17, 28, 208, 233
Proximity and price, 14, 200–203
Purchasing power, 35, 36, 38, 181
Put diagonal spread, 102, 103
Put ratio backspread, 103, 105

Q

Qualified covered call, 32, 78, 182, 239, 241
Qualified retirement plans, 242

R

Ratio backspread, 104
Ratio calendar combination spread, 69, 104, 107, 108
Ratio calendar spread, 104, 107, 109–111, 132
Ratio call spread, 109, 112, 113
Ratio put spread, 113, 114
Ratio spread, 82, 103, 104, 113, 132
Ratio write, 22, 33, 113, 115, 120, 136, 195, 210
Reputation risk, 48–49
Return calculations, 77, 78, 213, 215, 223
Return if closed, 223–226

Return if exercised or unchanged, 220–223
Revenue test, 231
Reversal, 34, 51, 115, 166, 185, 224
Reverse calendar spread, 116, 132
Reverse hedge, 116–118
Risk tolerance, 20, 36, 45, 209, 210
Rolling, 31, 32, 34, 35, 43, 55, 56, 73, 102, 117–119, 206

S

Sage, Russell, 7
Securities and Exchange Commission (SEC), 29
Short call, 12, 19, 21–23, 31–35, 42, 57, 60–64, 67, 70, 71, 73, 75, 77, 78, 80, 84–89, 91–93, 102, 104, 107, 109, 111, 113, 118–124, 126, 129, 131, 133, 136, 206, 208, 211, 216, 218, 227, 237–240
Short call butterfly, 120, 121
Short call condor, 121, 122
Short combo, 122
Short iron butterfly, 86, 87, 122–124
Short put, 19, 21–23, 34, 37, 57, 58, 60, 62, 65–68, 73, 75, 78, 80, 84, 85, 92–95, 97–99, 103, 104, 109, 113, 115, 119–125, 129, 131, 133, 136, 206, 209, 211, 238, 240
Short put butterfly, 124, 125
Short put condor, 125, 126
Short stock (synthetic), 23, 122, 126–128, 136
Short straddle (covered), 128, 129
Short straddle (naked), 128, 130
Short strangle, 130–133
Simulated straddle, 116, 132
Single-option speculative strategies, 20–21
Speculation, 2, 4, 6, 7, 20, 28, 46, 89, 94, 120, 124, 227
Spreads, 8, 33, 55, 141, 206
Sprouts, 47
Standard & Poor's 100 index (OEX), 8
Standardized terms, 7, 11, 13
Stock selection, 207, 208, 226–235
Straddles, 22–23, 42, 72, 86, 87, 89, 92, 94, 102, 116, 120, 122, 124, 132, 133, 210, 241
Strangle, 23, 82, 132, 133, 210, 229
Strap, 133, 134
Strategic considerations of taxes, 241–242
Strategy ranges, 20
Strike price, 7, 11, 12, 14, 20–22, 31, 43, 56, 60, 62, 65, 68, 70, 72, 73, 77, 78, 82, 89, 91, 94, 102, 104, 109, 113, 119, 124, 132, 133, 136, 191, 199–202, 204, 206, 209, 210, 218, 219, 221, 223, 238–240
Strip, 134, 135
Substantially identical positions, 240
Successor positions, 241
Support and resistance, 234
Swing trading, 21, 28, 46, 89, 94, 119, 124, 205
Synthetic long call, 100, 135
Synthetic long stock, 23, 92, 98, 135
Synthetic positions, 23, 36, 98, 99, 127
Synthetic put, 135
Synthetic short call, 136
Synthetic short put, 136
Synthetic short stock, 23, 122, 136
Synthetic straddle, 136

T

Tax put, 136
Tax risk, 32, 35–38
Technical selection indicators, 233–235
Thales the Milesian, 5
Time spread, 132

Time value, 10, 15, 16, 28–31, 34, 35, 42, 56, 61, 62, 70, 73, 75, 77, 79–81, 102–104, 113, 116–118, 128, 130, 132, 133, 192, 202–206, 211, 218
Trading costs, 55, 56, 68, 69
Trading range, 15, 16, 34, 49, 142, 182, 193, 200, 233–235
Tulipmania, 6, 7
Types of options (calls and puts), 92

U
Uncovered calls, 75, 194
Uncovered option, 194
Underlying security, 1, 2, 6, 7, 11–13, 16, 17, 19, 26, 28, 195, 200, 201, 230
Unqualified covered call, 32, 78, 239–240, 242
Unrealized losses, 33

V
Value Line, 8
Vertical spread, 64, 82, 132, 136
Volatility risk, 27
Volatility value, 16

W
Wal-Mart, 47
Wash sales, 37, 136, 196, 237, 240, 241
Whole Foods, 47
Working capital test, 231

Options traders rely on a vast array of information concerning probability, risk, strategy components, calculations, and trading rules. Traders at all levels, as well as portfolio managers, must refer to numerous print and online sources, each source only providing part of the information they need. This is less than ideal, as online sources tend to be basic, simplified, and in some cases incorrect. Print sources, on the other hand, are mostly focused on a very narrow range of strategies or trading systems. Up until now, there has been no single source to provide a comprehensive reference for the serious trader.

The Complete Options Trader is that much-need comprehensive reference, a compilation of the many attributes options traders need.

Thomsett lays out a rich and complete guide to 100 strategies, including profit and loss calculations, illustrations, examples, and much more. A thorough evaluation of these strategies (and the rewards and risk involved) demonstrates how a broad approach to analytically using options can and does enhance portfolio profits with lower levels of risk.

The book also features a complete glossary of terms used in the options industry, the most comprehensive glossary of this nature currently available.

All too often, the attributes of options trading are poorly understood; risk is ignored or over-simplified; hedging is not folded into a strategic evaluation; and options traders shun the value of holding equity positions. No longer—if options traders rely on this comprehensive guide as the reference for the industry.

Michael C. Thomsett
has been writing for a living since 1978 and has published more than 90 books. These include 12 options books. His best-selling *Getting Started in Options* has been published in nine editions and sold more than 300,000 copies. He also has developed and presented options webinars, and coaches on a live trading room every day and is a frequent speaker at trade shows and investment conventions. He blogs on his website, https://thomsettsguide.com/ Seeking Alpha, Options Money Maker, and social media.

palgrave macmillan

The manufacturer's authorised representative in the EU is Springer
Nature Customer Service Centre GmbH, Europaplatz 3, 69115 Heidelberg,
Germany. If you have any concerns regarding our products, please
contact ProductSafety@springernature.com

Printed and bound by CPI Group (UK) Ltd, Croydon, CR0 4YY
30/09/2026
02225654-0009